THE
FORMATIVE YEARS
1607–1763

By

CLARENCE L. VER STEEG

The Making of America

GENERAL EDITOR: DAVID DONALD

LONDON
MACMILLAN & CO LTD
1965

MACMILLAN AND COMPANY LIMITED
St Martin's Street London WC 2
also Bombay Calcutta Madras Melbourne

Foreword

THE HISTORIAN of colonial America faces formidable difficulties. Even if he begins his account with the first English settlement, the period he must cover is nearly as long as all subsequent epochs of American history combined. He is obliged to know in detail the politics, economics, social structure, and intellectual life, not of the American colonies alone, but of England and, to a lesser degree, of the continental states as well. Unless he confines himself to an arid account of colonial administration as seen from London, his history has no single, uninterrupted thread, for he has to trace the individual stories of more than a dozen quite different, or even conflicting, colonies. It is not surprising, therefore, that there have been so few satisfactory comprehensive histories written of our colonial experience.

Undeterred by these mountainous problems, Professor Clarence L. Ver Steeg, of Northwestern University, set for himself the task of making a meaningful pattern out of our colonial past, and, as *The Formative Years* demonstrates, he has brilliantly succeeded. Bringing to this study the expertise that has made him widely regarded as one of our most eminent historians of the colonial and revolutionary periods, he has produced a sweeping and insightful reinterpretation of the first century and a half of our history.

Professor Ver Steeg's central concern is with the forces that converted "transplanted Englishmen" into "provincial Americans." In developing this theme he has carefully avoided the crude environmentalism that has characterized too much writing on the colonial era. Recognizing the "invaluable legacy" the colonists brought from Europe, he shows how cultural conditioning, not mere geography, caused the pattern of New England settlement to differ from that in Virginia. At the same time, in analyzing how abundant land, expanding trade, and immigration modified the European heritage, he persuasively argues that Frederick Jackson Turner's frontier hypothesis, now so often controverted by historians, is valid when applied to the settlement of the Old West.

To an extraordinary degree Clarence Ver Steeg's book is based upon his own original researches, often in hitherto unexploited sources. Of course he has mastered the voluminous secondary literature, but *The Formative Years* is not a rehash of other books but a fresh exploration of the most important, and the most controversial, topics in our colonial history. In attacking these difficult problems Professor Ver Steeg has made use not only of the conventional tools of the historian but of insights derived from social psychology, sociology, and other related social science disciplines. As a result, even experts will find in each of his chapters original interpretations and new theses. Perhaps the most striking of these is his juxtaposition of the almost simultaneous Bacon's Rebellion in Virginia, Leisler's revolt in New York, and the Salem witchcraft episode in Massachusetts as manifestations of the social instability that accompanied the metamorphosis of the colonies into provinces.

While specialists will delight in, and probably argue about, Professor Ver Steeg's exciting new ideas, the general reader will find in these concise pages the best introduction to our colonial history. *The Formative Years,* therefore, precisely fulfills the objectives of The Making of America, a six-volume series designed to present new historical interpretations with clarity and compactness.

DAVID DONALD

The Johns Hopkins University

Contents

Maps

Table

THE FORMATIVE YEARS
1607 – 1763

1

England and the Age of Discovery

THE COLONIAL PERIOD of American history is the formative period because concepts and institutions later characterized
as distinctively American were developed in the first century and
a half of American experience. The roots of these institutions and
the source of these concepts are firmly entrenched in the mainstream of Western civilization as transmitted through England
of the early seventeenth century.

The diversity of faiths and the long history of predominant
Protestantism in the United States are legacies of the colonial
period, which in turn reflected the religious ferment of Europe
in the sixteenth and seventeenth centuries. Present-day local and
state governments, each with its assigned sphere of power, are
rooted in colonial America, to which English practices and institutions were transplanted. The formation of the English colonies
coincided with the rise of modern capitalism in the Western
world; no wonder then that the origins of American capitalism
are to be found in the first century and a half of provincial development. Even the nationalism of western Europe, defined as
the creation of a national state, was eventually imitated by the
English colonies in North America, for they entered into a union
and became one nation rather than thirteen separate states, a result now taken for granted. These examples are merely representative of innumerable patterns of thought and action which

underscore the strength and pervasiveness of the inheritance of the Western world, and which make the colonial years the formative years.

In Europe the Age of Discovery was also the Age of Humanism, as man exercised his talent and imagination to penetrate the unknown. The world of Leonardo da Vinci, Michelangelo, and Erasmus also embraced a Christopher Columbus; indeed, each man in his own way fulfilled the expectations implicit in the Age.

The Age of Discovery was strikingly different from that which characterized Europe on the eve of the Crusades or the era when the Norsemen sailed the northern Atlantic. The limited commercial enterprise of 1100 had given way to the revival of trade and the rise of the city; a limited intellectual outlook had flowered into the Renaissance mind; and the political fragmentation of feudal times had been transformed into dynastic consolidation. Still, American historians have been inclined to construe the medieval bequest too narrowly, thinking exclusively of feudal land policy and neglecting the historical force of the Christian faith, emphasizing constrictive feudal fees and overlooking the consequences of the university curriculum, finding examples of political rigidity but slighting the legacy of liberty. Out of the society of the Middle Ages emerged the seed of new life.

When Columbus' fleet cleared the sand bar at Palos, Spain, in August 1492 and caught the fresh sea breeze that was to carry the fleet to the Canary Islands and thence westward, the event marked an extension of the humanistic spirit. Columbus' contribution ranks with the timeless contributions of his great intellectual contemporaries, because his successful voyage marked a shift in the course of history. In ancient times, the Mediterranean Sea served as the center of the Western world, the channel of communication between peoples; in modern times, the center of the Western world has shifted to the Atlantic. Control of the Mediterranean assured ascendancy during medieval times; control of the Atlantic has assured ascendancy in modern times.

Voyages of discovery and explorations by Europeans in the Western Hemisphere were made possible by skills acquired in the late Middle Ages: the ability to tack against the wind, the improvement of vessels to withstand ocean voyages, and the development of technical tools for navigation—the compass and the astrolabe. The significance of the astrolabe, at least in Columbus' voyages, has been exaggerated; Columbus depended upon dead reckoning and seldom used celestial navigation.

The relationship between these practical skills required for an Age of Discovery and theoretical scientific discussion and thought as expressed in the Age of Humanism was direct, as advances in astronomy, mathematics, geography, and physics were transformed into better navigational practices, improved cartography, and the like. The learned scholar attempting to apply stringent criteria to insure the accuracy of a Biblical or scientific text was not unlike the bold captain verifying the coast line and contours of an unknown continent in the course of his discoveries. For scholar and seaman, theory and practice were harmoniously combined in the questing Renaissance mind.

Yet the nation-states along the Atlantic coast and not the Italian cities—the periphery of the Renaissance and the commercial revival, not the center—were destined to carry Western culture to the New World. Because Portugal, Spain, France, Holland, and England became the instruments of transmission, the Old World legacy bequeathed to the New was distinctive from that which might have occurred if the Italian city-states had attempted to explore and, no doubt, exploit America. The New World reflected the competition between nations and not cities, between peoples, policies, and faiths of respective countries, not of Aragon, East Anglia, or Burgundy.

Immediate access to the Atlantic is significant in explaining why the countries of western Europe took the lead in colonizing America, but location is only one of several factors. The initial discoveries were prompted by the earnest desire of Atlantic countries to escape the tolls exacted by the middlemen of the Italian cities. Portugal's explorations and eventual triumph in exploring and circumnavigating the continent of Africa to secure a direct route to India, Spain's sponsorship of the voyages of Columbus and Magellan, and England's expeditions, of John Cabot to America and of other adventurers to the Northeast to find a route to Asia by outflanking northern Europe, exemplify the universality of this objective.

The ability to colonize once a discovery had been made depended in large measure upon the political stability of the mother country. The thesis that the entrance of a particular European nation into the spirit of expansion depended more often upon political tranquillity than upon economic capability is well founded. Freed from internal political questions by the time of the fifteenth century, Portugal led in the exploration of Africa. The defeat of the Moors at Granada the year of Columbus' sailing defined Spain's territorial limits after a century of wearing and complex consolidation through marriage, negotiation, and conquest. In contrast, an unsettled England failed to follow up the discoveries made by Cabot in 1497 and 1498, even though Henry VII, the first Tudor, was reputed to be the richest monarch in Christendom. Indeed, the principal concern of the Tudors for a century was the consolidation of a dynasty.

In so many ways Portugal serves as an excellent example of the mergence of motive, experience, learning, stable political institutions, and leadership which made possible the entrance of a country into the mainstream of European expansion. Portugal, having resolved many of its internal problems after its final separation from Spain in the fourteenth century, turned to external opportunities. No period in Portuguese history was quite so vital as the reign of Prince Henry the Navigator, when he attempted to realize two ambitions: to extend the Christian faith and to circumnavigate the African continent. The impetus given to the study of astronomy and cartography in Portugal by Prince

Henry gave the nation an enviable reputation among the learned men of Europe. His training school for sailors and his emphasis on maritime skills translated learned debate into practical application, a fifteenth-century demonstration of science wedded to technology. Lisbon became a cosmopolitan court, rich in the merchandise brought in from an uninterrupted series of expeditions and voyages along the West African coast, whose final objective was to find a short all-water route to India. This experience enabled Bartolomeu Diaz to round the southern tip of Africa in 1488 and Vasco da Gama to complete the voyage to India in 1498. The Treaty of Tordesillas of 1494 with Spain, giving the Portuguese the new lands discovered east and south of the longitudinal line drawn 370 leagues west of the Cape Verde Islands, represented the fulfillment of Portuguese ambition and indicated the direction of Portuguese interest toward Africa and Asia.

Spain did not fit the pattern of experience, learning, and leadership exhibited by Portugal quite so neatly, yet in motive and dynastic stability parallels can readily be observed. Although merchants of means sat at the court of King Ferdinand and Queen Isabella, the country was not so deeply influenced by either the rise of modern capitalism or the Renaissance as were the Italian cities or Portugal or France or, at a slightly later period, England. Yet Spain was destined to sponsor the voyage of Columbus and to establish the first colonial empire in the New World.

In many ways, Columbus' voyage was supported by Spain as an act of desperation, in the spirit of nothing to be lost except a modest outlay of money. Spain was being seriously outpaced by Portugal in the race to find a new all-water route to the Orient. When Diaz rounded the southern tip of Africa four years before Columbus' voyage, the triumph of Portugal was predictable. Spain gambled on an Atlantic voyage on the slim chance that Columbus' analysis of the distance between the Iberian Peninsula and Cipangu (Japan), based on the errors of Ptolemaic geography and *The Book of Marco Polo,* might be accurate, in contradiction to the counsel of learned men who we now know correctly estimated the circumference of the earth. Yet Spain was able to capitalize on Columbus' discovery, to introduce a colonial establishment within a decade after the discovery, and to extend its authority over much of Central and South America within a quarter of a century. This result can only be explained by the drive and vitality of Spain at the opening of the sixteenth century.

That Spain was to become the foremost power in Europe during the course of the sixteenth century was a consequence of the treasure found in the New World. The treasure financed additional Spanish adventurers and advanced its New World frontier; in the Old World, this treasure enabled Spain to become a strong maritime power and enhanced its influence throughout Europe. The decision of the Spanish monarchs to pursue an ambitious plan to dominate Europe rather than to make capital investments within Spain set the stage for the eventual diminution of Spanish power. Once the source of treasure from the New World dried up, Spanish influence in Europe receded; yet the Spanish colonial system in Central and South America endured more than three hundred years, a longer period than any other empire in modern times. Its achievements were many, but its exploitation of New World resources—a policy accepted by all nations—without serious reinvestment crippled the growth of an indigenous economy in Central and South America, an enduring consequence that no amount of rhetoric or good will can dispel.

Western culture was first transmitted to the New World via Spain. The result was not merely that Spanish America reflected a stage of European civilization frozen at a given point of time (around 1500) but that patterns emerged characteristic of the homeland. The language, the political institutions implementing the absolutism of the Spanish Crown, and the Catholic Church as an instrument of education and faith contributed to this distinctive society in Spanish America. Feudal institutions were transplanted to Spanish America rather than the institutions of a developing commercial capitalism, a contrast to English America. Moreover, fundamental decisions, that only those receiving royal assent could transport themselves to America and that natives were to be regarded as subjects of the Crown, introduced a social system unlike that which was to develop in English America.

In the same way that the societal patterns developed in the Spanish colonies reflected time and place, the peculiar legacy of English America was the result of the special conditions prevailing in the mother country in the late sixteenth and early seventeenth centuries. That interval of a century between the voyages of John Cabot in 1497 and 1498 and the establishment of England's first permanent colony in 1607 was all-important, for it produced a nation so singular in character in terms of religious diversity, of commercial experience, and of singular political thought and practice—the culmination, to be sure, of centuries of evolutionary change—that England's colonies in the New World, reflecting these traits, were not only set apart from the Spanish colonies but were vastly different from what they would have been if England had been able to plant colonies in the wake of Cabot's voyages. Western civilization had assumed a different shape by 1600, and in filtering through England to America the results were, in many respects, distinctive.

During the fifteenth century, England was torn between two giant rivals, the factions of Lancaster and of York, each laying claim as the legitimate line for the English monarchy. For nearly a quarter century the York faction seemed destined to rule, but losses on the field of battle and bitter internal quarrels weakened its grip on the throne. In 1485 Henry Tudor, at the head of a few thousand men embodying the Lancastrian aspirations, gained the Crown in the decisive battle of Bosworth Field. However, more than a century was required to achieve internal

stability and strength sufficient to enable England to engage in
the expansion and fulfillment of the Atlantic community, defined
as those countries of western Europe and those New World
satellites of western Europe which bordered on the Atlantic
Ocean.

The Tudor reign, from 1485 to 1603, reinforces the thesis that
the pace of expansion of a given country often depended upon
political stability. During the sixteenth century, the development
of this stability was slowly but assuredly coming about in England, and the character of the English expansion along the western shores of the Atlantic was profoundly affected by the direction of developments within England which bound together the
English people.

One English historian has observed that the Crown acted as
the innovating force in English life in the sixteenth century, in
the same fashion that Parliament acted as the generating force in
the seventeenth century. Perhaps it is not too much to say that,
in the sixteenth century, the Crown fixed its star to the aspirations of the English people while Parliament gained this initiative in the seventeenth. In part, the success of each can be understood in terms of riding the tides of fortune. Certainly, the Tudor
monarchs linked their fortune to the rising eminence of the mercantile classes at the expense of the nobility, the source of dis-
unity and royal dependence, and the Tudors unified the English
people by linking the Crown to the people through the agencies
of local government so that the national will and national policy
reached into every shire in the land.

The shire—the English county—and the sheriff, the principal
local official, had attained high importance by the time Henry
VII, the first Tudor, ascended the throne in 1485. When Henry
traveled to London to take his place at the head of the government, he was escorted within the boundaries of each shire by the
sheriff, whereupon the sheriff of the adjoining shire met the
King's party, a practice not unlike the modern-day political
ritual which expects local politicians to accompany political fig-

ures of national reputation who travel through their districts, a token, in a sense, of their mutual dependency. This practice at the time of Henry VII acknowledged that local political institutions had achieved maturity and power. It remained for the Tudors to use these institutions to advantage.

By making the sheriff, the principal officer of the county, more responsive to royal policy, the tie between the central government and the local government was strengthened, and the vitality of each level of government was thereby enhanced. Appointed directly by the King from one of three candidates submitted by the Privy Council, the sheriff supervised the county courts, the collection of taxes, the execution of the decisions of the justices of the peace, and the election of candidates to Parliament.

An innovation of the Tudors was the creation of a second important county official, the lord lieutenant. Customarily a man of wealth and position, the lord lieutenant, too, received his appointment and his authority directly from the Crown. The lord lieutenant supervised the training of local militia; in this service, he became the military arm of the monarch, which again freed the Crown from excessive dependency upon the nobility, thus promoting a unity symbolized by the monarch.

In the same way that the central authority represented by the Crown extended its political ties through the sheriff and its military ties through the lord lieutenant, so the Crown extended its judicial ties by way of justices of the peace. The office of justice of the peace was a legacy inherited by the Tudors, but the Tudors clothed the justice with authority. During Tudor times over three hundred statutes described the specific jurisdiction of the justices of the peace; this official became the foundation stone upon which much of the political-legal institutional structure rested.

The significance of these developments in English government can be measured in several ways. Not only did the strengthened institutional ties bring greater unity and stability to the country,

thus preparing the English people for a future role in the Atlantic community, but the vitality of local government in England made possible its transmission to the New World. The
county sheriff, the justice of the peace, and the county coroner
of modern America can trace their lineage to sixteenth-century
England. Future chapters will delineate the changes brought
about by transfer across the Atlantic, but the heritage of local
government in the United States is a product of Tudor England.
No other group of colonies, founded by the nations of western
Europe, received such a bequest.

In addition to shaping and vitalizing the political structure of
England, the Tudors were willing to employ other means to secure dynastic stability. Pretenders to the throne who were backed
by the declining York faction were swiftly disposed of. The fear
that families of noble birth might yet prove a threat, a disin-
tegrating force, drove Henry VII to secure the enactment in 1487
of the Star Chamber Act, thereby reorganizing the judicial
powers to obtain for the monarchy special jurisdiction in cases
of livery, maintenance (meaning the retaining of a private army
by a noble, under the guise of employing ordinary servants), or
civil disorder. By this means, Henry VII curtailed the power of
those nobles who attempted to insulate themselves from the royal
authority. At the same time the Court of the Star Chamber,
which was to become infamous as the arbitrary instrument of
the King, was originally visualized by the gentry, and indeed by
the populace, as their champion against the arbitrary actions of
the nobles, the King and the people pitted against the highborn.
   Henry VII was also remarkably successful in adding to the
Crown's financial resources. Eliminating corruption and waste
in the collection of royal accounts, confiscating property of
political offenders, finding old laws to enforce and obtaining
new laws from Parliament to fatten the royal treasury were
among the devices effectively employed, but none exceeded in
importance the Book of Rates setting specific valuations on

goods involved in English trade. Increase in trade provided an increase of funds; promotion of trade, therefore, received priority.

In this regard, England reflected the concept of mercantilism, a set of economic ideas held by countries of western Europe during the fifteenth to eighteenth centuries, ideas whose fundamental assumption was that nation-states should regulate their economic life to strengthen themselves in competition with other nation-states. Mercantilism was to economic life what the rise of nations was to political life. The ideas held by the mercantilists were not pure theory but the product of experience. A policy that appeared to produce prosperity and national strength in one country was seen by competitor nations as the policy to imitate if they were to share in the struggle for power in Europe. Yet each nation, although it thought in terms of imitation, in practice emphasized different features of mercantilism because of the special historical conditions applicable to them. In Spain bullionism was emphasized; in France internal trade and subsidy of luxury goods; in Holland external trade.

In England the principal emphasis in the sixteenth century was on internal regulation; the principal emphasis in the seventeenth century was external regulation, notably the definition of the economic relationship between England and its colonies. In the sixteenth century, for example, production of woolen goods was promoted to avoid exporting raw wool to Flanders where it would be made into cloth. The Statute of Artificers passed in 1563, together with the Poor Laws, was designed to harness men's labor to national goals. Idle men meant more than personal tragedy; idle men represented the squandering of a national resource, a notion that sounds strangely modern. Because Spain's rise to the status of an international power coincided with the extension of its colonial possessions, Englishmen such as Richard Hakluyt theorized in the late sixteenth century that the founding of colonies was imperative to national strength, and these mercantile concepts led eventually to the establishment of English colonies in the New World. Colonies could supply the raw materials required by the mother country, thus eliminating dependence upon other nations.

During the sixteenth century, however, mercantile ideas became an instrument to strengthen England's relative position of power within the Atlantic community. The maturation of the English economy was reflected everywhere: in its production of finished goods, in its development of powerful trading companies, in its use of relatively sophisticated financial devices, in the emergence of an indigenous English mercantile community. The practice of carrying on trade in foreign vessels was slowly changing, although English superiority in shipping was not achieved for almost two centuries. This economic maturation was not only largely responsible for the successful expansion of England overseas in the early seventeenth century but determined the agencies of settlement: the joint-stock trading company, the mercantile nature of many colonial enterprises, and the transfer to the English colonies in the New World of a market economy.

The economic revolution of the sixteenth century which transposed medieval, manorial England into commercial, capitalistic England can best be illustrated by the trade in raw wool and in woolen cloth. When the Tudors gained the throne, trade in woolen cloth was already rising rapidly in proportion to trade in raw wool, an obvious reflection of the gradual metamorphosis within England which was to make it a supplier of finished products rather than raw materials, thus converting England from an economic appendage of Flemish, German, and Italian enterprise to an economic entrepôt.

The demand for wool encouraged its production for market, bringing about an agrarian movement known as the enclosures. Enclosures took many forms. Land previously available for grazing by all the people on the manor was diverted exclusively to the landlord. The strip farms characteristic of the medieval manor were consolidated to make land available for grazing. The precise statistical extent of the enclosures has been hotly debated, but few historians disagree with two conclusions: (1) that the movement represented the application of capitalistic practices in agricultural production and (2) that a dislocation of population resulted.

These dislocations encouraged political economists of the period to conclude that England was overpopulated, an assumption resulting in a theory that exportation of people to colonies was a national asset, that the labor of those Englishmen who migrated would be more productive from the point of view of national welfare. Coupled with the theory was the fact: thousands of Englishmen were forced off the land and unwelcome itinerants became a common sight in Elizabethan England, constituting a problem which the Poor Laws solved only in part. Colonies, concluded the poet John Donne, would not only serve as "a spleen to drain ill humours of the body [England], but a liver to breed good blood." The displacement of population produced a group of men and women willing to turn to opportunities in the New World.

Dislocation was not the only factor that created unrest. England's economic transition jeopardized the status of the gentry, the landed middle class. Perhaps the most direct relationship can be seen in the extraordinary general price rise of 350 per cent that began in 1500 and extended until the middle of the seventeenth century, primarily accounted for, so scholars have determined, by the American treasure brought by Spain to the Old World during the sixteenth and early seventeenth centuries. The English gentry, living largely on fixed incomes, could not maintain their customary standards. Moreover, the fear that they would be unable to offer their sons opportunities equal to theirs provoked individual crises. For example, John Winthrop, first governor of the Massachusetts Bay Colony, listed the limited opportunities for his children as an important reason for his decision to emigrate.

Another factor of supreme significance was the emergence of the English commercial classes. At the beginning of the Tudor reign, the Italian and particularly the German merchants, the Hanse, controlled the major proportion of the English trade. Indeed, the German merchants received special concessions enabling them to pay less duty than English merchants on goods brought into England. During the sixteenth century the control of the foreign merchants was reduced. By 1550 the Venetian merchants were shunted aside, and during the reign of Queen Elizabeth the Germans were forced to relinquish their favored position.

On the other side of the coin, an indigenous English mercantile community was achieving maturity. The Merchant Staplers, organized as early as the thirteenth century to market specified commodities through a designated port, foreshadowed this major development, but the Merchant Adventurers, a semicorporate group that protected individual merchants primarily engaged in the cloth trade, demonstrated decisively the vitality and determination of the English enterpriser. After 1550 chartered English joint-stock companies flourished; the Muscovy Company (1555), the Levant Company (1581), and the East India Company (1600) represent perhaps the best known and the most prosperous enterprises of this nature, but the full statistics of several hundred companies large and small in existence by 1600 gives a better measure of the dimensions of the entrepreneurial spirit. Charles M. Andrews has correctly stated that the English colonial empire was built upon the foundations of the English trading empire, or more accurately the trading experience of the second half of the sixteenth century. The chartered company, a commercial instrument virtually unknown at the beginning of the Tudor reign, became the principal instrument for planting colonies in the seventeenth century, and the commercial, capitalistic tempo of early seventeenth-century England was transplanted to America, not the medieval, manorial environment of the late fifteenth century.

It seems idle to suggest that expansion had to wait until the early seventeenth century because of economic reasons. By the end of his reign, Henry VII (1485-1509), through diligence, shrewdness, and parsimony, had become a wealthy monarch; his son and successor, Henry VIII (1509-1547), after confiscating the church lands, had the funds necessary to finance limited expansion. But these monarchs directed their attention to more immediate issues. Henry VII was engrossed in the establishment and consolidation of a dynasty, and Henry VIII was caught up in a political-religious revolution at home. Their immediate successors, Edward VI and Mary Tudor, were preoccupied with domestic issues, notably the insecurity of their position during a period of transition. Only during the time of Elizabeth (1558-1603) did English interests begin to turn outward. Domestic preoccupation and deliberate decisions involving the centralization of political authority, therefore, determined when expansion was to take place.

An instrument used by the Tudors to strengthen the dynasty and to unify England was Parliament; the decision to seek the support of Parliament resulted in a dramatic change in the balance of power of England's political institutions which produced lasting effects quite beyond the intentions of the Tudors, reaching eventually into the English colonies in America. The vital concept of representative government and a limited monarchy was transplanted to the New World by emigrating Englishmen, a perspective not shared by Europeans migrating to colonies established by other countries.

The catalyst for this dramatic development in English constitutional history was the break between Henry VIII and Rome, marking the formal enlistment of England in the ranks of the Protestant Reformation, the consequences of which produced more than a century of religious upheaval within England itself and gave to the English colonies within the Atlantic community a distinctive character that was to permeate the entire history of what was to become the United States of America. The Protestant Reformation, beginning unofficially in the fourteenth and fifteenth centuries with clerics such as John Wycliffe and John Hus and beginning officially in 1517 with the defiant act of Martin Luther at Wittenberg, Germany, in issuing the Ninety-Five Theses condemning the church, spilled over into every aspect of life in the Western world in the sixteenth century. Initially, the consequences of Luther's action had relatively little effect upon England. Although some learned men read Luther's numerous pamphlets and writings with approval, Henry VIII, who had mounted the English throne in 1509, barred the literature of the Reformation from his court. Eventually Henry VIII modified his position, not because he was convinced of the rightness of the Reformation, but because the movement presented him with unexcelled personal advantages: it allowed him to free himself from the bonds of an unpromising marriage and to remarry with the object of fathering a male heir to the throne, and it enhanced the monarchical authority by making the King the ecclesiastical as well as the civil sovereign.

Disappointed that Catherine of Aragon had not produced a male heir to the throne, and knowing that she was incapable of bearing additional children, Henry sought a solution to his dilemma. Attracted by an Englishwoman, Anne Boleyn, the King in 1527 applied to the Pope for an annulment of his marriage on the grounds that the marriage tie had never been properly sanctioned. The Pope, under the influence if not the dictate of Charles V of Spain, the nephew of Catherine, refused Henry's request.

In 1529 Henry VIII summoned Parliament; Parliament's role in the ensuing crisis produced a constitutional revolution that historians of Tudor England frequently designate as the turning point in English history, government by consent rather than government by decree. Whatever the degree of "revolution," the importance of this reviving and strengthening of Parliament can scarcely be overestimated from the point of view of the colonies, for it meant that the concept of government by consent was transplanted to the New World. The image of Parliament would forever be the mirror into which the colonies would look to judge their own performance.

The constitutional revolution separated England from Rome, created a national Church, and placed the King at the head of the Church. Parliament, guided by the King, acted against church abuses. As early as 1531, in a convocation of the clergy, the clerics were forced to acknowledge the King as the Supreme Head, with the modest qualification "as far as the law of Christ allows." A year later, in an act entitled the Act in Conditional Restraint of Annates, Parliament approved the request of Henry VIII to prevent the payment of certain fees to the Pope, transferring such payments instead to the Crown.

In the years that followed, Parliament passed a procession of enactments to create a national church: the Act for the Submission of the Clergy (1534); the Act Concerning Ecclesiastical Appointments (1534); the Act Concerning Peter's Pence and Dispensations (1534); the famous Act of Supremacy (1534), making the monarch without reserve the Supreme Head of the Church; the Act of Succession (1536), giving the King a relatively free hand in deciding upon his successor, one of the objectives being the preservation of the new Church establishment; a series of acts confiscating, initially, the small church monasteries (1536) but eventually reaching out (in 1539) to secure all the church lands, thus placing in the King's hand one sixth of the land in England, valued at hundreds of thousands of pounds.

These events reflect not merely the whim of Henry VIII but the fundamental change in the structure and pattern of religious and political-religious development in sixteenth-century England. Fundamentally, the break with the Catholic Church was a political act, a means to an end, the end being the centralization of political authority. No longer were the English people faced with a divided loyalty, a political loyalty to the Crown as head of the secular State and a religious loyalty to the Pope as head of the

Church. Now these offices were united in a single person, the King, the secular and ecclesiastical head.

Three underlying forces help to account for Henry VIII's success in creating a separate English religious establishment without a revolt among the populace: First, the Church of England during Henry's time did not represent a marked departure from the religious beliefs and the doctrinal convictions and conventions held by the Catholic Church; for the average Englishman the major change was not in the daily religious practices and rituals, but in the oath of supremacy acknowledging the King as Head of the Church. Second, the groundwork for the English Reformation had been prepared by widespread dissatisfaction with the practices of the Catholic Church. In this regard, the evidence suggests that Henry VIII was a follower rather than a leader. Third, the indefinable but significant rise of national feeling, of discontent with a status of economic dependency in Europe, resulting in the elimination of the Italian and German mercantile interests, had its ecclesiastical counterpart in the Reformation in England.

The Reformation in England permanently influenced the character of the English settlements in the New World. Like any revolution, the Reformation, once started, was difficult to stop. In specific terms, the Church of England represented only a slight departure from the Catholic Church. The Puritans, an impassioned and vocal minority, believed that the Reformation had stopped short of its goal. They advocated additional reforms within the Church of England. The separatists, the "left wing" of Puritanism, took the position that each congregation should become its own judge of religious orthodoxy. In the seventeenth century "freethinkers" such as Quakers took an additional step asserting that each individual was a church unto himself. By advocating this position, they threatened all religious organizations, bringing upon themselves abuse born of fear and insecurity. The separatists represented a potent political threat, for in defy-

ing the centralization of religious authority, they stood, by implication, opposed to the centralization of secular authority. In
the eyes of the Crown, the separatists were fully as dangerous to
the political-religious establishment as the Catholics.

This religious fractionalism was reflected in the English colonies at the outset, making them distinctive from the colonial
establishments of Spain and France. Except for the colony of
Virginia, the first English colonies—Plymouth, Massachusetts
Bay, and Maryland—were products of the divisive forces created
by the Reformation within England; these colonies embodied a
diversity in religion, primarily Protestant in orientation, which
characterized the peoples in the English settlements and the nation they eventually created.

England's colonizing activities of a half century were consum-
mated by the establishment of the colonies of Virginia (1607)
and Plymouth (1620), two English footholds in the New World.
Previous expeditions, notably those of Sir Humphrey Gilbert to
Newfoundland and Sir Walter Raleigh to Virginia, had been
encouraging, but they failed. Why did earlier colonizing attempts
fail, and why did Virginia and Plymouth succeed?

The preoccupation of the Tudor monarchy, the concentrated
effort devoted to strengthening of the nation-state, and the transition in English religious and economic life provide a ready
answer, but the specific expeditions, particularly those of Raleigh
(Gilbert's effort, though it established a precedent, was, after all,
short-lived), reveal that the prospective colonizers were the pris-
oners of fifteenth-century England. In preliminary planning and
in implementation, these expeditions failed to employ effectively
the new instruments, the new monies, the new zeal, and the new
conditions developing in Tudor England. Raleigh's charter was
principally a proprietary grant. The acquisition of land was to
serve as the magnet for settlers, and despite all of Hakluyt's
propagandizing on the usefulness of colonies to "rayse trade,"

the colonizing concept in practice was essentially the establishment of a self-contained agrarian settlement.

Three separate attempts were made by Raleigh to found a
settlement in the New World. The third attempt, the famous
lost colony of Roanoke sent out in 1587, receives the most attention, but the second expedition, sent out in 1585, was the most
significant. Led by Sir Richard Grenville and Ralph Lane, the
second expedition eventually settled on Roanoke Island. Through
the pen of Thomas Hariot, the author of the first English accounts of the New World, and through the eyes of John White,
whose sketches of the Indians of the sixteenth century were responsible for the Western image of the Red Men, the experiences
of the expedition were recorded. When Grenville returned to
England to secure supplies, he left two hundred men on Roanoke
Island; by the time he returned the following year, Sir Francis
Drake, appearing at the colony after a marauding mission against
the Spanish, had offered to take Grenville's men to England, an
offer they had accepted, even though no unusual hardships were
suffered during their winter in the New World. Grenville left a
token force at Roanoke, but they perished, an omen of the fate
of Raleigh's third and final colonizing effort.

The more elaborate undertaking of 1587 included women and
children. Their governor, John White, returned to England,
expecting to bring back fresh supplies the following spring
(1588), but this was the year of the Spanish Armada and help
was unobtainable. When White finally returned to the New
World in 1591, he could find no trace of the colonists who had
been left in the New World four years before, and the legendary
lost colony of Roanoke became a symbol of well-intentioned but
misdirected colonizing efforts.

These colonizing failures reveal the significance of sustaining
a link with England and the folly of using outmoded techniques
to plant a settlement. Once the link with England was broken,
either by misfortune or inadvertence, the colony withered and
died. A proprietor, a Raleigh, or even a combination of pro-

prietors, lacked the resources and experience to sustain a New World settlement.

That the first attempts to found a colony were made before the English defeat of the Spanish Armada in 1588 suggests that this dramatic clash was not a prerequisite to English colonization; instead, the defeat of the Armada was an indication of growing English power, a growth which lifted the expectations of English enterprisers who looked to the New World, encouraged theorists and publicists to urge the Crown to play its proper role in the expansion of the Atlantic community, and spurred the efforts of the established English trading companies in competing with other commercial areas of the world.

The story of the establishment of a colony at Jamestown in 1607 is, fundamentally, the narrative of a business enterprise seeking to trade in the New World for self-enrichment and for the glory of England, two objectives seen as indistinguishable. But the adventure also reflected the prudent employment of the techniques made available by the transformation of the sixteenth century: the joint-stock company, the mercantile experience of the important enterprisers, and the role of local government. In 1606 James I, by a single charter, established the London and Plymouth Companies, the London Company to receive the land between the 34th and 38th parallels and the Plymouth Company between the 41st to the 45th parallels, the intervening space subject to colonization by either company. The grants extended two hundred miles inland, a restriction eliminated in a second charter of 1609.

Early in 1607 three vessels under the command of Captain Christopher Newport carrying one hundred men and four boys entered the Chesapeake. Captain Newport's background as a veteran of the Mediterranean and Asian trade illustrates the tie between the commercial experience of the sixteenth century with the colonial experience of the seventeenth century. In the same way, Sir Thomas Smith, the leading merchant of the Virginia Company of London also played a prominent part in several major trading companies, including that majestic enterprise, the East India Company, demonstrating the logical relationship between the English expansion to America and to other parts of the globe. In view of England's previous experience, the first group sent to Virginia was not as well equipped for the enterprise as would be expected. A list of the personnel included not only gentlemen who were unaccustomed to hard labor, but craftsmen whose skills were unsuitable to the agricultural tasks confronting the infant colony. Gold refiners, perfumers, and the like were in ample supply, but the number of agricultural workers and tool-makers was limited.

In general, the first settlers followed the directions given by the parent company in London. A settlement was founded on a waterway. It was established in the interior so that the risk of Spanish detection was minimized and so that further explorations and trade with the Indians were encouraged. The decision to settle in a low, somewhat swampy area, however, was not desirable from the point of view of health, and it directly contravened the instructions from London.

From the first, the Virginia settlement was in trouble. Political direction was confusing and the purpose of the colony, though theoretically explicit, was, in practical, everyday operation, disarranged. To administer the day-by-day affairs of the settlement, a local council had been appointed by a council in London composed of influential stockholders of the company. Disputes among the members of the local council, who learned of their appointment only after their arrival when sealed instructions were consulted, arose at the beginning when John Smith was barred from accepting his post by his colleagues on the council. More significant, the principal questions were not satisfactorily answered: What crops should be planted? What explorations should be undertaken? What trade should be initiated? For the first five years of settlement the colony lived in a state of anxiety. Not until late in the second decade of the seventeenth century did conditions improve sufficiently to encourage the hope that the

colony would endure, and not until the colony withstood a
dangerous Indian assault in 1622 was this hope confirmed.

In the main, success was due to the resources of the London
adventurers. Again and again provisions and supplies were made
available to the New World settlers just as conditions within the
settlement appeared hopeless. During these periods when conditions in the colony discouraged migration, thus reducing the
number of immigrants to the infant settlement, the chance of
survival improved, for the large reinforcements of people who
usually arrived short of provisions and after the end of the growing season intensified the problems of maintenance. The "starving time" of 1609–10 is a case in point, for it resulted from one
of the largest migrations to Virginia, coming late in the season
and without sufficient provisions.

Stern and purposeful leadership assumed control of the colony
at a critical stage in its evolution. The first of the strong men
was Captain John Smith, whose account of these years, for all its
misrepresentation, is still important in understanding the development of the colony in the early years. In 1611 Sir Thomas Dale
was given dictatorial authority. The beat of drums ruled the
schedule of each day, summoning the settlers to the fields at six
o'clock in the morning, to morning prayers at ten, to the noon-
day meal, to the fields at two in the afternoon, and to evening
prayers at four.

Until the dissolution of the Virginia Company in 1624, the
enterprise was hard pressed to secure new capital to reinvest in
the Virginia venture. To improve their advantage the company
received a charter in 1609 which included the provision that the
Virginia territory extended from "sea to sea" and in 1612 a third
and final charter included the Bermuda Islands, over six hundred miles off the North American coast. Land without the
capital to develop the land, as enterprisers and speculators
throughout American history were to learn, was almost valueless.
To raise new resources, lotteries were held in England, with only
modest success. The base of stock ownership was broadened by

c

encouraging new investors and by allotting to adventurers willing to go to the New World a share of stock. A trading monopoly was contemplated, but these remedies were inadequate to the task.

A fortunate by-product of the company's effort to strengthen the Jamestown settlement was the introduction of an enlightened and far-reaching governmental system. In 1619, through the efforts of Thomas Smith and Sir Edwin Sandys, the Jamestown settlement received instructions to establish the first assembly in English America, the House of Burgesses. Although the precise instructions have been lost, historians generally agree, after reconstructing the evidence, that every adult male was allowed to vote, including indentured servants. These specifications were far more democratic than anywhere else in the world, including England itself. Meeting in the church building, this first assembly exercised legislative, executive, and judicial authority, but its jurisdiction was naturally confined to local problems.

This example, in 1619, of self-government in the first English settlement in America is an outstanding representation of the impact of the developments within England during the sixteenth century and their direct relationship to the English colonies in America. It would have been unthinkable for the Spanish sovereign in the 1500s to have permitted this degree of self-government within the Spanish settlements and, indeed, almost unthinkable for the England of Henry VII. When the Spanish colonials moved tentatively in the direction of limited self-government in the 1530s, the Spanish sovereign, Charles I, banned representative bodies in the New World. In contrast, the concept of the limited power of the monarch was widely accepted in England by the concluding years of the sixteenth century, and this product of the English mind and experience was transmitted to the English settlements in the form of self-government, an enlightened idea that was eventually to lead to a severance of the tie between mother country and colony.

Self-government was not an American creation; it was an invaluable legacy. The development of self-government in America
eventually took a course divergent from what it took in England,
not, as some historians insist, because Old World ideas were too
impractical for New World conditions, but because similar ideas
planted in two areas of the world are obviously subject to historical experiences peculiar to that area. In the case of Virginia, Englishmen were responsible for the establishment of an assembly;
indeed, Englishmen were responsible for all the original concepts
of self-government, from the Mayflower Compact to Roger Williams' Rhode Island charter to William Penn's constitutions for
Pennsylvania.

When the Virginia Company failed financially in 1624 and the
Crown took over the colony, the company bequest was enduring:
a permanent English settlement in America; a staple crop, tobacco, around which the colony's economy was to be organized;
and finally, self-government. Although the first English settlement in America, made possible by English trading and commercial enterprise in the beginning of the seventeenth century,
was modified by the Crown over a period of more than a century, these three principal factors never changed.

The Plymouth Colony, the northern beachhead of the English
invasion of the New World, was also an outgrowth of English
trading enterprise. The Scrooby congregation in England, devout
advocates of separatism with its underlying threat to the newly
established Church of England and to the Crown, moved to
Holland to escape persecution. Moving first to Amsterdam, the
congregation settled eventually in Leyden. Although the Leyden
congregation had no difficulty in worshipping as it pleased, its
members were dissatisfied. William Bradford, later to become
governor of Plymouth colony in the New World, was explicit
in describing the causes of their discontent. The economic hardships for the English separatists in Holland were so severe, said
Bradford, that men of separatist conviction preferred to remain

in England and be subject to persecution rather than to join the congregation in Holland. Moreover, Bradford declared, the Leyden congregation was concerned about the future of the children, who were leaving the self-contained separatist community, finding opportunities elsewhere, too often, thought the elders, tending "to dissoluteness and the danger of their souls." Finally, Bradford mentioned the desire to propagate the gospel in the New World. None of the reasons given by Bradford can be associated in any way with freedom of worship; only if freedom to worship could be combined with more encouraging economic prospects could the congregation flourish.

How were these impecunious separatists to get to the New World? By using the resources which a trading company could provide. Refusing an opportunity to be transported to the New World under Dutch auspices—the Leyden congregation wished to preserve its English ways and heritage—the Leyden separatists made an agreement with merchants in London. Members of the congregation who agreed to migrate to the New World automatically became stockholders: the toil of one's hands in exchange for a share of stock. Merchants in England could invest to the limit of their expectation of profit, twelve pounds, ten shillings for each share. The price was exacting when the settlers at Plymouth were eventually compelled to buy their way out of their agreement with the London merchants who, from the point of view of the colonists, exploited them unmercifully.

The small band of separatists, self-styling themselves Pilgrims, who boarded the vessel *Speedwell* in Holland for the first leg of their journey, comprised less than one half the Leyden congregation. The full complement of adventurers who eventually sailed from England aboard the *Mayflower* was composed of one-third Leyden separatists and two-thirds company men, the latter including such men as John Alden, hired as a cooper, and Miles Standish, employed to protect the company and the colony.

The Pilgrims arrived much too late in the year to plant crops or to prepare adequately for the experience of a New England winter. The colonists intended to settle on a patent in Virginia, but the landfall of the *Mayflower* was Cape Cod, which some historians maintain was a deliberate attempt by the Pilgrims to avoid the restrictions that Virginia might impose and the fulfillment of a secret objective to settle in New England. However these subtle motivations are interpreted, the *Mayflower* turned south to make for Virginia after landing near the tip of Cape Cod, but foul weather and the fear of reefs along the southern shore of the Cape forced the vessel to return to the shelter of the Cape. Disembarking at Plymouth, the Pilgrim ranks were depleted by one-half during the first winter by deprivation and disease.

Before disembarking, the men aboard ship drew up and signed the celebrated Mayflower Compact which, in essence, extended the church covenant to embrace civil circumstances. "We, whose names are underwritten . . . do . . . covenant and combine ourselves together into a civil Body Politick. . . ." They promised "all due submission and obedience" to such laws and ordinances which might be passed from time to time "for the general Good of the Colony. . . ." The compact was signed by forty-one adults, nineteen from Leyden, sixteen from London, two sailors, and four servants. Because Plymouth was never able to obtain an independent charter, the Mayflower Compact became the foundation of that colony's government.

This document has become something of a symbol of self-government, but the motivation which prompted the signing of the compact has often been misunderstood. Finding themselves in an area without an authorized English government, the Pilgrims, who were outnumbered, feared that their control of the colony might be jeopardized. Without sanction for rules of conduct they wished to enforce, the Pilgrims could easily have forfeited one of their primary objectives for migrating, to establish an attractive separatist refuge free from "licentious conduct," Church of England doctrine, or popish heresy.

Plymouth Colony developed very slowly. The separatist views

of the colony discouraged prospective nonseparatists, and the Spartan economy discouraged fellow separatists. As late as the 1640s, Plymouth Colony could claim only one plow. Domestic livestock was always limited, in large part because scarcity of money prevented the necessary importation of breed stock. Although fur was the only cash commodity of any consequence, the expected revenue from this trade never fully materialized. Yet the Pilgrims clung faithfully to their purpose, never doubting that God's will had placed them and their heirs in the New World, in Governor Bradford's words, "as one small candle may light a thousand, so the light here kindled hath shone to many, yea in some sorte to our whole nation." Plymouth's incorporation within the colony of Massachusetts Bay in 1691, only a few years after the death of John Alden, marked an end of an era. Yet nothing could ever erase the memory of the Pilgrim undertaking, the northern beachhead of England's expansion into the New World.

Virginia and Plymouth were the products of the English trading experience and enterprise, the rise of modern capitalism in England. Virginia as a Church of England colony and Plymouth as a separatist colony were products of the Reformation as it affected England. The seeds of self-government in the House of Burgesses in Virginia and the Mayflower Compact in Plymouth were the products of the constitutional evolution within England of the sixteenth century. These transplanted ideas were eventually to be modified and molded into institutions, in some cases so distinctively as to embody eventually an American character.

2

England Expands Into
Continental America

ALTHOUGH THE SEMINAL THEME during the seventeenth century continued to be the transmission of English civilization to the colonies, the New World environment often influenced the direction of colonial expansion and the development of colonial society. Subtle forces, impossible to measure with precision, operated to create a colonial Englishman who did not live and who did not think precisely as his English counterparts who, as one adventurer asserted, "dare not go farre beyond their owne townes end." Some men came to preserve a changeless structure of beliefs that events in England appeared to endanger. Other men came to pit their lives against the hardships of the New World wilderness, gambling that they could achieve for themselves or their progeny brighter prospects than England presented.

Conditions in the New World influenced the development of the English colonies. Some of these influences operated immediately, whereas others operated over centuries. Waterways and access to waterways often determined the priority, and assuredly the prosperity, of settlement, for watercourses served as a lifeline to the mother country, without which a colony withered and died. The hospitable harbors along the Atlantic coast, with majestic inlets and numerous navigable rivers, invited settlements: Cape Cod, the port of New York, Delaware Bay, Chesapeake Bay, and Charleston Harbor. By the same token, reef barriers along the Atlantic coast south of Virginia permanently influenced the development of North Carolina, and the absence of protective harbors along the Jersey coast placed that colony in an unhappy dependency upon the ports of New York and Philadelphia, a factor which explains, in large part, New Jersey's position on many intercolonial issues—including its support in 1788 of a strong national government.

Navigable rivers determined the location of many settlements and the depth of inland penetration for at least a century. In Virginia, colonials clustered around the rivers flowing into Chesapeake Bay—the James, the York, the Rappahannock—in order to facilitate the transportation of tobacco to market. In New York, Albany, although located some 150 miles upriver, was founded immediately after the Dutch arrived, whereas many towns a few miles from the coast line were not founded for a century because land travel was impractical. In Massachusetts, where the rivers were too shallow for extensive upriver transport, towns were bunched near the coast; western Massachusetts was more accessible from Connecticut, the Connecticut River serving as a convenient artery into the interior, thereby affecting the economic and political character of the region.

The Fall Line, marking the end of the inland sweep of coastal plains, also affected interior settlement. The Fall Line extended less than one hundred miles inland in the New England area, whereas in the lower South it extended several hundred miles inland. As a result, the settlers in Carolina, although a half century late in colonizing, were the first to penetrate deeply into the interior of the North American continent. Traders from South Carolina had reached the Mississippi by 1700, a feat not duplicated by other colonies for several decades.

Conversely, the continental shelf, the underwater ledge extend-

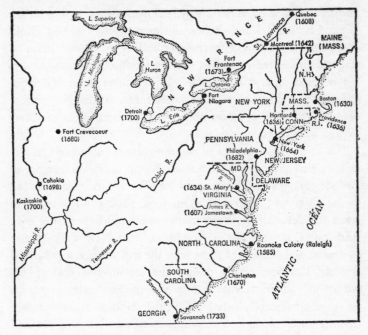

Early English Settlements in North America

ing into the Atlantic Ocean, was broadest along the New England–Newfoundland–Nova Scotia coast line, narrowing along the Middle Atlantic coast, to broaden once again in the South Atlantic waters. Adjacent to New England, the cool Labrador currents, in combination with the continental shelf, provided a natural habitat for a variety of fish, primarily cod, again affecting colonial development by making fisheries and the sea the cornerstone of mercantile operations in New England in the same way that plantation agriculture was the base of capital formation in the Chesapeake colonies.

The massive dense forests, so striking as to capture the attention of every explorer and traveler, produced an environment of fresh-water abundance and plentiful timber products, fully as influential in the life of the colonial settlers as the lack of water and trees was to be in the life of later Americans settling on the Great Plains. Fuel and shelter, the exposure of the Log Cabin Myth notwithstanding,* were dependent upon timber; commercial enterprise—the fur trade, lumber products, and naval stores —was based on a vast woodland. On the other hand, the abundance of trees discouraged intensive farming, making the conventional agricultural practices of England impractical in the New World wilderness.

The forest was a barrier to communication and travel. As late as 1723, Benjamin Franklin, leaving Boston to try his fortunes in Philadelphia, traveled by water to New York City, then overland to the Delaware, where he again took passage on a vessel to reach his destination. Water routes were much preferred over land routes. In 1701, Sarah Knight took the New York–Boston post road, and because of its novelty the trip merited a published account. Communication during the seventeenth century between an individual colony and the mother country was as strong and frequently stronger than the communication between colonies—note the lack of communication between Virginia and South Carolina—reinforcing the principal relationship, colony-mother country. Improving communications in the eighteenth century was one of many factors that strengthened intercolonial ties.

Climate and soil were important, although the degree of their influence is frequently overrated. It is true that the English colonies were a giant agricultural experiment, that the climate prevented the production of those staples most wanted by colonial planners—such as citrus fruits, mulberry trees for the silkworm—and that the climate encouraged production of maize in all the colonies, making it the chief cereal in the American diet. Yet it is as highly debatable to suggest that the combination of harsh climate and rocky soil produced a "New England character" as to suggest that a warmer climate and more fertile

* Frame houses rather than log cabins sheltered the first settlers. Log cabins were first introduced in the middle colonies later in the seventeenth century.

soil in Virginia and the Carolinas were destined to lead to large landholdings, secularism, and slavery. In fact, the concept of a self-contained religious community might more easily have been sustained in an area of agricultural plenty, because fisheries and trade, which developed in New England, led inevitably to outside communication, eroding intellectual, social, and religious isolation. The purpose propelling colonists to migrate to New England and the type of land system that was developed to subserve this purpose produced the distinctive community character; soil and climate were, at best, secondary factors. On the other hand, soil and climate were probably more influential in the Chesapeake colonies, where the objective of each settlement was ill defined. Settlers accommodated themselves to the natural environment, for they were not motivated to create a selective environment which they could control.

A part of the wilderness setting was the American Indian, whose influence upon colonial society is at once obvious and yet subtle. Whereas a small number of Spanish conquistadors under Hernando Cortez were able to dominate Mexico by conquering the Aztecs, who held lesser tribes in subordination, the English in North America faced a different situation which produced a decidedly different result. Powerful Indian tribes blocked the westward expansion of the English settlers: the Hurons in the triangular area between lakes Ontario, Erie, and Huron; along the spine of the Appalachians, the Iroquois in New York and Pennsylvania, the Susquehannas in Pennsylvania and Virginia, the Cherokees in the Carolinas; in the Mississippi valley below the Ohio River, the Chickasaws and, farther south, the Choctaws. And there were many other tribes interspersed throughout. However, no single nation had achieved ascendancy; to subdue one was not to subdue all. From the beginning, the English treated groups of Indians as separate nations or separate tribes, never as subjects of the Crown. Warfare and negotiation involved two nations, England and the particular tribe or nation in question. In contrast to the fusion of cultures that took place under the Spanish colonial system, the white and Indian cultures remained separate in English America, a policy that profoundly influenced society.

Moreover, the most powerful Indian nations in English America did not dwell along the Atlantic seacoast, so that the first white settlers from England faced the weaker tribes, often those who were on the periphery of power. As a result, the tribes near the coast were frequently more friendly, or, if warlike, more easily defeated. If the Indians had allied themselves to drive the English from North America at any time during the first half century of colonization, they could have succeeded. Lack of will, of unity of purpose, not an absence of power, explains the turn of events.

The limits to the Indian level of culture contributed to this indecision. Although the Iroquois and the Cherokees, for example, had relatively sophisticated political organizations and fairly advanced economic systems, they had not achieved a status equal to that of the Aztecs of Mexico or of the earlier Mayas. In consequence, as the white man moved inland, the Indians yielded territory—slowly, it is true, but unmistakably—until the Indians, in combination with the natural defenses of the Appalachian Mountain range and the presence of New France west of the Appalachians, were able to erect a formidable barrier that slowed expansion westward for a good part of the eighteenth century.

Remembered today is the Indian with his blanket, his simple pottery, pans, and trinkets, and his ornamental war paint; this image represents the Indian of the nineteenth, not of the seventeenth, century. English trade gave the Indian the blanket that replaced his coat of fur; English trade furnished the iron kettles that replaced his useful but crudely constructed cooking utensils; and, the final irony, English trade supplied the war paint to adorn the bodies of the Indian brave. It is often assumed that from the moment the English settlers arrived, the Indians, pushed aside by the white man, began moving west. In the seventeenth century and early eighteenth century, certain tribes, attracted by English goods, moved east *toward* the coastal plain rather than west toward the mountains. By falling under the spell of English commerce, the Indians contributed stability and strength to the white settlements, and thus contributed to their own downfall.

Conditions in the New World, ranging from waterways to Indian warriors, from physiographic features to forests, influenced the formation of colonial society.

Into this wilderness environment the English settlements in New England, led by the Massachusetts Bay Company, expanded. The Massachusetts Bay Company formed in 1629 was the product of a decade of development. First, the outmoded proprietary colonizing organization of the Plymouth Company was replaced by an enterprising joint-stock company, led by men of experience and purpose: the Council for New England, composed largely of landed proprietors, void of merchants, was created in 1620 by a charter from the Crown. The common mode of implementing a proprietary organization—issuing patents to influential individuals with the expectation that they would plant colonies—had failed, for no individual had the capital or organization to sustain a colony. In 1623–24, the newly organized Dorchester Company received authorization from the Council for New England to fish and trade in the area, and in 1626 this company founded a small, somewhat marginal settlement at Salem, used largely by fishing fleets to dry their nets, although a number of semipermanent settlers, including women and children, established homes. Except for this modest migration, the Dorchester Company was not successful; but prominent Puritans within the Dorchester Company foresaw the possibility of founding a Bible Community in the New World, using the company form of organization as the instrument. Encouraged by this prospect, in 1628 a group of Puritans organized the New England Company, which obtained a patent from the Council for

New England. Led by John Endicott, an advance group of colonizers, Puritan in faith, took tentative steps to found a Bible Commonwealth.

Several considerations threatened to undermine the experiment: the disposition of land granted by the Council of New England was so confused that it placed land titles, including that of the New England Company, in jeopardy; the degree of independent political authority to be exercised by the New England Company was uncertain; and, finally, the colonizers feared that additional support from other Puritans in New England would not materialize. To avoid insecurity of land titles and to clarify the issue of independent political authority, a new company was formed in 1629, the Massachusetts Bay Company, which received a charter directly from the Crown, thereby eliminating the Council of New England as an intermediary. Composed of three principal groups—merchants and fishing magnates of the Dorchester Company, a small selection of London merchants, and a number of the Puritan gentry—the stockholders of the company possessed the power to govern the colony, including the right to elect a governor, lieutenant governor, and eighteen assistants to serve as the day-to-day ruling body.

To assure the Puritans of control of the colony's destiny, a document known as the Cambridge Agreement was signed by Puritan stockholders who agreed to migrate to the New World, provided the charter was legally transferred to America. This provision was crucial. For some reason which historians have been unable to discover, the charter awarded to the Massachusetts Bay Company, either because of an oversight or because of some clairvoyant principal in the company, did not specify that the document should be retained in England. Yet the location of the charter determined the meeting place of the company stockholders, and thus the location of the seat of power. By taking the charter to the New World, the Puritans assured themselves that they alone would control the Massachusetts Bay Company. If the charter had remained in England, the danger would have been ever present that merchants hostile to the Puritans would acquire shares of stock, gain control of the colony's management, and create conditions intolerable for the colonial Puritans.

Although the establishment of a Bible Commonwealth was the principal purpose of the Massachusetts Bay Company, individuals involved in the migration were attracted to the enterprise for a variety of reasons. In a pamphlet prepared by John Winthrop, who was to become governor of the colony, emphasis was placed upon the availability of the land, upon trade, and upon staples in the New World that would be important in trade.

Winthrop was personally motivated by a number of considerations. First, he believed that the success of the Puritan plantation depended upon the quality of leadership of those Puritans willing to migrate, and he was sensible enough to recognize that he belonged to this select group. Second, Winthrop believed that his economic position in England was deteriorating. As a member of the gentry class whose income was largely fixed, he was hard hit by the inflationary price rise. Third, Winthrop experienced a sense of personal frustration. He was convinced that his talents were not fully employed in England and never would be; in Massachusetts his energy and capacity, he reasoned, would find expression, which proved to be an accurate prediction. Fourth, the future governor was sincerely moved by the purpose of the settlement, the establishment of a Bible Commonwealth; and, fifth, Winthrop's wife and children were disposed to migrate to the New World. Winthrop left such a full record that his motives can be thoroughly documented, but there is every reason to believe that he reliably represents the main body of Puritans, who, within the larger purpose of creating a Bible Commonwealth, were impelled as well by individual considerations.

The migration of the Puritans to the New World was the largest single expedition in the history of seventeenth-century English colonization. In 1630 seventeen ships, carrying more than one thousand persons, provisions and supplies, livestock and equipment, sailed for Massachusetts. England had taken more than a century to match the first major Spanish migration led by Nicolás de Ovando in 1502.

The Puritans set to work immediately to create a prosperous commonwealth, for they were never beguiled by the notion that it was in the nature of man to substitute the life of the spirit for food and for opportunity. A lively trade in furs and, to a lesser extent, in lumber products, diversified farming, and an extension of fisheries, begun before the Puritans reached American shores, together with the introduction of modest manufacturing, transformed Massachusetts into a thriving colony, though scarcely an opulent one. The new settlements in Massachusetts never suffered a starving time as did Virginia or a winter of horror as did Plymouth. In part, this favorable beginning was the result of intelligent, extensive preparations and planning on the part of the Puritans. In part, the result reflected the experience of the first settlements which educated latecomers to the problems and perils of New World establishments.

Significantly, the great migration to Massachusetts marked a definite turning point, a maturity, in the history of English colonization in America. From this date forward, English settlements ceased to be a gamble. It is somewhat ironical, therefore, that Massachusetts Bay was the last colony to be founded as a company enterprise, in large measure because the first colonies had not proven to be profitable ventures. English commercial interests could invest more advantageously elsewhere. The influence of the company enterprisers was permanent, none the less; they were responsible for the creation of three thriving settlements, and they transplanted to English America the spirit and basic institutions of commercial capitalism.

With the purpose of the Massachusetts Bay Colony clearly defined—to set up a Bible Commonwealth based on Puritan religious beliefs—transplanted English institutions and concepts were employed to achieve this objective: political practices based on English precedent, economic practices based on English experience and theory, and a social and intellectual framework carried from England.* Yet disagreement arose because Puritan beliefs were subject to debate; the noblest theories must accommodate to human frailties and everyday practice.

Transferring the charter to the New World had placed the government of Massachusetts Bay in the hands of the governor, the lieutenant-governor, and the seven assistants who migrated, for they were authorized, under the terms of the charter, "to make, ordeine, and establishe all manner of wholesome and reasonable . . . statutes," subject only to the restriction that these statutes not be repugnant to the laws of England. Such limitless power to be exercised by a few men raised many questions. A substantial body of Puritans in the colony, in excess of one hundred adult males, had no voice in the colony's management. Confronted with this problem, the Puritan leaders made two decisions. First, Winthrop and his colleagues, at a general meeting of the settlers in 1631, agreed to enlarge the base of government by altering the meaning of the term "freeman." Whereas it was previously used to designate a stockholder in the Massachusetts Bay Company, the term now was to designate those who were eligible to be citizens of the colony with the power to vote and hold office. The freemen, now citizens rather than stockholders, elected the assistants, who, in turn, were transformed into a legislative assembly. The assistants together with the governor and the lieutenant-governor made up the General Court. Second, membership in the church was to serve as basis for freemanship. Making political participation dependent upon church membership fulfilled the principal objective of the colony, to found a Bible Commonwealth, but it also seriously strained, if it did not violate, the terms of the charter.

Twentieth-century Americans, accustomed to easily acquired church membership, find the demanding requirements for church

* New England Puritanism and an analysis of the social-political framework it inspired is discussed at length in Chapters 3 and 4.

membership in Massachusetts Bay difficult to comprehend. To be received as a church member, a man was compelled to prove before his doubting neighbors that he was God's elect. Consider the town of Dedham, whose record begins in 1637. Some thirty families, about 120 persons, originally settled near Dedham, many of them strangers to each other. Weekly meetings were held, usually in various homes, to discourse and consult upon the questions related to a peaceful civil society and to a spiritual communion. Although an understanding of the elemental questions affecting the civil society—on a local not a colonial level—was reached with relative ease, the establishment of the church society required two years of meetings and soul searchings.

To form a church, seven pillars, that is, seven men, had to be selected to serve as the core of the congregation. In Dedham, John Allin was urged to become the first candidate and he in turn chose a neighbor, Ralph Wheelocke, as the second candidate. The two men opened their "spiritual conditions" to each other and, finding mutual approval, selected a third and a fourth man until ten candidates were picked as candidates for appointment as the seven pillars. At this stage, after much fasting and prayer, each man appeared before the people of Dedham to reveal his spiritual experiences, to recount his sins, to bare his soul. After deliberation and prayer, the seven pillars were chosen. One man failed to win acceptance because of "rash carriage and speeches savoring of selfe confidence"; another was judged "too much addicted to ye world"; still another man failed to win approval because he had sold meal in excess of the accepted price. Repentance failed to save him, and he was considered unfit for foundation work and dropped "with grief." To the seven pillars who were chosen an eighth was added, and these men, in a "sweete consent of judgment" drafted a covenant announcing the establishment of the church of Dedham. More meetings followed, in which men of Dedham testified as to the "breathings of their souls after Christ," thus entering the church and eventually the body of the electorate.

Historians, following the lead of J. T. Adams, frequently assert that the right of becoming a freeman, obtained only by church membership, was restricted to the minority of male settlers, but Samuel Eliot Morison and more recently Edmund S. Morgan have suggested that in permitting 116 persons to become freemen in 1631, the authorities—Governor Winthrop, Lieutenant-Governor Thomas Dudley, and the assistants—were probably including most if not all of the adult males in the existing colony, exclusive of servants.* As the tide of migration swelled during the decade, the number of adult males excluded from political participation probably increased, but the research on this point has been so badly in error in the past that a final judgment cannot be made. Church membership, and thus freemanship, did become more selective until internal resentment and the threat of interference from England forced the door of church affiliation ajar.

It should be noted that suffrage based on church membership applied only to colony-wide elections and thus to colony-wide issues. In local matters participation did not necessarily depend upon being a freeman. In many towns nonfreemen as well as freemen voted, and sometimes nonfreemen held local office. What proved to be an interesting and little understood phenomena was that some church members refused to become freemen, presumably to avoid the duties and responsibilities which being a freeman entailed.

In 1632 the freemen gained the power to elect the governor directly, and in 1634 a most significant step was taken when the freemen in each town were empowered to select two or three from their number, designated as deputies, to represent them in the General Court. The deputies gained the right to participate in legislation, including the right to levy taxes, previously considered within the competence of the governor, the lieutenant-

* Morison and Morgan are much closer to the truth than Adams. Morgan's estimate is perhaps a bit generous, if the contemporary formula for estimating population is applied, that is, four times the number of tithables.

governor, and the assistants. These deputies continued to be elected annually by the freemen.

Although Governor John Winthrop had encouraged the extension of freemanship, he fought tenaciously but without success against the next logical step: permitting the freemen to elect deputies to represent them at the General Court. This step, in Winthrop's judgment, granted too much power to the deputies; for this opinion, Winthrop paid a price, the temporary loss of the governorship.

A revolution by the freemen or by their deputies was not, however, in the making. The General Court, composed of the deputies, the assistants, the lieutenant-governor, and the governor, made church attendance compulsory in 1634, solidifying the Puritan church-state establishment. Another landmark was reached when a bicameral legislature was instituted in 1644, the upper house composed of the governor, lieutenant-governor, and the assistants and the lower house composed of the deputies. For legislation to be enacted a majority vote was needed in both houses; each house thus held veto power over the acts of the other.

By the 1640s Massachusetts had completed the metamorphosis from a chartered trading company into a self-governing Bible Commonwealth. It had also been responsible, either directly or indirectly, for the formation of additional New England colonies, constituting the first sectional grouping in American history.

Maryland, the extension of England's settlement in the Chesapeake area, marked a departure in English colonization. The instrument of settlement was a proprietary grant rather than a joint-stock company, and the composition of the colony was more diversified than the other colonies, which were generally characterized by a homogeneity of background in religion and in social thought.

George Calvert had been granted the title Lord Baltimore by James I, despite Calvert's decision to adhere to Catholicism, which forced him to resign as the King's principal Secretary of State. An investor in the Virginia Company and in the New England Company, Calvert had originally succumbed to the contagion of colonization in an abortive attempt to plant a settlement in Newfoundland (1627), but because of the bitterly cold winters he turned his attention to a more hospitable climate. He attempted to obtain a land grant in Virginia, but his religious affiliation and his refusal to take the Anglican oath of supremacy forced him to leave the colony. The outcome was a direct grant from the Crown in 1632 to the northern half of Chesapeake Bay, with a westerly boundary on the Potomac River. The colony was called Maryland in honor of the Queen. The extent and location of the grant annoyed many Virginia planters and stirred up resentment which was to linger for the better part of a century.

Ample precedent existed for the extensive grant of power given to Baltimore. As proprietor he was given exclusive title to the land to be disposed of as he wished; exclusive rights in the trade of the colony; political sovereignty tempered only with the admonition that Maryland laws must conform to those of England and be enacted with the "advice, assent, and approbation of freemen," a term presumably to be defined by the proprietor. Gilbert, Raleigh, and to a lesser extent the Council for New England, to mention the most obvious examples, had enjoyed these privileges, only to have them evaporate as their colonizing schemes collapsed. Maryland, however, was a success, and the mother country was to learn that a prospering proprietary with such extensive powers could contravene the best interests of the Crown and country.

The first Maryland contingent, sponsored by the second Lord Baltimore because of the death of his father prior to the fulfillment of the project, settled at St. Mary's, an attractive region of high bluffs with a good anchorage and fresh water. Supplies were purchased from Virginia where the welcome was warmer than expected; in addition, the colonials raised a crop of maize before winter. They made immediate use of rude shelters and cleared land vacated by the neighboring Indian tribes who had sold their land to the colony and moved south of the Potomac to avoid harassment by their enemy, the Susquehannas.

Maryland was planned as a refuge for Catholics as well as an income-producing property for the Calverts, but from the outset more Protestants than Catholics came to the colony. The artisans and agricultural laborers were primarily Protestant, whereas the leadership of Maryland and the most prominent families were Catholic. Some religious rivalry appeared, but no serious problems arose until the middle of the century. In fact, serious religious bigotry, which took the form of the persecution of Catholics by Protestants, was largely an eighteenth-century phenomena. Early in the life of the settlement several priests of the Jesuit order acquired excessive land grants for the church, but Lord Baltimore personally intervened to curtail the ambition of the clerics.

Maryland's success as a proprietary rather than as a joint-stock operation depended on several factors. First, the stability acquired by Virginia after a quarter century enabled it to assist the new settlement. Second, Maryland was located in a sheltered area, where Indian hostility and the problems of an exposed frontier were minimized. Third, by the early 1630s, merchants had learned that colonies were overrated as investments, and they looked to more lucrative enterprises. Fourth, the Puritan migration of 1630 marked the dividing line between colonies as joint-stock enterprises and colonies as outposts of empire. After 1632, with the founding of Maryland, the King frequently gave land to his favorites to promote colonies for the benefit of England rather than granting this privilege to companies. Parenthetically, mention should be made that the willingness of imperial authorities to validate the Maryland enterprise was the result in part of England's desire to counter the Dutch activities in New Netherland and elsewhere.

Lord Baltimore administered his colony with skill. He was

particularly successful in anticipating developments in England and in the colony which threatened to damage the growth of the settlement. According to the terms of the charter, the proprietor was the sole source of authority, legislative and judicial, but in practice the institutional framework responded to the realities of New World environment, with the result that the organization of government gradually began to resemble that of Virginia.

Lord Baltimore appointed his brother Leonard as the first governor, who, with three advisors, was to rule the colony according to the instructions he provided. Within three years of the founding, an assembly had been called; by 1638 the assembly had taken a stand rejecting "legislation" sent over by Baltimore, proposing instead that, until the will of the proprietor be known, the assembly frame the laws. Although the governor refused to accept this proposal, the assembly, in the ensuing years, gained limited power. And although the proprietor continued to initiate, he was seldom able to win acceptance of his proposals without modification by the assembly. In certain cases, the proposals of the proprietor were blocked altogether.

The term "freeman," that is, those permitted to vote, originally included all adult males, but eventually. as the number of indentured servants increased, the possession of land defined the qualifications for suffrage. A novel practice arose in which freemen, if they were unable to attend the assembly session, gave their voting proxy to another member. In 1641, for example, Giles Brent, a planter with political talent, held sufficient proxies to control a majority of the votes. The practice of proxies, as a result, was abandoned.

New England rather than the Chesapeake region experienced the greatest expansion in the first half of the seventeenth century. During the decade 1630–40, twenty thousand men and women migrated to New England; in 1640 only six thousand colonials lived in the Chesapeake colonies. The explanation for this unequal growth lay primarily in England, where Puritan-

ism was on the rise but where its expression was curtailed by
ecclesiastical as well as political authorities. To publish Puritan
views and to follow Puritan practices invited reprisal. Massachusetts Bay in particular and New England in general were
recognized as havens. When Puritanism gained supremacy in
England during the 1640s, migration to New England abruptly
declined.

The direction of expansion in New England was mainly determined by two factors, geography and the rigorous religious
conformity required of colonials living in Massachusetts Bay. Accessibility to the Atlantic waterway definitely dictated coastal expansion into the areas that became known as Rhode Island,
Connecticut, New Hampshire, and Maine. The valley of the
Connecticut River, for example, offered fertile fields for farming.
The valley also had the advantage of a direct water route to England and a protective waterway to Boston, the economic hub of
New England. The issue of religious conformity in Massachusetts also affected the character of New England expansion.
Groups from England coming to New England were sometimes
diverted from Massachusetts Bay upon arrival when they realized that they would play secondary roles in the formation of
policy. Moreover, dissenters from within Massachusetts Bay,
many of them extremely articulate, contributed to the expansion
of English settlement.

Despite the heroic efforts of historians such as Charles M.
Andrews and Perry Miller to set aright the conditions controlling
action at the time, no point seems to be more misunderstood
among historians of liberal thought in America than the character of these dissenting groups. The dissenters of Massachusetts
Bay were not moved by a concern for freedom of religion, by a
humanistic movement in religious life and thought, or by a dis-
taste for religion passionately and vigorously practiced; on the
contrary, the issue, from the point of view of the dissenters, was
in many cases the impurity, the imperfection, of ecclesiastical and
civil polity in Massachusetts Bay. As viewed by the most per-

sistent dissenters, the Bay Colony was too worldly, too ready to compromise truth. In their judgment, Massachusetts authorities failed to read the Biblical injunctions correctly.

The two principal figures associated with forced migration from Massachusetts Bay, Roger Williams and Anne Hutchinson, amply illustrate the principles that were at issue. Roger Williams, because of his even-tempered, charming, persuasive personality, enjoyed a remarkably loyal following not only in Massachusetts Bay but also in Plymouth Colony. William Bradford's estimate of Williams has often and properly been quoted: "A man godly and zealous, having many precious parts, but very unsettled in judgmente." Williams had arrived in Massachusetts in February 1631, and been offered a temporary post as teacher in the Boston church, for which his training in divinity at Cambridge University in England made him eminently suitable. But he refused the post on the grounds that the congregation had not repented of its former practice of attending services within the framework of the Church of England, thereby worshipping with the unregenerate. As Williams asserted, "I durst not officiate to an unseparated people."

Williams was a separatist of the most virulent type, a contagion that was eventually to impel him, along theological lines —and the word "theological" should be underscored—to religious isolation, and to cause his eventual banishment from Massachusetts Bay. Throughout his career, Williams remained an outspoken Calvinist, untiringly inspirited with the doctrines of predestination, irresistible grace, and the perseverance of the saints. His quarrel with the churches of Massachusetts Bay, and even with the separatist colony of Plymouth, was that they failed to adhere faithfully in practice to the teachings of the Bible and to the rigorous tenets of the Calvinist theology.

Massachusetts Bay, in the eyes of Williams, was acting out a gigantic hypocrisy. The churches of Massachusetts Bay, in failing to renounce completely the Church of England with its devotion to the concept of an unregenerate and regenerate membership, were falling short of pure Christian principles. Moreover, the civil magistrates, by enforcing the Ten Commandments, violated the essential concept of congregational church polity. By 1634 Williams was publicly preaching that the King's patent to lands in the New World was invalid—he called the King a "liar"—thus bringing into question the security of individual land titles in Massachusetts Bay. He also resumed his contention that the authority of the civil government in religious affairs defied scriptural evidence, and he found the Massachusetts churches so imperfect that he asked his Salem congregation to renounce the other churches of New England for their many unseemly religious practices but particularly for permitting the unregenerate to worship with the regenerate, that is, God's elect, the natural outcome of compulsory church attendance. Following his theological probing to its logical conclusion, Williams arrived at the conclusion that if the church in Massachusetts was impure, the obvious solution was to withdraw from it and to form a church composed of regenerate members only. But who could truly prove that he was numbered among this select group? This question tested the most lucid mind. Finding an answer impossible to determine, Williams eventually took the position that he could be assured of only two regenerate people, his wife and himself.

These theological principles expounded so fervently by Williams contained consequences for the colony and for the man. The authorities in Massachusetts were taken aback by the heretical views on the impurity of the Puritan colonial church, the plea for separatism, the denial of civil authority in religious affairs. If each congregation could decide upon its own objectives, if separatism were unleashed, the commonwealth would be shattered. The response of the magistrates was to banish Williams from the colony in 1635, though apparently John Winthrop's timely, secret warning saved him from the more ignominious fate of being shipped to England. Williams in mid-winter fled to the Narragansett region where the colony of Providence, under his guidance, was finally founded.

The consequences for the man were equally, if not more, momentous. Williams' theological isolation forced him to acknowledge that a "pure" church was an unobtainable goal; each man was indeed an island. So he reacted in what to him seemed the logical manner. No church could attain purity; therefore, all faiths striving toward purity should be welcomed. In the words of John Winthrop, Williams, "having, a little before, refused communion with all, save his own wife, now he would preach to and pray with all comers."

In a sense, therefore, Williams backed into the principle of religious freedom, not as one who would liberalize religion, but as one who would strive for a purer faith. His approach and his solution were theological. In his time, Williams was neither considered nor recognized as an advocate of religious liberty, but he was adopted by later generations, who more often than not misunderstood his premises, as the prophet of religious liberalism.

From the point of view of the Massachusetts Bay Puritans, Anne Hutchinson also fell into dangerous courses. The wife of William Hutchinson, Anne Hutchinson arrived in Boston in 1634, a voluble woman of spirit, superior intellectual gifts, and a dominating personality. She quickly attracted followers who came to hear her weekly and semiweekly discussions of theological questions. Her model was the Reverend John Cotton of Boston, who received her blessing—which eventually proved a curse—as one of the few ministers in the colony who was definitely included in the covenant of grace, one of the men assured of a place in heaven, a distinction she also granted to her brother-in-law, John Wheelwright. She hinted that the remaining clergy fell under the covenant of works, men as yet unproven as God's elect.

Anne Hutchinson and those who followed her were labeled antinomians. Defined in terms of theology, antinomianism asserted that God could be immediately and directly revealed to an individual without previous application of good works and without intervention of the clergy. Defined in terms of Massachusetts Bay, antinomianism meant someone who challenged the existing clerical and civil establishment.

To the twentieth-century mind, the convolutions of the Puritan theology appear alien; occasionally modern historians have dismissed the contention over fine points of doctrine as so much froth, hiding more deep-seated motivations and obscuring more significant long-term developments. But these disputes over theological issues must be examined and comprehended, for they represent the language in which the issues of the day were discussed. In the case of Anne Hutchinson, the issue concerned the acceptable framework for the ecclesiastical-civil society. The discussion of this issue centered on a theological question, preparation for grace. Could grace be received by instantaneous conversion? Or was a period of preparation required? If instantaneous conversion were possible, preliminary preparation such as church attendance, sessions of prayer, and living a Godlike life were not prerequisite to achieving God's grace. Conceivably a man could live licentiously and, by the magic of conversion and divine revelation, become, at an instant, God's elect. Under such an interpretation, the Bible Commonwealth, the city on a hill, would be smashed. Moral and spiritual conduct inimical to the purpose of the undertaking would have to be tolerated, for a man living in sensuality and sin, punishable under the laws of Massachusetts Bay, could become God's elect. A nonchurchman could be numbered among the regenerate, for present conduct was not a prediction of future salvation.

Such a dangerous doctrine, undermining the tenets of the civil religious establishment, required radical measures. Anne Hutchinson, after a public prosecution in which she skillfully parried her critics until boldness tripped her into the heresy of confessing that her convictions were obtained by "an immediate revelation"—God speaking directly—was banished from the colony.

This brilliant, talented, harassed woman first fled to Portsmouth (1638) and eventually to Long Island where, in an Indian uprising, she was killed. But Anne Hutchinson was also to join the American pantheon, though she, no doubt, would have shuddered to learn that in defying the Puritan magistrates she was opening the door to freedom of religion so broad in scope as to tolerate agnostics.

Although the expansion in New England is associated with Roger Williams and Anne Hutchinson, congregations under other leaders account statistically for the substantial majority of people who migrated. William Coddington and his followers founded Newport; Samuel Gorton, who was banished from Massachusetts Bay, and his group settled at Warwick. Despite the enmity between them, Newport and Warwick combined with Portsmouth and Providence to secure a charter for Rhode Island in 1644, reconfirmed in 1663. Thomas Hooker led his Newton (Cambridge) congregation to Hartford, Connecticut, in the summer of 1636, and two other congregations from Massachusetts migrated to Windsor and Wethersfield to supplement preliminary settlements. In 1638 John Davenport and Theophilus Easton established the colony of New Haven, to which surrounding settlements became attached. Connecticut, including New Haven, eventually obtained its charter in 1662. Within a five-year period, 1635-40, the English settlements in New England, confined originally to a small segment of its eastern shore, spread along the Atlantic shore line as far to the southwest as New Netherland and northward into New Hampshire and Maine.

The expansion of New England is worthy of several brief observations. First, the dissenting elements, represented particularly by Roger Williams and Anne Hutchinson, constituted a minority segment of the total expansion. Second, historians have justifiably emphasized the minority migration because of its association with principles of religious liberty that were to develop later. Third, the expansion of New England would have occurred in the 1630s even if Roger Williams and Anne Hutchinson had not lived, and the direction of that expansion along the Atlantic coastal waters and inland along the inviting fertile river valleys would have been identical. Fourth, expansion was carried out chiefly by church congregations, even those not involved in the internal disputes of Massachusetts, thus giving all of New England a religious character. The dissenter groups, indeed, were often more zealous than the Puritans of Massachusetts Bay. Fifth, group migration, the religious character of the migration, the intercommunication between settlements, and the mutual dependence upon trade gave New England an overall unity. New England can properly be called a section as early as the middle of the seventeenth century, whereas the Chesapeake colonies cannot be properly called a section until very late in the eighteenth century or early in the nineteenth century.

3

Englishmen Transplanted

WHEN THE FURNISHINGS of the English mind and the fabric of English social, political, and economic institutions were transplanted to the American colonies, a subtle screening process eliminated some institutions incapable of transmission. The new environment modified many other institutions during the course of the seventeenth century until the transplanted Englishman became, in the eighteenth century, the provincial American. In the simplest acts—the cultivation of crops and animal husbandry —the pattern of change was immediate, and its outline is relatively easy to delineate. In the area of social structure, social values, upward mobility of status, economic change, and local judicial-political institutions, the information is limited and the work of historians in some cases has been so scanty that only educated approximations rather than precise assessments can be made.

The earliest accommodation to New World conditions involved the simple acts of sustaining life. Old World grain could not at the outset of colonization be grown in the soils of the New World, so Indian maize was substituted as a staple cereal. Englishmen were accustomed to raising sheep, and in some measure cattle, but in the New World the colonials were forced to depend heavily upon pork for meat. Cattle and particularly sheep required extensive care and protection, while the pigs, tough-skinned and corpulent, could defend themselves against the elements. Corn presented in a variety of forms, such as cornmeal and corn bread, together with salted pork became staples in the American diet for two centuries, the direct result of the early adjustments to New World conditions.

What was true of animal husbandry was equally true of farming techniques. Because of the shortage of labor and capital and the abundance of land, extensive farming was practiced. Instead of clearing the land, which would entail excessive labor costs, trees were girdled, causing them to die; then the dying timber would be burned to afford a clearing. Trees or stumps were seldom removed, for this process required additional labor. Seed, usually corn, was planted around the stumps by poking a hole into the ground with a stick and dropping in fertilizer, often a dead fish, with the seed. The elaborate cultivation practiced in England—plowing, harrowing, and careful preparation of the soil for seeding—was impractical in the New World. If the practices carried on in the settlements exhausted the fertility of the soil in a short time, no one was concerned, for the supply of land appeared, in relative terms, to be limitless.

As late as the eighteenth century, the colonials were criticized for being wasteful, but in reality the charge was quite meaningless. Compared with the New World, land in England was scarce, labor was abundant, and capital was available. These factors were precisely reversed in the New World, where no money could be spared to invest in tools or equipment, where labor was dear, but where land was abundant. Therefore, land was exploited to save scarce capital and labor. Fundamental conditions, not indolence or improvidence, made exploitation an American characteristic.

The ownership of land was treasured in England. Even merchants who acquired wealth in trade bought land to confirm their newly won position of privilege. In English America, where land was the principal resource, its acquisition and its distribution profoundly influenced the development of the New England and the Chesapeake colonies.

In Massachusetts Bay, land was distributed in townships, a procedure imitated by the other colonies of New England. A group of people, usually a church congregation, petitioned for a grant of land from the General Court, the Massachusetts legislature. If the grant was approved, it was given in fee simple, meaning that it was granted without any restrictive feudal obligation. A township was created, and a community or village was established within the township. After a portion of the land had been set aside for the village green, for the church, and occasionally for a school, town lots were distributed in a variety of ways: by sharing equally; by portioning according to need, with large families receiving a larger lot; and, more rarely than would be expected, by awarding the lots according to economic and social station. Outside the village, but within the township, lands were allotted for farming and grazing. Individual titles were secured, but the essence of the system was the preservation of a community.

The method of distributing lands in Massachusetts Bay served as a powerful check, a censor in a sense, upon religious deviation. The land grants were made by the General Court; the General Court represented the views of churchmen. Obviously the chances of a nonconformist obtaining a land grant were few if any. Control of the colony and preservation of its purpose was maintained by controlling the distribution of land.

In the Chesapeake colonies land was granted to individuals instead of to groups. The colonists took up settlement separately rather than in villages, following the contours of the waterways, the essential link with outside markets and sources of supply. Procedures varied slightly in the distribution of land, but these conventional steps were generally followed: A man interested in obtaining land requested a warrant from either the governor's office or the official clothed with the governor's power of granting warrants. A survey was made, and, if confirmed, the land patent was granted.

The system was open to abuses. Surveys were carelessly made;

E

on occasion this step was eliminated altogether. A grant of fifty or one hundred acres, when finally surveyed decades later, was frequently found to include many times the amount of land specified in the grant. Aggrandizement of land by favorites of the officials was not unknown, although this development was far more characteristic of the early eighteenth century than of the first settlements. Disputes were endless, because boundaries were defined in vague terms—a group of trees, a clump of stones, a tributary, a trail, many of which became unidentifiable within a few years. In Virginia, as in many other colonies, the law required the property owner to walk his boundary every few years to counter the unreliable definition of boundaries, but despite this precaution, land titles and boundary disputes were staple fare in county courts for two centuries.

Headrights became the most advantageous avenue to the acquisition of land in the Chesapeake colonies. During the final stages of the Virginia Company period, a man who agreed to migrate to the New World was automatically rewarded with a grant of fifty acres of land. After Virginia became a royal colony in 1624, this concept was gradually enlarged so that a person who brought in servants or slaves was entitled to the fifty-acre headright per person. Abuses were widely practiced. Ship's captains received headrights for persons transported; if the individuals involved were servants, their masters would also claim headrights, thereby instituting a system of multiple grants. By making the journey many times, a ship captain could accumulate substantial landholdings, and some of the early Virginia positions of privilege were gained in this way. Maryland imitated the practice of headrights, for land was almost the sole resource available to attract colonists. Whereas land was granted in fee simple in New England, quitrents were required in Virginia and Maryland. Quitrent was a feudal remnant in which the grantee paid an annual fee to the grantor, frequently a sum of two shillings for each hundred acres. It is often mistakenly suggested that quitrents were seldom if ever paid. Quitrents, in fact, served as an important source of revenue; although a definite study has not been made of quitrent revenue, sample investigations indicate that quitrents were paid much more often than not, despite the obstacles placed in the way of sheriffs, whose duties included collection of the quitrent, and the chicanery practiced by owners in using devices to keep their property off the quitrent rolls. It was not uncommon, for example, to change ownership on a piece of property just before the quitrent could, by law, be collected.

Historians are agreed, especially after the researches of Thomas J. Wertenbaker in Virginia, that the amount of land granted to individuals in the Chesapeake colonies during the seventeenth century was small. The word "plantation" (connoting to the nineteenth- and twentieth-century mind a staple-producing, market-minded agricultural unit of the ante-bellum South) has in itself been misleading, for any grant, whether it constituted twenty-five acres or a thousand, was called a plantation in the seventeenth century. Grants in Virginia and Maryland were, however, larger than those given in New England, although the reservation must again be made that only a small proportion of any grant in the Chesapeake colonies was cultivated. A man could clear only a few acres of land a year. To have more than five or ten acres under cultivation during the middle of the seventeenth century was rare.

In the Chesapeake colonies, the land system constituted the law and the prophets because it determined the development and direction of most social, economic, and even intellectual institutions; the exploitation of land led to a privileged status and to wealth. In New England the land system constituted a buttress and a shield, for the law and the prophets had already been revealed in the ideal of a Puritan commonwealth founded on the principles of a utopian Biblical community. In New England the land system did not dictate the New England town or determine the development of the Puritan ideal; rather, the Puritan ideal dictated the New England town and land system.

Once adopted, the implications of the New England land system were outreaching. The town became the center of life. The church, the spiritual core, was readily accessible to all residents, and the proximity of settlement enabled each person not only to enjoy the conversation of his neighbor but to watch his spiritual well-being, a powerful sociological check upon behavior; no man wanted doubt cast upon his right to be included within the divine covenant. Social life and family life was grouped around the town. Children played on the village common. School attendance was made easy, although chores or work in the fields occasionally kept students from their books. Families visited, worked, and prayed together. The town served as the base of political representation. The town system of land distribution reinforced the central purpose of the commonwealth, the establishment of a covenanted people.

Contrast this system with the experience of Virginia and, to a more limited extent, Maryland where settlement was decentralized. Churches as well as schools were difficult to attend because of the distances involved. Irregular school and church attendance became the common practice, and a second generation of colonial-born, without knowledge of the practices and customs of school and church in England and with little or no experience in the colony to guide them, often remained unknowing. An itinerant clergy became a Chesapeake institution.

Without towns to serve as centers for a social life, a sense of community was created by entertaining guests for extended periods, the beginning of the celebrated Southern hospitality that placed special emphasis on the home. As an economic and social elite developed in the Chesapeake colonies, the architecture of the family residence, still gloried in by tourists of the twentieth century, reflected the emphasis on the plantation home as the center of social life. Other substitutes filled the absence of a physical sense of community: Sunday church meetings, a prim and solemn occasion in New England, became for the Chesapeake colonies—when people attended—a day for business, for conversation, and for frolic and fun, in part because the Anglican faith did not discourage such use of the Lord's Day, but in large part because of infrequent community-wide social occasions; court day, when decisions on local issues such as boundaries and the building of roads were made, combined good company with necessary business.

Despite the social disruption attending the migrations of peoples to America and the temporary disorganization produced by starving times and other immediate experiences of the wilderness environment, the family, as the basic social organization, was strengthened in the Chesapeake colonies and in New England, although the forces molding the role of the family were quite distinct. The family as a social unit was, of course, a characteristic transplanted from England, but in early Virginia, with the emphasis on the migration of males rather than families, the danger of changing the role of the family was decidedly present, a far cry from New England, where family migration was encouraged from the outset, and if a married man arrived without his spouse, he was generally ordered to bring her to the New World as soon as possible or return to England.

Puritanism prided itself on family devotion and family cohesiveness, second only to God's love as man's earthly treasure. A host of Puritan concepts were involved in elevating the importance of the family. The family was, after man's fall into sin, the Christian answer to social organization, the "mother hive" out of which more advanced institutions, the church and the state, issued. A man and woman married not out of passion or romance, a reference to earthly lusts and idolatry, but out of a rational love. Of course, this concept suited the rationalization of marrying within one's own social and economic station, as valid a practice for non-Puritans in England and the Chesapeake colonies as for New England. The Puritans conceived of the family as the social unit to train and educate children for God's grace and to train and discipline servants, a concept not unrelated to the role of the family in the Chesapeake colonies. Puritanism held that the family was not merely a handy social organization to provide for material considerations but primarily a spiritual center, and the layman was frequently admonished for being "very careful for the shine, and take[ing] no care for the foot."

In the Chesapeake colonies the family as the principal cohesive, social force was preserved by the scattered method of settlement. The family was isolated and by necessity made the social and economic unit of the colony. As in New England, not only the children but the servants, and eventually the slaves, were considered a part of the plantation family, whose care was entrusted to the owner, the head of the household. Care included food, shelter, clothing, training in skills, and religious as well as secular instruction. In the Chesapeake colonies, though migration by families seldom occurred in the earliest settlements, the legacy of English family life survived the first abrupt modification by the wilderness environment, to flourish under a regime of isolated settlement.

Of course, during the seventeenth century the attractions of cheap land close at hand encouraged children to move away from the homesite to try their fortunes elsewhere. As a result, the family circle was usually reduced in size from that of its English counterpart and perhaps the tie of family kinship was somewhat weakened. This development of children settling elsewhere to form their own families was to become characteristic of an expanding America. However, it is easy to exaggerate the differences between the family in England and in America; the family homesite in the seventeenth century, in many cases, was still the family homesite in the eighteenth.

The land system in New England and in the Chesapeake colonies also affected the role of the artisan. As ships' lists show, workers with a great variety of skills arrived at the English settlements in the early years, but the labor supply in New England during the seventeenth century, in general, differed from that of the Chesapeake colonies. The town system made available a ready market for the talented artisan—bootmaker, blacksmith, or cooper. Indeed, if a town lacked a workman with these skills, the conventional practice was to advertise for such a person, often offering inducements of a house, a grant of land, or even a modest initial subsidy.

The scattered settlements in the Chesapeake colonies during the seventeenth century created conditions that made it nearly impossible for the skilled workman to practice his trade. The market for the service he provided was decentralized. A skilled workman could become an itinerant, traveling from plantation to plantation to ply his craft, but this unattractive prospect encouraged him to migrate where his prospects were more attractive, notably town-centered New England. The Chesapeake region, as a result, was forced to develop its own skilled labor force. Some of the men and women brought in as indentured servants were assigned tasks that would develop them as skilled artisans, such as bricklayers or cobblers.

Indentured servants were common to both New England and the Chesapeake, although in proportion to population, indentured servants are more properly identified with the Chesapeake colonies. In exchange for their transportation to the New World, these people sold their services for a given period of years, seldom less than four and seldom more than seven. The procedures followed in these contracts varied. The money for transportation was sometimes advanced by a colonial who engaged a factor in England to obtain an indentured servant. Ships' captains often carried boatloads of migrants unable to pay passage to the New World, and upon arrival, sold their services. Convicts were also brought to the colonies, although this form of labor became more common in the late seventeenth century and early eighteenth century. Hired servants accompanied the first settlers; fewer servants seemed to accompany later settlers, although the evidence is not conclusive. Many servants eventually entered the mainstream of colonial life, becoming responsible citizens in their community and occasionally achieving elevated political positions.

The land systems introduced into the New England and

Chesapeake colonies varied because of a difference in social objectives; once adopted, the land systems became a historical factor that affected many phases of colonial life, in many instances forcing modification of conventional practices and customs.

The colonial economies of the New England and the Chesapeake regions contrasted rather sharply in detail, although in general English capitalism affected both areas. In each case, production for market became a predominant theme. New England, using its resources to best advantage, entered into enterprises based upon shipping and fisheries; the Chesapeake, utilizing its resources most effectively, developed a marketable staple, tobacco. In one case, capital was applied to trading enterprise; in the other, capital was applied to agriculture.

The pattern and development of these two economies merits attention, for, once established, the pattern was fixed for two centuries. In many respects, Massachusetts Bay was the offspring of maritime enterprise, and therefore it is not unexpected that traders were active in the decade preceding 1630. Yet this commerce was a rather feeble affair. When the Puritans migrated to New England in such overwhelming numbers between 1630 and 1640, several of the saints (another term for the elect), most of them more experienced in the life of the gentry than in the life of the merchant, engaged in trade. A brief spasm of fur trade brought profit to a few, but by the second decade of settlement this commerce subsided. Minor merchants reaped small profits as distributors of imports from England, and other enterprisers, searching for some way to obtain a marketable commodity, convinced English investors to support industrial ventures, notably the Saugus Iron Works.

The pattern for future trade, based on the export of fish, began to take shape in those decades when England was involved in civil discord, 1640–60. Indeed, English preoccupations at home gave Puritans in New England an opportunity to explore the establishment of fisheries, previously dominated by merchants in

England. In time the Puritan populace would have turned to such an obvious resource, but the precise timing was prompted by the vacuum created by conditions that forced the retrenchment of English merchants after 1640. Twenty years later the New England fisheries were strong enough to withstand competition.

By 1660 a merchant group, including prominent Puritans, had developed in New England, a group whose influence was to increase in importance and power. The direction of trade was clearly evident. Finished products, chiefly owned by English merchants, were imported from England, and outgoing staples, particularly fish but occasionally lumber, were shipped to the English West Indies, an area whose economic productivity and specialization had leaped forward between 1640 and 1660. Sugar was shipped to England from the West Indian islands, to complete the circle of trade. The early trade was frequently advanced by fellow Puritans from England who had settled in the West Indies.

The trade was fully dependent upon England for capital, for credit, and for trading experience. For the Puritans who wished to fashion and preserve a Bible Commonwealth of Saints, this intrusion, welcomed in the interests of economic well-being, often served in practice as a secular wedge, of which the Puritan fathers were properly suspicious. Edward Johnson in his *Wonder-Working Providence,* published in 1654, reveals:

> . . . whereas He [God] hath purposely pickt out this People for a patterne of purity and soundnesse of Doctrine, as well as Discipline, that all such may finde a refuge among you, and let not any Merchants, Inkeepers, Taverners and men of Trade in hope of gaine, fling open the gates so wide, as that by letting in all sorts you mar the worke of Christ intended.

But the wedge was widened as the years advanced, for the merchant-enterprisers of New and Old England were riding the wave of the future, the surge of modern capitalism, while the Puritans were caught in the swirls of the past, religious rather than secular supremacy. The issue, however, was not by any means decided at so early a date. The years were to witness intense controversy over this point; finally, theological thinking was rationalized to accept the world of enterprise as it was.

Trade in the Chesapeake colonies in the early years offers a distinct contrast to New England. A marketable commodity was developed early, and trade quickly became the lifeblood of the colony. But no merchant group developed in the Chesapeake to administer the trade. The reason for this does not lie in the people who came or who were interested in the colony. Virginia was, after all, an offshoot of English commercial enterprise. The explanation rests, fundamentally, in the geography of the region and the patterns that developed because of geography. Once established, these patterns were not easily changed.

The waterways, the Chesapeake Bay itself, and the numerous rivers which emptied into the bay, permitted a direct link with England. An oceangoing vessel could anchor near the wharf of the colonial planter, his tobacco easily loaded aboard ship. The planter corresponded directly with the merchant in England, from whom he purchased goods, or with the merchant's agent, who accompanied the vessel to the New World. Credit was secured on the basis of the year's crop. If the current crop was not sufficient to pay for the goods the planter wanted, credit was extended, in anticipation that the planter's next crop would be ample to meet present and future obligations. As a matter of course, the planter was then forced to buy through the merchant to whom he was indebted. His choice of correspondent, indeed, his bargaining power, was seriously undermined.

So began the pattern of Chesapeake trade. Not until an expansion of population later in the seventeenth century forced new planters to settle *near* rather than *on* a navigable river did the need for an intermediary arise, either for the distribution of goods imported or for the export of tobacco. With the wave of migration and issuance of new land grants late in the seventeenth century and in the beginning of the eighteenth century, the larger planters on the navigable rivers became planter-merchants, a trend that foreshadowed the development of an individual merchant class later in the eighteenth century.

The development of a merchant class in New England as well as in the Chesapeake rested upon the premise of a back country. In Massachusetts, oceangoing vessels could not penetrate the interior; thus the need arose for the services of merchants in residence along the seacoast, Boston serving as the hub. In Virginia, the services of a resident merchant were unnecessary because the English merchant had a direct tie to the producer-consumer.

In the seventeenth century, the transplanted Englishman in America lived in a society whose social framework resembled that which he had known at home, but the extremes of the English social structure had been eliminated. The top level of society, the nobility, did not migrate. Their status at home, based on extensive landholdings and the accident of birth, gave them a position of privilege. Members of noble families held political positions of responsibility at the pleasure of the King. Although the nobility was as frequently troubled by debts as by opulence, and infected by boredom and even dissipation fully as often as by a contagion of creativity, they had little or no incentive to migrate. Occasionally an adventurous younger son, whose prospect for inheritance was slim and who saw little virtue in the traditional careers of the church or the military, left for America, but in the main the families of privilege remained at home.

At the other extreme, the lowest class in English society, the idle and the destitute, did not migrate because they did not have the means. This social group, of course, ranked lower than the Pilgrims, who were poor, and thus required financial aid, but who were not destitute. Not until the introduction of indentured servitude was it possible for a man to sell the future work of his hands to pay the costs of transportation. Even then, many Englishmen in the lowest orders of society were unable to qualify as indentured servants.

The English migration to America was, therefore, composed of the middle and lower classes. The leadership in this migration, especially in New England, was frequently supplied by the gentry, country gentlemen whose estates ranged from a few acres to substantial landholdings. In England the gentry comprised the backbone of government, forming the largest single group in Parliament and controlling many key positions in county government. Obviously, most of the gentry remained in England, content with their lot and their estates. Many English gentry saw greater advantages in allying themselves with the "new" money made by the emerging merchant groups, and their sons, with luck, could always achieve status by positions in the church, in the military, or in the universities. When gentry families did migrate to America, as in Massachusetts Bay, they naturally assumed positions of leadership. Moreover, for the first few decades of settlement they were the topmost group in the society, although in the course of the century they frequently failed to retain this position of prestige and privilege.

The English yeomanry—defined as men who held freeholds with annual incomes of forty shillings, but whose precise qualifications in fact varied greatly from this arbitrary norm—contributed the largest numbers to the migration to English America. If the gentry provided the backbone of the political system, the stalwart yeomanry, men of simple taste who farmed with frugality, provided the tradition of English resourcefulness and nationhood. One of the Western world's outstanding scientists and *the* great man of the seventeenth century, Isaac Newton, was the son of a yeoman. The yeomanry constituted the great middle class of English America in the seventeenth century, and characteristics which have often been extolled as distinctively American—impatience of formality, optimism and self-confidence, capacity for simple but deep loyalties, directness—are identical with those which historians have used to describe the English yeomen.

The English working classes varied greatly, ranging from the skilled artisan, who often made his living as a small shopkeeper, to the journeyman, a semiskilled artisan, from the apprentice learning a trade to the hired servant. Transportation costs to America automatically tended to discourage the migration of the working classes, but the gentry and even yeomen brought servants, and indentured servitude was to provide an additional means to get to America. Since highly skilled artisans were not in great demand in the new settlements, the semiskilled and the servants comprised the larger segment of the working classes who came.

From the beginning, therefore, the structure of society in English America differed from that of the mother country. A screening process determined not by policy but by historical forces operating at the time reduced the range of the social structure by eliminating the wellborn and the impoverished, thereby magnifying the importance of the middle- and lower-class segments of society. Out of this relatively narrow spectrum of society, a social structure rather distinctively American was eventually to evolve.

This is not to say that class divisions failed to be recognized and honored in the first settlements. They were. The son or daughter of a gentry family did not marry below his or her status. A craftsman was expected to live according to his station —but not beyond it. When these barriers were occasionally breached, a cry of protest was raised.

The degree of mobility between levels of the society in the early years of settlement is debatable because studies have not been made with sufficient precision to warrant unequivocal generalization. However, it is clear that indentured servants upon completing their terms became yeoman farmers, that accessible land invited servants to become landholders, that the dearness of labor limited apprenticeship, and that, where apprenticeship was employed, the length of the contract was of necessity reduced.

The most important single determinant in social position by the mid-seventeenth century, regardless of the status of a person upon arrival in America, was possession of land, and its very abundance no doubt encouraged class mobility. Nowhere is this more clearly demonstrated than in the Chesapeake colonies. The vast majority of colonials in that region were yeomen or indentured servants who were able to rise to the status of yeomen by becoming landholders after completing their terms of servitude. It is true that during various crises of the seventeenth century, especially after the Restoration of the Stuarts in 1660 following the Puritan Ascendancy in England, members of gentry families and, more rarely, younger sons of noble families migrated to Virginia, but they acted as no more than leaven to the loaf.

Although a gentry class began to emerge in the Chesapeake colonies, it was made up primarily of men who had risen to this status in America; it was not the English gentry transplanted to America. By the end of the seventeenth century the emerging Chesapeake gentry was beginning to imitate the ways of their English counterparts: encouraging the practice of leisurely learning and taking an amateur interest in science and writing; serving as vestrymen in the Anglican Church, the established church; participating in gaming, sports, and riding; opening their homes to travelers, in part because of necessity but in part to play the role of a country gentleman.

A colonial elite began to develop in seventeenth-century America, but in each colony it was composed of families who over several generations had achieved a modest position of privilege by gaining wealth in America, mostly through land but occasionally, especially in the New England port towns, through trade. The emerging elite late in the seventeenth century, regardless of the colony, was indigenous to that colony and not an English transplant.

Social mobility was affected by the choice of careers in America, which differed greatly from that in England. In England professional advancement could be achieved, for example, through the church, the military, or the law. In America the profession of law was out of favor and in little demand, and the military, based on a militia rather than on a permanent establishment, offered no inducement. Only in New England, not in the Chesapeake colonies, could place and position be attained through the ministry. A number of New England country boys with talent and ambition completed preparatory school, graduated from Harvard College, entered the ministry, and achieved positions of importance. John Wise, for example, a most celebrated divine near Ipswich, was the son of an indentured servant. In the second half of the seventeenth century, business enterprise, especially trade, opened new gates to affluence, but the full force of this development was not experienced until the eighteenth century. In contrast to New England, as noted earlier, a mercantile community failed to develop in the Chesapeake colonies. Men of talent and ambition achieved status through land ownership and tobacco plantations. By the second half of the seventeenth century, indeed, formal learning became less important as an avenue to success in English America. "Culture" was to manifest privilege, once it was achieved.

The transplanted Englishmen also brought to colonial America institutions of local government common to England, but, during the course of the seventeenth century, these institutions were modified. The modifications took different forms. In some instances the jurisdiction exercised by local courts was altered; in others local officials in the colonies gained or lost power as compared to their English counterparts. As has been noted, most of the transplanted Englishmen came from the yeomanry and lower classes, and in America some of them rose to privileged positions at a local level. Frequently they were unfamiliar with the precise duties of local officials in England, never having attained such status before coming to America. As a result, they performed these tasks with an eye to fitness rather than to formality, to practicality rather than to precedent.

In the New England and Chesapeake colonies local government flourished. To trace this development in individual colonies requires more space than this volume allows, but the experience of Virginia offers an excellent representation of the mainstream. Recognition should be made at the outset that the local government of each colony possessed certain special characteristics attributable to its people or its environment, but these individual traits are overshadowed by the massive fact that the practice of local government in English America set the English colonies apart from the colonial establishments of other countries.

As early as 1619 a form of local government had emerged in Virginia, but local government as distinct from colonial government did not take shape until the expanding population forced the creation of subordinate courts to exercise authority outside Jamestown. By 1624 the House of Burgesses passed an act creating two local courts outside the seat of government in order to avoid the expense and inefficiency of bringing the principals, not to mention witnesses, to Jamestown; by 1632 five monthly courts were provided, each court to be composed of commissioners, who were instructed to model their proceedings after those of the justices of the peace in the English Quarter Sessions. Two years later Virginia was divided into eight counties, in character fashioned after the English shires, with appropriate county officials. The county commissioners became known as the county court, and the provost marshal was rechristened the sheriff, after his English counterpart. Within ten years, a system of county courts had been created in several New England colonies, including Massachusetts Bay, and the beginning of a county court system was founded in Maryland patterned in large part after that in Virginia.

The expanding jurisdiction and power of county government is impressive. By 1645 justices of the peace composing the county court in Virginia were authorized to hear civil cases involving any sum of money, but they were the final authority only in those cases in which the amount in dispute did not exceed twenty pounds, approximating the sum which a person could earn in a year. Interestingly enough, twenty pounds was also the limit set for the local courts in New England. At the same time

(1645), the county courts in Virginia were officially authorized to serve as probate courts, although it should be noted that this enactment confirmed accepted practice rather than introduced new jurisdiction. Assigning to the county official such duties as recording wills and deeds and making inventories of estates set a pattern for American history; county courthouses throughout the nation would continue to compile the social record of people's lives from birth to death.

The county court was entrusted with other duties. It became an orphan's court, holding in trust the estate of orphans, or, if the orphan children were destitute, placing them as apprentices or as servants until they reached their majority. The contractual arrangements with an indentured servant were also recorded. Permission was required from the court to move out of the county, a measure to prevent avoidance of debt. To the court belonged the duty of licensing taverns, of enforcing price and wage regulation, of seeing that the roads were kept in good repair, of authorizing ferry service—peculiarly important to Virginia, which was intersected by waterways. Most important, the county courts were to enforce enactments passed by the House of Burgesses. Local government was directly related to colonial government, and men who became burgesses often served an apprenticeship as justices of the peace of the county court.

Obviously, the justices of the peace were important men on the local scene. They were in practice a self-perpetuating body, although they received their commission from the governor. In many if not most cases, they were unfamiliar with the precise procedures of their English counterparts, so they were urged to consult Michael Dalton's handy volume *Justice of the Peace* or some similar instructive book on judicial responsibilities. In the main, however, the justices attempted to apply common sense appropriate to the particular case. They were advised by statute not to trouble about "any imperfection, default or want of forme in any writt" but rather to "give judgement according as the right of the cause."

F

In the evolution of the county court in the colonies, the image held up as a model was always the English county court, but the responsibilities of the New World did not always permit direct imitation. In England, for example, the jurisdiction of the county courts included criminal cases affecting life and limb; in the Chesapeake and New England colonies the jurisdiction of the local courts did not extend that far. As the Virginia House of Burgesses declared in 1656: "Wee conceive it no ease nor benefit to the people to have their lives taken away with too much ease. And though we confesse the same to be done in England, yet wee know the disparity between them and us to be so great that wee cannot with safety follow the example."

Other county officials, such as the county clerk, who recorded deeds, wills, and issued licenses, became fixtures in our history, but in the seventeenth century the sheriff held the greatest power. He collected taxes, for which he was paid a commission; he generally enforced the decisions of the county court. His duties as tax collector made him an especially important person to know. When the position became extremely burdensome in the eighteenth century because of increased population and fewer compensations, the prestige of the office declined.

Of the key officials in an English county, the only one whose position was not duplicated in the New World was the lord lieutenant, the King's military arm. A colonial militia was summoned by the governor and placed under local commanders. In time, the militia frequently elected its own officers. The position of lord lieutenant simply failed to fill a need in colonial America.

What has been observed of the evolution of local government in Virginia applies to the other colonies. In Massachusetts, for example, county courts were established in Suffolk, Middlesex, Essex, and Norfolk within a decade after the founding of the colony. The jurisdiction over cases and the creation of county officials paralleled that of Virginia. In New England, however, the towns rather than the counties were the basis for representation in the colonial legislature; moreover, enforcement of economic regulations and poor relief were also more commonly exercised by the towns.

The consequences of the emergence of local government in colonial America cannot be exaggerated. First, Englishmen transplanted to America agencies of local government which became the base of a complex structure of social institutions that has endured to the present. So pervasive was this influence that even in those colonies which were not originally under English auspices, such as New York, and where local self-government was unknown, the structure of local government was eventually introduced. In those English colonies where attempts were made to deny local government, the attempts failed.

Second, the establishment of local government provided an unshakable base when political storms shook and even altered colonial political institutions. Rebellions might come and go, but local government provided an anchor that enabled the colonials to weather the storm. Indeed, the fact that local government in America has survived a revolution, a civil war, an industrial revolution, and global responsibilities is one of the most impressive yet most neglected aspects in the history of American political institutions.

Third, America's local government in the formative years served a purpose distinctly different from England's. In England local government related the people directly to the central government, to the King and Parliament, and thus acted as a unifying force. In the colonies local government related the people directly to the decentralized provincial governments—not to the King and Parliament. By reinforcing and strengthening the different colonial governments, local government acted as a divisive force within the English empire. In this distinctive role, local government in colonial America planted the seeds that were to produce a provincial American rather than a transplanted Englishman, seeds that were eventually to flower in the American Revolution.

4

The Colonials in an Age of Faith

(IN THE AGE OF FAITH of the late sixteenth and early seventeenth centuries, Western man's relationship to God was not the subject of idle philosophical speculation but the fulfillment of life.) Prayer and piety were devoted to posing searching questions: How does God's grace intervene in the course of a man's life? What degree of free will can man exercise? What is the church? Who is fitted for membership? What is man in the eyes of God? These and like questions had been raised consistently by Christians for centuries past, but in defining the ultimate meaning of the Reformation in England they transcended the boundaries of the life of the spirit to infuse the mind and character of society itself.

This quest was transplanted to English America. Too often historians associate the Age of Faith in the colonies exclusively with New England, but it was equally influential in the Chesapeake colonies, although its manifestation and direction differed. Concern with spiritual questions was common to all the colonies. English religious practices, convictions, and institutions, not the least being the vitality of a vigorous church-state relationship, together with the divisions that existed in the English mind, such as the split between Puritanism and Anglicanism, were transferred to the New World. In New England and in the Chesapeake colonies these beliefs, practices, and institutions were

74

slowly modified under the wilderness environment. Whereas this transformation can often be traced in theological and doctrinal disputations in New England, in Virginia the impact can be best evaluated through church practice. This is another way of saying that, during the seventeenth century, ideas, in a pure sense, played a more significant role in the New England than in the Chesapeake colonies, but that a common heritage bound the English colonials together.

Few subjects in early American history have generated greater controversy than the nature of the Puritan religious establishment in seventeenth-century New England. America's first historians visualized New England as the wellspring of American life, attributing to it every conceivable virtue: hard work, good judgment, faith, uprightness, unimpeachable motives, and the seat of representative government. In the popular mind, the Puritans became the purest of men, the embodiment of all that was best in humankind. Although a few of the nineteenth-century authors, notably Charles Francis Adams, cast a shadow upon this glowing image, a more modern historical view, presented particularly in the debunking 1920s, ruthlessly and supposedly realistically exposed the Puritans as selfish rather than selfless, authoritation rather than democratic, brutal rather than kindly, deceiving and pious hypocrites rather than vessels of faith. These historical "realists" concluded that New England's contribution to the mainstream of American life was not made until the control of the Puritans was broken. In more recent years the Puritans have been the object of a re-examination that attempts to comprehend the circumstances surrounding Puritan society rather than merely to praise or to condemn it. Significantly, in order to gain this fresh perspective, New World Puritanism has been studied in relation to its English roots.

Puritanism in England gained momentum during the latter half of the sixteenth and the first part of the seventeenth centuries as members within the newly established Church of England from all ranks of the society began to advocate the modification of church practice and doctrine to free them from the forms carried over from the Catholic Church. Puritanism cannot be definitively defined, but belief in a conversion experience, a spiritual rebirth, was at its root. Puritanism was radical in religious rather than in social terms. The manifestation of Puritanism in church government, in church practice, and in theological tenets varied greatly, ranging from inspired, extemporaneous prayers as opposed to fixed prayers in the worship service, from self-governing church congregations as opposed to a fixed ecclesiastical hierarchy.

Church government, as a single example, clearly illustrates the spectrum of diversity within English Puritanism. One group of Puritans, the Presbyterians, followed the Calvinistic line of a close church-state relationship in which each congregation would be linked to its counterparts by synods, and each synod then responsible to a general synod. Though a clerical hierarchy was eliminated and churchmen selected their own ministers, policies adopted by the church were to be enforced among the individual congregations by means of the synods. The Presbyterians became identified as the "right wing" of Puritanism because they represented the element which departed least from Church of England practices.

A second group, the nonseparating Congregationalists or Independents, constituted the middle ground of the Puritan movement. They held that the individual congregations should rule themselves, that church doctrine and practice should be enforced by individual congregations and not by a superior church hierarchy, but they also believed, as did the Presbyterian Puritans, in a vigorous church-state tie. Indeed, the Congregationalists and Presbyterians were willing to remain within the Church of England to achieve their reforms.

A third group, the Congregational separatists, the least influential group among the Puritans, believed that the task of reforming the Church of England was impossible. They firmly subscribed to the practice that each congregation was independent and self-governing. Ecclesiastical separation implied secular separation, and the separatists, as a result, were identified as the "left wing" of the Puritan movement.

The differences among the Puritan groups extended quite beyond these external forms. A profound division existed in defining those men and women who should be included in the church membership. The Presbyterians held that the church should include the nonelect—that is, the unregenerate—as well as the elect—that is, the regenerate, the saved, the saints, all interchangeable terms. The Presbyterians found themselves incompetent to judge who was truly God's elect. In contrast, the Congregationalists, the nonseparating as well as the separating, believed that they could identify God's elect and that the church should comprise only the saints, although occasionally they conceded that "Close Hypocrites will creep in." In their view, the church of the invisible saints, God's chosen, and the church in daily operation, the congregation of visible saints, were one.

Puritans of all persuasions believed in the covenant theology, which in essence asserted that God made a contract with man that set down the terms of salvation. God pledged Himself to abide by these terms. This covenant in no way changed the doctrine that God elected the saints, but it explained why certain people were elected and others were not. The terms of the covenant, of course, were to be found in the Bible, and thus it became the rule of conduct. For this reason the Puritans searched the Bible incessantly for interpretation of passages when the meaning of the Scriptures was not self-evident or, in some cases, was contradictory. Each law, each act, each policy, because of the covenant theology, demanded literal Biblical support.

The covenant theology was intimately related to two additional concepts, the covenant of grace and the covenant of works. If a man lived according to God's injunctions as found in the Scriptures, he would give the appearance at least of leading a Christlike life, and he would live according to the covenant of works.

No one, however, could enter into the covenant of grace unless he experienced a conversion, a regeneration, and he could only receive such an experience if he were elected by God. Whereas many men might live within the covenant of works, only a few, presumably all of the New World Puritans, could live within the covenant of grace.

The Puritans in America were composed of the transplanted separatists (Plymouth) and the nonconforming Congregationalists (Massachusetts Bay), which explains why the New England Puritans for more than half a century fought savagely against Presbyterianism, not so much because of its conviction with regard to church government but because of its belief that the church membership should include the nonelect as well as the elect. It should also be noted that although Puritanism was to have a dramatic career in seventeenth-century England, only in English America were Puritan ideas transmuted into a distinct social organization, a wilderness Zion, a city set on a hill. As a result, in New England, somewhat in contrast to England, the covenant theory was applied to an entire community rather than conceived of exclusively as a contract between God and each individual. The Puritans in New England, therefore, considered themselves a covenanted people.

These New England Puritans were not shallow sentimentalists, but tough-minded men and women. They recognized the imperfections of the world; when they came upon evidences of man's infirmities they were not dismayed. The Puritan entertained a peculiar balance of zeal and skepticism. His inner life was dominated by his relationship with God. His external life was, in his eyes and the eyes of his fellows, a constant battle for self-restraint, a constant vigilance against the multifarious pitfalls of man's failings, his avarice, his lusts, his worldliness, his selfishness.

The condemnation of Puritan inhibitions and narrowness is misplaced, for in the Age of Faith most Englishmen were governed by rigorous rules of personal conduct. Puritans were first of all Englishmen, as their political practices, social concepts, and economic activities revealed. In the same way, 90 per cent of the Puritan mind was a reflection of the common mind of all Englishmen and only 10 per cent set the New England Puritans apart. In morals and piety, Anglicans as well as Puritans believed that man was born in sin, to be liberated only by God's grace,* that man was saved by faith rather than by deeds, that a learned ministry was required to find Biblical truth, and that God conversed with man through his revealed word, the Bible, though on this last point the Puritans were more literal and rigid than the Anglicans. The observation can also be made that the Puritans of New England more faithfully represented the English mind of the early seventeenth century, with its strong bent toward Puritanism, than did the colonies of the Chesapeake—in faith, in culture, in intellectual life. The 10 per cent divergence between Puritans and Anglicans included, of course, the elimination of the ecclesiastical hierarchy and making the relationship between God and the individual churchman more direct, a step that eventually opened a Pandora's box.

Although the inner, emotional intensity of the individual Puritan should never be discounted, the emphasis of the Puritan mind in New England was on reason. For the Puritans, scholarly disquisition and searching self-analysis were required. They abhorred an illiterate clergy and illiterate laymen, and they attempted to make provisions so that Biblical scholarship would be preserved. Leaders like Reverend Thomas Hooker and Governor John Winthrop conceded that the fine theological points were

* Whether or not the New England Puritans believed in predestination has been the subject of dispute. The historian Samuel Eliot Morison, relying upon the theory that the Puritans did not live or act as if strict predestination were operative, has suggested that predestination was not among the firmly held views of the Puritans. There is substantial evidence in the Puritan theology, however, to suggest predestination. Historically, orthodox predestinarians seldom act as if they believed what they preached. Although the Puritans consistently cited English theologians such as William Ames, they were Calvinists in the sense that they believed man was born in sin, saved only by God's grace, that God's grace is given to some but not to others, and, therefore, some are predestined to be saved and others predestined to be damned.

sometimes difficult for the layman to follow, but they also agreed that all churchmen should educate themselves in the Bible and attempt to master the fine distinctions of theological inquiry. Because of their premise of a reasoned religion, the Puritans stood firmly opposed to religious enthusiasm. Self-revelation was a degenerative force. God did not speak to just anyone who, thereupon, determined what God did and did not want. This is the pothole into which Anne Hutchinson stumbled; self-revelation could lead to every type of enthusiasm, even to Quakerism, viewed by both the Anglicans of England and the Puritans of New England as a debasement and a defilement of God's plan.

In church government, the Puritans of New England turned to Congregationalism, which is not surprising in view of their English antecedents. But Congregationalism posed a serious problem. If each congregation could make its own decisions with regard to doctrine and practice, the danger of separatism was a persistent threat, indeed, almost an inevitable result. Because of the premise held by Massachusetts Bay Puritans that the colony had established the pure church, the regenerate church, authority to enforce conformity was mandatory. Just as the Anglican Church wished to stabilize its Establishment short of what the English Puritans desired, so the New England Puritans attempted to stabilize and to preserve their establishment short of what some inhabitants of New England desired. Because the Congregational Church polity did not provide a central authority, the Massachusetts Puritans responded by using the civil authority to enforce religious conformity and thus to prevent separatism.

In this context, two terms, "oligarchy" and "theocracy," have been widely used to describe the relationship between church and state in New England, but the term "theocracy," which implies that the ministers held the reigns of power, has been generally and properly discarded, for the civil authority never relinquished control. Not the clergy but the lay leaders, the oligarchy, were primarily responsible for the banishment of the first principal nonconformists, Roger Williams and Anne Hutchinson (Chapter 3). The clergy were expected to teach and instruct, not to govern.

The dangers of nonconformity, therefore, represented a persistent threat not only to the church establishment but to the civil authority. The central fact was that a segment of the people— the size of which is as yet undetermined—who eventually settled in New England supposedly had an inconsequential voice in either the government of the church or the management of civil affairs. In many respects, historians have often distorted the meaning of this disenfranchisement, particularly in the early years when, as noted in the previous chapter, the vast majority of adult males except for servants were eligible to vote.

Indeed, somewhat too much emphasis has been placed upon the people versus the oligarchy. A penetrating examination is yet required to assess the contest for power between the deputies and the magistrates, between the deputies representing older wealth and position and the deputies representing new wealth and power, between one port town and another. The source of discontent in seventeenth-century New England, even with the evidence in hand, does not appear to be massive disenfranchisement. No other group of colonies experienced such an influx of immigrants, despite the fact that as early as 1631 church membership was the basis of civil government.

Valid comparisons have yet to be made between the relative percentage of disenfranchisement in New England during the first three decades of settlement and the situation in England, or between New England and other seventeenth-century English colonies. General comparisons, without benefit of detailed studies, indicate that the percentage of disenfranchised colonials in early Massachusetts was not so disproportionate for the period as has often been assumed.

For example, it is commonly cited that in 1643, when Massachusetts Bay had a population of 15,000, only 1,708 colonials were eligible to participate in colonial government. To translate these figures into meaningful terms, certain factors must be considered.

The population figure included men, women, and children. To ascertain population figures, colonial authorities customarily multiplied the number of tithables by four. Tithables included men between the ages of sixteen and sixty. In the case of Massachusetts Bay, to get a reasonably accurate estimate of those colonials of voting age, that is, men over the age of twenty-one, the total population figure should be divided by four, the result being an estimated 3,750 males between the ages of sixteen and sixty. Assuming the original figure of 1,708 voters to be reliable, probably at least one of every two adult males held the franchise, a high proportion compared with any area in England or elsewhere.

Aside from the episodes of Roger Williams and Anne Hutchinson, which occurred relatively early in the history of Massachusetts Bay, crises to signal that the movement of events seriously outpaced the established religious-political structure did not appear until the conflict with Dr. Robert Child in 1646. The ministers had given serious thought to the question of enlarging the membership of the church as early as the 1640s. Indeed, nonfreemen as well as freemen, you will recall, were permitted to vote in town elections. Many New England men, in fact, did not wish to become freemen. They did not wish to assume colonywide as well as local governmental obligations. The clergy, however, were concerned that the church would become divorced from the main body of inhabitants unless some of the perfectionist qualities—for example, a demonstration before the congregation by a prospective church member that he had undergone the conversion experience and thus had entered into the covenant of grace—could somehow be modified. Some preachers, most notably Thomas Hooker, thought that it would be enough merely to live a godly life, that such a manifestation, not in itself evidence of regeneration, would at least qualify a man to join the church. This issue was to be debated over several decades as the New England mind, represented by its spokesmen, responded to the changing conditions of the New World. Because political as well as church authority was at stake, the actions taken affected both.

Robert Child arrived in Massachusetts in 1645, although he had resided briefly in the colony a few years earlier. Child attempted to correlate the aspirations of the colonials in Massachusetts Bay who were nonfreemen with the emergence of Presbyterianism and toleration in England. He petitioned the General Court to allow the creation of a Presbyterian Church, asserting that if redress were not obtained from the General Court he would appeal to Parliament. This threat to the Congregational Church establishment and to the structure of civil authority in Massachusetts Bay was fought tenaciously by the magistrates. Child's petition was not only defeated, but as he prepared to depart for England, his possessions were seized and searched, revealing that he was carrying a petition to Parliament signed by more than twenty dissatisfied Massachusetts colonials. John Winthrop, in particular, used every ploy to present the action of the General Court in a favorable light to the civil authorities in England so that by the time Child arrived to press his case, his cause was hopeless, in part because in England the Puritan Presbyterians had lost power to the Puritan Independents (Congregationalists).

Two documents of significance were drawn up in 1648 in actions precipitated by the Child incident. The first was a codification of colonial laws, and the second was the Cambridge Platform, which can be described as an ecclesiastical constitution. Agitation by deputies for a code of laws had begun as early as 1635, motivated in the main by the deputies' desire to limit the authority of the magistrates, that is the assistants. Winthrop opposed such codification, arguing that judicial precedents would serve as a proper guide when an individual case arose and that a blanket code might prove inflexible. In addition, Winthrop feared that legislative action in defining a code would meet with disapproval in England and, as a result, that the Puritan cause would be hurt rather than helped. In 1641 a Body of Liberties was approved, and, somewhat augmented, it was confirmed in

1648 as *The Book of General Lawes and Libertyes*. It defined and codified current practice: monopoly was prohibited; land tenure in fee simple was approved; the upholding of moral behavior was clarified by enumerating all punishable crimes—idolatry, blasphemy, and adultery, as well as murder and witchcraft; election of officials by freemen was guaranteed; the relationship between church and state was defined, and civil authority over ecclesiastical affairs was confirmed; and finally, the procedural practice and jurisdiction of town governments was acknowledged.

The second document, the Cambridge Platform, defined the church government of the Massachusetts Congregational churches by "presbyterianizing" them, not in terms of belief but in terms of organization. Individual congregations were to be composed only of saints, in contrast to the Presbyterian prescription of elect and nonelect; yet these congregations were to be governed by synod action enforced by the civil authority: "If any church one or more shall grow schismaticall, rending it self from the communion of other churches, or shall walke incorrigibly or obstinately in any corrupt way of their own, contrary to the rule of the word; in such case, the Magistrate is to put forth his coercive powr, as the matter shall require." Although the Cambridge Platform was adopted in the General Court in 1651, 14 dissenting votes were registered against it, an indication that the deputies visualized a possible curtailment of their own powers through the alignment between the magistrates and the ecclesiastics.

The Book of General Lawes and Libertyes, confirming in writing the rights of individuals and the power of the deputies, seems at first sight to be in contradiction to the Cambridge Platform, which was greeted by the deputies with qualified reservation; however, these documents signify an underlying unity. In both cases, civil and ecclesiastical procedure, formerly taken for granted, were defined in writing, an acknowledgment that the accepted premises were in dispute. Although these documents, especially the Cambridge Platform, have frequently been consid-

ered the high-water mark of the civil-ecclesiastical tie in Massachusetts, it is more valid to suggest that both documents should
be interpreted as signs of weakness, that the civil-ecclesiastical
relationship had, by this date, become seriously endangered. Conformity could no longer be assumed.

The most dramatic adjustment the Puritans made in the
New World was the adoption in 1662 of the Half-Way Covenant by the Massachusetts Synod, confirming an agreement made
by the Ministerial Association in 1657. The Covenant enabled
members of the church, after professing a godly life, to have
their children baptized, and thus associated with the church.
The importance of this concession can only be comprehended if
seen against the backdrop of Puritan theology. A proved conversion experience or demonstrated regeneracy entitled a person
to membership in the church covenant. Children of church
members could be baptized, for they were assumed to be somewhat within the covenant, but baptism did not entitle the new
generation of Puritans to full membership unless they, too, enjoyed a conversion experience. Therefore, the question arose,
Should the children of these baptized members, in turn, be baptized? Under the terms of the Half-Way Covenant, baptism of
these children (third-generation New World Puritans) was permitted, giving them partial membership in the church although
they could not receive all the sacraments. This step signified that
the Puritan Church, henceforth, would not be composed exclusively of the visible saints, that is, those men and women who,
because of a demonstrated conversion experience, had presumably
entered into the covenant of grace and thus were the elect, the
saved.

Why was the concession of the Half-Way Covenant, this significant compromise, made in 1662? In perspective, this action
was the climax of a long discussion, begun as early as the 1640s,
which focused upon the restrictiveness of church membership.
Undoubtedly, one of the catalysts which produced a decision in
1662 was the peculiar political position of Massachusetts as a

result of the Restoration of the Stuart monarchy in 1660. Under
attack for "independency" even when the Puritans had gained
supremacy in England under Cromwell, the New England Puritans were fearful of reprisal, particularly because of their restrictive political-ecclesiastical practices. If the full weight of the
monarchy had been applied at this critical juncture in the 1660s,
the Puritan construct would unquestionably have been smashed,
but the Stuarts, after a somewhat superficial effort at investigation, accepted surface reforms. In this context, the Half-Way

Covenant represented not only an attempt to extend the influence
of the church in New England by including second- and third-
generation Puritans as well as late arrivals, but also an effort to
appease the authorities in England.

The Half-Way Covenant, it should be noted, was adopted over
stiff opposition—not from the clergy, as too often it is mistakenly assumed, but from the laity. With certain exceptions,
such as the Reverend John Davenport, the great majority of
clergymen supported the Half-Way Covenant because they
feared, first, that the influence of the church in the community
would be reduced unless the larger membership were admitted to
the congregation, and, second, that colonial society would present
a threat to the church if prominent figures and a large majority
of colonials lived entirely outside the discipline of the church.
The privileged laity, on the other hand, were obviously reluctant
to share their position of prestige and power, not only in church
government, but in civil government. The Half-Way Covenant
was adopted by the General Court in a close vote and recommended to the towns, thus transferring the struggle, which lasted
several decades, to the local level. The Old South Church, which
was to become famous in the decade preceding the American
Revolution, was founded when the First Church of Boston opposed the Half-Way Covenant and the dissident members
formed their own congregation.

After the introduction of the Half-Way Covenant, the bars to
church membership were consistently lowered until many

churches accepted professions of a godly life—the covenant of works rather than the covenant of grace—as sufficient evidence to warrant church membership. The clergy were compelled to rationalize the position they took and to exhort the laity. Actually, Puritan practices were adjusting to changing conditions in the New World: the immigration from England, the expanding trade, the rising prominence of individuals outside the establishment who had made their fortunes in the New World, and the migration to frontier areas. These developments were articulated as theological issues because theology was the language of Puritan society; the sermons of the ministers and the documentation of lay leadership record the struggle between the ideal of a church made up of visible saints, and the realities of retaining for the church and the ministry a determining influence in the evolution of New England institutions and society.

One important political implication of the Half-Way Covenant has never been satisfactorily settled. Preliminary studies have not provided indisputable proof of the Half-Way Covenant's broadening the political franchise. It is quite clear that a halfway member did not, at least initially, receive a vote in the governing of the church, but it is not equally clear whether a halfway member acquired the right to participate in colony-wide government. He was already permitted to vote on civil matters relating to the town, but whether he was permitted to vote on deputies and other provincial matters is a question requiring more exacting and penetrating investigation. It is entirely possible that after 1662 the franchise was much less restrictive in practice than has often been assumed, particularly in comparison with other parts of the British Empire, and that no surge of deep dissatisfaction on this score ever materialized within the New England colonies.

The so-called Fall of the Puritan Oligarchy with the revocation of the Massachusetts Bay Charter (1684) has been so exaggerated it qualifies as a myth. New World conditions consistently modified intellectual expression, but there is no abrupt break at the conclusion of the seventeenth century, either in the social institutions, in the political power and structure, or in the intellectual framework of New England. The intricacy of the church-state relationship in New England, its deep involvement in theological presumptions, shows the mind of the Puritan addressing itself to issues as profound as the meaning of life itself; ideas and environment subtly interacted as the transplanted Englishmen faced the American wilderness.

In contrast to New England, the religious adjustment of the Chesapeake colonies to the New World cannot be measured by an analysis of the trend of theological tenets or thought. In Virginia, the doctrine of the Church of England was transplanted intact, and church government and liturgy *in theory* remained unchanged. In practice, however, church government and liturgy were modified to meet wilderness conditions because neither the clergy nor the lay leadership was committed to the preservation of the Anglican Establishment as transplanted. New England Puritans, obsessed with the notion of a belief founded on reason, rationalized and intellectualized the change forced upon them by the new environment, but in Virginia a concentrated ministry, composed of seminal, creative minds, was not present during the seventeenth century.

Colonial issues, therefore, were neither posed nor discussed in terms of doctrine; accepted dogma was not challenged. Virginia, frequently considered to be directly related to the mainstream of English life in the seventeenth century, was in fact on the periphery, because England itself during the better part of the seventeenth century experienced a dramatic debate in church doctrine and practice which was seldom if ever reflected in the Chesapeake colonies. Once the Anglican religious institutions were transplanted to Virginia, interaction between the mother church and the colonial church was minimal until late in the seventeenth century. New World conditions alone determined the evolution of the institution; the adjustments caused by these conditions can be measured in church organization, church government, and an altered form of worship, but not in doctrinal determinations.

In Virginia two factors, the scattered plantations resulting from the land system and the remoteness of the Virginia church from its parent church in England, illustrate the process of adjustment. An absence of a clerical hierarchy within the Anglican Church in Virginia—an Anglican bishop was never appointed for the colonies and Virginia consistently opposed such an appointment —placed special ecclesiastical responsibilities upon the governor, who was already overburdened with his duties as the commander-in-chief of the militia, the executor of colonial laws, the head of the judicial system, and the Crown's representative in the colony. The Virginia church was placed officially under the supervision of the Bishop of London, which further confused the lines of responsibility. Thus the Anglican Church in Virginia exercised a remarkable degree of self-government, in part because of indigenous circumstances and in part because of the power vacuum in the central clerical authority.

The church vestries in Virginia became self-perpetuating during the middle years of the seventeenth century, although the exercise of such exclusive authority occasionally faltered later in the century when the governor called for an election of vestrymen in a particular parish. In any case, the vestry, composed for the most part of the social and economic elite of the parish, accepted and exercised ecclesiastical authority in the absence of a central church government. Ecclesiastical policy was often enforced in lay county courts, where once again the vestrymen exerted influence. To dominate the ministers, who in England customarily secured a degree of tenure and independence once inducted, the church vestry refused to "present" the clergymen to the governor for induction. Without this formal ritual a clergyman could not obtain tenure. Equally trying for the clergymen was their dependence upon the generosity of the congregation for maintenance. A parcel of land was of little value without servants to cultivate it, and receiving payment in tobacco and corn, the customary clerical compensation, had serious short-comings. The amount of tobacco allotted for compensation remained relatively fixed, whereas the price of tobacco fluctuated, usually with a downward spiral after 1660. Moreover, the minister found in many cases that though the amount of tobacco was fixed its quality was not. Clergymen, not unexpectedly, bent before the practical power of the vestry over appointments, tenure, and maintenance.

The resulting cycle was vicious. Only inferior clergy, especially in the second and third generations of settlement, were willing to migrate to Virginia. The ministers who did come were insufficient to fill the church vacancies that arose in rapidly expanding colonies. Parishes hesitated to endow a clergyman of inferior quality with permanent tenure, and good ministers hesitated to undertake a career in Virginia because of financial insecurity. The absence of a strong clergy during the formative years of the Anglican Church explained in large measure the success of the vestry in seizing ecclesiastical authority.

Scattered plantation settlement necessitated the creation of excessively large parishes, frequently crisscrossed by streams that made travel treacherous during the rainy season. Sabbath attendance was at best irregular. To meet the problem, chapels of ease were established throughout a parish and the clergyman became an itinerant, preaching at various chapels on successive Sundays, with lay readers filling the role in his absence. Second- and third-generation Virginians, unfamiliar with a rigorous church organization common to England, fell into secular habits not so much because of a lack of faith but because of an environment that loosened the hold of established practices.

The effect of the environment upon New World Anglican clerical practice was everywhere apparent. As itinerants on horseback, clergymen were often unable to transport proper church vessels and vestments normally required in the administration of rites. Moreover, the dead, for practical reasons, were seldom buried in consecrated church grounds but in family cemeteries at home; the lengthy journey from a plantation to the church, the uncertainty of the weather, and the absence of clergymen made immediate burial at home a necessity, and in violation of church law, laymen often read the service. Because ministers were not readily available, baptism was administered at irregular intervals; in extreme cases the wedding ceremony and the baptism of the fruits of the liaison were administered simultaneously. In colonial Virginia, weddings became almost a secular ceremony. For an entire wedding party to travel ten miles by horseback or rude carriage to church for the ceremony and then to return to the plantation to celebrate the wedding was impractical.

Religious toleration, a term too often mistakenly interchanged with religious liberty, was not among the virtues of the first colonials, even among the Chesapeake colonizers. In Virginia, the Catholic Lord Baltimore was asked to leave; part of the conflict between Maryland and Virginia was based upon religious rivalry between the Virginia Anglicans and the Maryland Catholics. In New England, Rhode Island alone tolerated a variety of beliefs.

Indeed, an excellent case can be made that toleration developed more rapidly in England than in the colonies during the seventeenth century, a consequence of the religious discord in the mother country. Not until late in the seventeenth century did toleration reach Virginia, and then only because toleration coincided nicely with economic enterprise. French Huguenots were invited to settle in Virginia, to be followed eventually by a settlement of Quakers, a true test of toleration. Even the star of Roger Williams, as noted in the previous chapter, arrived at its zenith by a most devious path.

The Maryland Toleration Act of 1649, hailed as a significant step toward religious liberty in America, was conceived not in a liberalizing spirit but as a means of self-preservation. Supposedly a Catholic refuge, Maryland very quickly became predominantly a Protestant rather than a Catholic settlement. To preserve the position of the Catholic minority from possible

Protestant oppression, Lord Baltimore insisted upon passage
of the Toleration Act, which the Maryland legislature honored.
But the date of the enactment in itself is of importance. The rise
of Puritan supremacy in England in the 1640s and 1650s constituted an immediate threat to the Catholic proprietor of Maryland, a threat readily overlooked by historians searching for the
origins of religious liberalism, and he was wise to appease the
Puritans holding power in England.

The frequent suggestion, therefore, that the New World
environment automatically produced tolerance promotes a mis-
conception. The examples of Rhode Island and the Maryland
Toleration Act, it is true, foreshadowed the future; the diversity
of religions transplanted to the New World did require a modification in attitude and policy. To carry the thought a step
further, the diversities of the eighteenth century, with the migration of non-English people to the English colonies, made
toleration a necessity. The liberalizing spirit produced by the
necessities of the colonial experience provided the precedents
that eventually resulted in the concept of religious liberty. Yet
each advance of toleration in America in the seventeenth century
had its counterpart in England; and in some parts of the New
World—note the Anglicans in Massachusetts and the Huguenots
in South Carolina—the English Act of Toleration, passed in
1689, was invoked to rescue minority religious groups.

Intellectual life in the Age of Faith, quite naturally had religion as its center, but its province extended beyond ecclesiastical
boundaries. Frequently, seventeenth-century intellectual life has
been characterized as utilitarian; this generalization is accurate,
but it oversimplifies. It is accurate in the sense that, despite the
philosophical and theological works in the New England
libraries, a book written about man's relationship to God was
not speculative but utilitarian, in exaggerated modern terms, a
religious "how to live" book. The Chesapeake colonials, more
readily classified as utilitarian thinkers, purchased a larger per-

centage of books on such subjects as the techniques of farming than did the New England colonials.

The generalization of seventeenth-century utilitarianism is oversimplified in the sense that it fails to answer much more penetrating questions. Did environmental conditions in the New World determine the direction of cultural life of the early English colonials? Or was the link with English cultural resources strong enough to predominate? Wilderness conditions were not identical for each colony, and different social values held by settlers produced divergent cultural results. For the New England Puritans, for instance, literacy and "culture" were a necessity. As the preceding discussion on religious life in the colonies suggested, a faith and a colony built upon a reasoned and logical theological system demanded not only penetrating intellects among the ministry but understanding among the laity of the reasoned argument based on Biblical truth. The often quoted Puritan saying that learning must be advanced to assure a literate ministry "when our present ministers lie in the dust" is equally applicable to the body of laymen. The Massachusetts Bay Acts of 1642 and 1647, making provision for elementary and grammar schools, were to the body of laymen what the founding of Harvard College in 1636 was to the Puritan purpose of a trained ministry. Education prepared a person for the incoming of God's grace.

No such philosophy animated the colonial leaders or laymen in the Chesapeake colonies, for the accepted social values did not place much emphasis upon knowledge or education. Except at the outset, when men of position and learning accompanied the earliest settlers, the principal migration to the Chesapeake colonies was composed of rank-and-file Englishmen until the upheaval of the 1640s and 1650s brought a few men from upper-class English families.

Late in the seventeenth century a colonial elite began to develop in Virginia. Culture then became an appurtenance to position, a mark of status. Dispersed settlements in the Chesapeake colonies still militated against intellectual activity, it is true, but, equally significant, the Chesapeake settlements lacked a cohesive philosophy which placed a premium on learning and on intellectual expression. Not until the eighteenth century with the emergence of the Enlightenment and its premise of right reason did learning become a necessity rather than an accessory; the Enlightenment made learning and reason the keys to nature and to nature's laws, thus the keys to a meaningful life.

A thesis which has been suggested earlier but which requires repetition at this point is that in the seventeenth century New England reflected more precisely the mind of the mother country, whereas in the eighteenth century the Chesapeake colonies, together with the other southern colonies, more accurately reflected the intellectual currents in England. As the seventeenth century progressed, the literate colonial in the Chesapeake colonies began to acquire an intellectual edge over his New England counterpart as he—and his sons after him—of necessity returned to the seat of culture, the mother country, for higher education. If he were so inclined, he could secure a level of learning superior to that offered at Harvard College, the intellectual center for New England; he could be exposed more easily to contemporary English and European thought.

Early colonial culture cannot be discussed convincingly in terms of art or architecture. The transplanting of the East Anglia Cottage to New England, thatched roof and all, and the modification of dwellings to accommodate to the available materials and to the new environment do reflect, in some measure, the interaction between patterns of experience in the Old and New Worlds. But colonial dwellings of the seventeenth century did not exhibit a predominant cultural pattern. Culture among the first colonials is better expressed, however feebly, in the prose and poetry, the publications, the educational system, the libraries, and certain components of everyday life.

The flood of prose and trickle of verse from New England, little of it enduring, exceeded in quantity and penetration the literature of the Chesapeake, but this discrepancy was the result of differing backgrounds, purposes, and social values rather than the product of pure intelligence. It has been estimated that Massachusetts Bay had more university graduates in relation to its population in the early part of the seventeenth century than at any time in Massachusetts history. Certainly the Chesapeake colonies in their first four decades could not make such a claim, though men of culture and station participated in its founding.

The absence of a noticeable output of writing in the Chesapeake colonies was the consequence of the system of settlement, which made concentrated groups of people, a ready-made audience, a rarity. Moreover, the secular objectives of the Chesapeake settlements did not attract literary figures: the clergy in Virginia and Maryland, to cite an example, were not deeply engaged in intellectual pursuits. In New England, in contrast, sermonizing was cultivated as an art; sermons provided a staple fare for the press and populace. The contribution of the sermon was, of course, primarily theological, but the sermon also contributed to clarification of the constitutional structure of the church, and, especially with election day sermons, "instructed" the populace on secular as well as sacred matters. Famous sermons reached audiences in England as well as in New England; and many a country parson was introduced to the magic of a wider reputation when called to deliver a sermon in Boston or Cambridge, thereupon to burst into print.

Literary expression, although not always literary grace, was given voice through prose and poetry. The transplanted generation of colonials had something to say. William Bradford's *History of Plymouth Plantation* and John Winthrop's *Journal,* both unpublished in their own time and thus unread by contemporaries, represent for New England the type of contemporary narrative published by Captain John Smith for the Chesapeake settlement. Smith's account was read by his peers, though his veracity has often been questioned. Not so with Bradford's *History,* whose charm and integrity set it apart as a literary work of rare quality and insight. Edward Johnson's *Wonder-Working Providence,* another contemporary production, reflects the Puritan view of manifest destiny, but as a literary work it cannot compare with Bradford. Later colonials, children of the transplanted generation, made their most effective and durable contributions in describing firsthand experiences. Mrs. Mary Rowlandson's astonishing account of her capture by the Indians had no precise counterpart in the Chesapeake colonies, but Robert Beverley's *The History and Present State of Virginia,* though an early eighteenth-century publication, reflected the literary trend of the seventeenth-century colonials in Virginia: descriptive contemporary or nearly contemporary history.

The Chesapeake colonies had no press in the seventeenth century, but in 1639 the New England colonies introduced their own press, a part of the Puritan drive to articulate an intellectual gospel and to promote learning. The first publication was, fittingly enough, the Bay Psalm Book (1640). The development of the press in New England is unusual in comparison with other colonies. The French colonies in America never introduced a press, and the only other English colony to respond promptly to the challenge of a press soon after its founding was Pennsylvania, where once again the intellectual level and background of the founders, in combination with the urgent need for an outlet to present the Quaker views, often in reply to harsh New England critics, made publication desirable.

Although settlement by towns explains in part the early founding of a press in the Massachusetts Bay Colony, the demands for a rational, thus an intellectually oriented faith on the part of the Puritan leaders and the need for an outlet to publish Puritan concepts were paramount. Puritans in England during Archbishop William Laud's tenure, which coincided with the early years of Massachusetts Bay, frequently found English presses closed to them on the premise that Puritan ideas undermined the Anglican Establishment. Puritans, therefore, were often forced to seek publication elsewhere, in Holland, for example; frequently the King applied diplomatic pressure to reduce these outlets. A press in New England, where Puritanism reigned supreme, could give Puritan theologians in England as well as New England a voice. Of course, the ascendancy of Puritanism in England after 1640 reduced the need for a press in New England. In addition, by 1660, when the Stuart monarchy was restored to the throne, the Puritans of Old England and New England had taken divergent intellectual and constitutional paths; thus, the press in New England never truly fulfilled one of its original purposes, to serve as the intellectual outlet for English Puritan divines. But the Puritan press in New England did become a mirror of the religious establishment.

Statistically, the output of the press in Boston during the seventeenth century exceeded that of Cambridge and Oxford in England, and the Boston press published much, though not all, of the early New England verse. Intensive training in Latin verse in grammar schools encouraged crude imitation, of which the efforts of Michael Wigglesworth are the prime and most unfortunate example. That such a mild, pensive, beloved Harvard tutor could compose such harsh images unrelieved either by literary grace or spiritual comfort in his *Day of Doom,* a 224-verse epic describing the Day of Judgment, is indeed a vivid commentary on the Puritan mind. *The Day of Doom* struck a responsive chord among the Puritans and became the outstanding best-seller of seventeenth-century New England; this grim hymn for adults, this strange lullaby for the young, was read, so it is estimated, by one half of the populace.

Critics agree that among the first colonials the most durable contributions to poetry were made by Edward Taylor, recently rediscovered, and by Anne Bradstreet, whose verse was first published in England and a few years later in Boston. Edward Taylor, a pastor at Westfield, Massachusetts, was fired with an intense devotion to his beliefs and to poetic expression. He instructed his children not to publish his verse, so that his work was hidden from his contemporaries. The work of Anne Bradstreet, who came to New England at the age of eighteen, already a wife and mother, was known to her contemporaries. It is little less than remarkable that a woman who reared a family of eight and attended to the numerous chores of the household could compose such attractive verse, simple in structure, combining a warmth of understanding, sensitivity, and a choice of subject matter almost unique for the Puritan mind.

> Some time now past in the Autumnal Tide,
> When Phoebus wanted but one hour to bed,
> The trees all richly clad, yet void of pride,
> Were gilded o're by his rich golden head.
> Their leaves and fruits seem'd painted, but was true
> Of green, of red, of yellow, mixéd hew,
> Rapt were my senses at this delectable view.
>
> .   .   .   .   .
>
> I heard the merry grashopper then sing,
> The black-clad Cricket, bear a second part,
> They kept one tune, and plaid on the same string,
> Seeming to glory in their little Art.
> Shall Creatures abject, thus their voices raise?
> And in their kind resound their Maker's praise:
> Whilst I as mute, can warble forth no higher layes?
>
> .   .   .   .   .
>
> Under the cooling shadow of a stately Elm
> Close sate I by a goodly Rivers side,
> Where gliding streams the Rocks did overwhelm;
> A lonely place, with pleasures dignifi'd.
> I once that lov'd the shady woods so well,
> Now thought the rivers did the trees excel,
> And if the sun would ever shine, there would I dwell.

What was published in early America is known, but what was read by the first colonials has been the subject of much speculation. To answer this question, historians have consulted wills, inventories of estates, and book vendor's advertisements. Individuals in both the Chesapeake and the New England colonies possessed extensive libraries: William Byrd, William Fitzhugh, and Ralph Wormeley in Virginia and John Winthrop, William Brewster, and John Harvard in Massachusetts. Perhaps the libraries of the Chesapeake men were a bit more secular in orientation than those of the New England men, but the similarity of the titles is more striking than the differences: religious books, historical works, Latin grammars, classical literature, and some English literature. A generalization made for Connecticut seems universally applicable: the smaller the library, the greater the percentage of books on religion. The most modest inventories usually included a Bible, a prayer book (in the Chesapeake colonies), or a psalm book (in New England). The larger individual libraries embraced a broader range of titles, including books on science, philosophy, history, and literature. In the Chesapeake colonies books were purchased directly from England; in New England books were often purchased from local booksellers, which no doubt restricted the range of titles available.

The question has been raised, is a library a good index of the mind of a man or a society? No one can certify how frequently a particular book is used or read; no one can truly assess the assimilation or influence of the material; no one can estimate accurately whether a book is read for pleasure or for utility; no one can judge precisely whether a library is merely an ornament, an index of the social and economic position of the owner, or the result of an awakened intellect. Books do not necessarily produce a cultivated and speculative mind, but cultivated and speculative minds do purchase and read books. Among the first colonials, it is safe to generalize that the existence of libraries indicates a recognition that culture was desirable; a library was a symbol of civilization even in the New World wilderness. Moreover, the letters of the first colonials make clear that intellectual currents in England were frequently followed with intense interest, though this curiosity about English intellectual developments in the colonies south of New England is intensified in the eighteenth century.

The school systems within the English colonies also offer an insight into the scope and dimension of intellectual life. A few grammar schools were founded in New England within a decade of the Great Migration, but legislation throughout the region (with the exception of Rhode Island, which, strangely enough, seemed to eschew all learning) followed the pattern of the well-known Massachusetts Bay enactments of 1642 and 1647. The first enactment required the establishment of elementary schools in towns of fifty or more families, and the second required the formation of grammar schools (secondary schools) in towns exceeding one hundred families. These enactments indicate that the voluntary system of education had failed, a serious matter in a community based on the philosophy of a literate laity.

The elementary schools of New England taught reading and writing, whereas the grammar schools prepared students for advanced learning in a college or a university. Parents were not forced to send their children to elementary schools, but they were compelled through some alternate program to teach their children to read and write. Exercises in the elementary schools were based upon religious subject matter. The curriculum of the grammar schools imitated that of the grammar schools in England, with their emphasis on Latin.

Historians who have written about the New England school system have generally disagreed on the purpose of the schools and the quality of learning. Some historians regard the curriculum as narrow in scope, restricted by the inhibitions of Puritanism, whereas others view the school system as the instrument which preserved the humanistic tradition. Samuel Eliot Morison is unmistakably correct in asserting that the support of the school system was secular. He has also demonstrated beyond doubt that the curriculum compared favorably with that in England and that the emphasis on religious exercises was not excessive in an age where faith—Puritan, Anglican, Catholic—was the center of life. Yet the secular and religious impulses cannot be separated so easily. The schoolmasters in many of the towns were candidates for the Puritan ministry, and when a vacancy in the ministry occurred they changed from teaching to preaching. In addition, the town, though by no means identical with the church, was usually controlled by leading Puritans, who operated as a pressure group in much the same way that pressure groups operate today. Although nonchurch members could vote in town affairs and sometimes possessed influence, available teachers were definitely of a kind—pick your Puritan. There was freedom of choice, therefore, but the choice was limited.

The New England school system, then, was secular in terms of its support, and humanistic and scholarly in terms of its curriculum, because the Puritans followed the only example they knew, the image of England. The school system was also an extension of Puritanism, for it upheld the concept that learning was paramount in a society based on a reasoned religion, and that education, in effect, was part of the preparation for entering into the covenant of grace.

It has been asserted that the New England school system of the seventeenth century was the basis of the public school system of the nineteenth century, but it is well to note that no studies have yet shown that a continuous thread specifically links the two centuries or that a vigorous and vital public school system existed in New England at the time of the Revolution. The public school system of the nineteenth century arose out of different circumstances and for a different purpose. The American Revolution, in many respects, broke the thread of continuity.

So far as it can be ascertained, the school system of New England was enforced during the seventeenth century, although this point has been contested by J. T. Adams and Charles Andrews. In many cases a schoolmaster taught the elementary school and, if scholars appeared, also taught grammar school pupils. In certain towns the minister taught the scholars preparing for college, indicating that, in practice, training at the grammar school level was not far removed from the church leaders. Evidence of such an arrangement was often accepted as compliance with the law requiring a grammar school.

In the Chesapeake colonies distance between plantations made a centrally located school unrealistic. Groping for a solution to the problem of education, the Chesapeake colonies substituted family responsibility for community responsibility. The family's sense of values and its finances guided individual responses. Interest in education for the young is amply documented by numerous wills making provision for education, but the opportunities available for attaining a modest learning were readily exhausted. One avenue was the "old Field Schools": a school would be located near enough to several plantations so that children from a number of families could assemble, to be taught by a clergyman, a lay reader, or the wife of a planter. A few free schools, that is, schools with endowment to pay for upkeep, were also established, one as early as 1643, a benefaction of Benjamin Symes. The curriculum and student body of the free schools in the Chesapeake colonies have not been properly investigated, but it appears that they served as modest grammar schools. Another alternative open to a family or a group of families was either to hire an indentured servant to teach the children in the family or, if possible, to secure the services of a clergyman. It is interesting to note that the Virginia governors were instructed by the Lords of Trade to license every schoolmaster; the governors were not only to evaluate the quality of the teacher's character and his mastery of subject matter, but also to ascertain whether he conformed to the teachings and practices of the Anglican faith. The effectiveness of this licensing system has never been thoroughly examined, but the establishment of a system to select an individual within each county to honor this obligation does indicate its enforcement.

How many of the alternatives in the Chesapeake colonies led to the equivalent of a grammar school education is uncertain. Families of affluence often sent their children to England for preparatory training and in some cases for professional training or for advanced work at an English university. Consideration was given to founding a college in the Chesapeake colonies, but nothing developed until the end of the century. The education of William Byrd II (1674–1744) is an excellent example of the process in practice. Byrd's earliest schooling was indifferent, but his father sent him to England where he was placed in the Felstead Grammar School in Essex. The headmaster, Christopher Glasscock, had also tutored the sons of Oliver Cromwell, an ironical circumstance suggesting again the interweaving of the secular and the sacred in the seventeenth century. Byrd later was sent to Holland to learn about mercantile matters, and for a time he was associated with the mercantile firm of Perry and Lane in London. Finally, he acquired training in law at the English Inns of Court and was admitted to the bar. A Virginian by birth and inclination, Byrd cultivated political and intellectual ties in England which proved to be enduring. Byrd represents the general trend in the Chesapeake colonies: the indigenous elite becoming English in orientation, intellectually and culturally, in the late seventeenth and early eighteenth centuries. New England, on the other hand, initially the best reflection of English cultural and intellectual life, had become by the late seventeenth and early eighteenth centuries provincial and self-contained, which proved to be a source of weakness as well as a source of strength.

Undoubtedly, the proportion of well-educated men in the Chesapeake colonies at the mid-seventeenth century was lower than that in New England. Preliminary studies have indicated that the inability to write was more prevalent in the Chesapeake colonies. Yet the concern for education in the Chesapeake colonies was more intense than has often been depicted, though the prevailing intellectual milieu, unlike that of the Puritans, was not predicated on a learned, literate populace.

The College of William and Mary did not receive a charter until 1693, and it did not operate successfully until the eighteenth century, but Harvard College was founded by a vote of the Gen-

H

eral Court of Massachusetts Bay in 1636. Officially named Harvard in 1639, following John Harvard's library legacy, the college was formally incorporated in 1650. The college nearly foundered at the outset when the followers of Anne Hutchinson, advocating the tenet of immediate revelation, threatened the concept of a learned ministry and a literate laity. However, the college survived the earliest theological storms and the periods of financial crisis, in one case by an assessment of produce from each Puritan family. By 1650 Harvard was able to enlarge its curriculum and to offer a four-year rather than a two-year course.

Harvard College served as an intellectual instrument transmitting to the English colonies in the New World the classical learning of Europe. The idea of a community of scholars, the broad curriculum including the arts and philosophies, the humane learning embodied in the instruction and the books studied, and the use of Latin as the language of instruction reinforce this generalization. Formal instruction, it is true, emphasized the ancient arts and philosophies, but the commonplace books of the young scholars reflected an appetite for contemporary literature. This is not to say, of course, that Harvard did not train clergymen. One half of the alumni of seventeenth-century Harvard entered the ministry, and by the end of the century most New England churches were served by Harvard graduates. The influence of Harvard College reached into every New England town, an influence that has not yet abated. According to Harvard's historians, the broad construct of knowledge included in the curriculum lighted the lamp of learning in English America.

College education was not confined to the wealthy, but the road for a poor boy entering Harvard was strewn with obstacles. Who would maintain him in grammar school so that he could prepare for college? Once a boy reached college, he could work, and many a youngster of modest means offered sides of beef and bacon, bushels of wheat and corn, kegs of apples and casks of butter to pay expenses. A Harvard degree could lift a young man from the journeyman to professional class.

What is perhaps most significant is that throughout the colonies, formal learning became by the late seventeenth century less and less the avenue to success, and therefore formal learning received less emphasis. When new wealth in America produced a new colonial elite, authority and learning once again became bedfellows.

It is a mistake to conclude either that the Puritan experiment failed or, as is less often affirmed, that it succeeded; this is to construe history as narrowly as the Puritans themselves wished it construed. For historians, the important consideration is to perceive the evolution of institutions and ideas shaped by the forward thrust of events, to trace and analyze the modification of church policy and doctrine, to delineate the shift of purpose and intent. In the largest sense, the Bible Commonwealth never collapsed; its leadership never fell. Rather, the commonwealth responded to new values and purposes as conditions changed.

In the Chesapeake colonies, New World conditions left their imprint upon the English colonials; their livelihood, their land and labor, their trade, their intellectual life, their emphasis on family, their social values—all were directly influenced by the New World environment.

5

Outposts of Empire

DOMESTIC DEVELOPMENTS within England dramatically influenced the outposts of empire. Diplomatic policy often touched the colonies in vital areas, for, as outposts of English power, they became the battleground between international rivals. In domestic and diplomatic developments, the relationship between the mother country and its American colonies introduced innovation in the exercise of authority. Theoretically, all authority was concentrated in England, but unlike other European colonial systems, authority in practice was divided, with the individual colonies assuming certain powers of self-government, thus taking the first steps toward a federal system of government. Of the continental colonies, the Chesapeake colonies, particularly Virginia, became the jewels of the imperial diadem, although none of the continental colonies could equal the luster of the English West Indian colonies, whose products fulfilled the intent of the imperial theorists.

Political upheaval within England strongly influenced the colonies as outposts of empire as the contest between Parliament and the Crown intensified during the reign of the early Stuarts beginning in 1603. Less gifted in parliamentary government than their Tudor predecessors, the Stuarts relied heavily upon an appeal to the divine right of kings, an increasingly outmoded and impractical defense. The struggle between Parliament and the Crown reached its climax in the period of cruel discord (1640–60), that began with the seating of the Long Parliament and extended through a stormy series of events including the execution of Charles I (1649) and the establishment of the Puritan supremacy. In 1660 the Stuarts were restored to the throne.

This titanic struggle provoked an uneven response in the colonies, some of it unpredictable. The expectation that New England would strengthen its tie with the mother country because of the Puritan supremacy at home was misplaced. Migration to New England dwindled because English Puritans now had less reason to abandon the motherland. The Bible Commonwealth itself chastely maintained a neutrality. Too intimate an association with the English Puritans, the New England Puritans feared, might involve them in actions that could destroy their ecclesiastical experiment. Moreover, Puritanism in England had taken a divergent course from Puritanism in America. If the Puritan rule in England was upset and the authority of the Crown re-established, Massachusetts Bay in particular could suffer reprisal.

The reservations of the Puritans in America were well founded. When the turn of the wheel restored the Stuarts to the throne, the investigations by English authorities of the Puritan mistreatment of non-Puritans lacked direction and determination. Only in less obvious ways did the contest between King and Parliament accelerate change, most prominently in trade. As discussed earlier, the decrease in English trading resulted in the stimulation of New England fisheries and increased trade between New England and the Puritans who had settled in the English West Indies.

Surprisingly enough, the period of Puritan Ascendancy in England, at least on the surface, imposed a more striking imprint upon Virginia and Maryland than upon New England. Maryland, controlled by a Catholic proprietor, was a natural target for an ultra-Protestant English government, and Parliament assumed control of the colony in 1652. If domestic affairs had not distracted English policy makers in moments of critical crisis, Maryland could conceivably have become a royal colony instead of being returned to the Baltimore proprietors in 1657, when Cromwell took the side of Baltimore. During the period of unrest in England in the 1640s but before the takeover by Parliament in 1652, the proprietor adjusted to the shifting currents by appointing a Virginia Protestant as governor and by instituting the celebrated but often misunderstood Toleration Act of 1649.

There was less turmoil in Virginia. As a royal colony and as an Anglican establishment, Virginia had supported Charles I. An expedition sent to Virginia by the English Puritans received the peaceful capitulation of the colony, but Royalist sentiment never died and the Restoration of the Stuart monarchy was not only welcomed but anticipated. Yet two subtle influences during the period of the interregnum produced enduring results. First, Virginia experienced some measure of independence during the English domestic preoccupation; and, second, the composition of Virginia society was modified when younger sons of English Cavalier families migrated to the colony. Although these men were seldom from families of the highest rank, a number of individuals from this group of Virginians none the less sired family groups that gained significant political power in terms of social status. They eventually ranked among the first families of Virginia.

During the period of parliamentary supremacy, the Navigation Act of 1651, the foundation of the English colonial system, was passed. This Act provided that: (1) goods grown or manufactured in Asia, Africa, or America which were brought into England or its possessions could be transported only in ships of which the proprietor, master, and majority of mariners were English; (2) goods of foreign growth or manufacture could be brought to England only from the place of production, thereby eliminating the middle man; (3) goods grown or manufactured in Europe could be brought to England or its possessions only in

English vessels or in vessels belonging to the country that had produced the goods, again reducing competition with outside carriers.

The Act of 1651, according to Charles M. Andrews, perhaps the leading authority on this question, was directed primarily toward the Dutch, who had achieved supremacy in the Caribbean trade and a favored position in much of the English colonial coastwise trade, especially in the transport of staple commodities such as Virginia tobacco. English vessels, English seamen, and English merchants were not profiting from the English colonial possessions, and, from the mercantilist point of view, the nation was suffering. If the commercial power of the Dutch were to be reduced and that of England enlarged, then regulations to insure English primacy in the trade of its colonies must be assured.

The thesis that the trade enactment was directed at the Dutch can be questioned, because precedents for regulating colonial trade extended back specifically over four decades, and in more general terms for several centuries. This English experience was composed of three parts: (1) the influence of mercantilist thought; (2) the relationship between England and its early dependencies, notably Scotland and Ireland; and (3) the accumulated experience of managing the first royal colony in the New World, Virginia.

Mercantilist thought, with its emphasis upon colonies as sources of supply, its concept of colonies existing solely for the benefit of the mother country, and its view that no nation could achieve greatness without colonies, has already been discussed. The point to be remembered here is that English policy makers, regardless of their political or religious persuasion, held the mercantilist view. Drastic political upheaval, such as that experienced in England between 1640 and 1660, in no way affected long-term colonial policy: trade enactments have an unbroken history unaffected by 'political change. Commercial relationships between England and its subordinate territories, particularly Ireland, were exceedingly restrictive, and the long-standing regulation of that

trade for English advantage reflected a point of view easily translated into a generalized policy for colonial possessions in the
New World. The royal relationship with Virginia included the
same category of precedents. As early as 1621 tobacco regulation
was instituted in Virginia, and this legislation was frequently
supplemented in the years following.

From the English mercantile point of view, the Navigation
Act of 1651 contained certain shortcomings. This act, for example, did not prevent the American colonists from exporting goods
directly to Europe, nor did it prevent them from acquiring
manufactured goods on the Continent and transporting these
goods directly to the colonies for market. With the Restoration
of the Stuarts, the legality of the Navigation Act of 1651 was
questioned, since it had been passed during the period of Puritan
Ascendancy. In 1660, therefore, it was re-enacted with substantially the same provisions but modified somewhat to make it
more effective and enlarged to meet new issues. The Navigation
Act of 1660 included the following principal provisions: (1) all
goods, regardless of origin, could be imported into or exported
from an English plantation only in English vessels, thereby
closing the loophole which permitted the colonials to import
directly from Europe; (2) three fourths of the crew of these
vessels were to be Englishmen, and the master of the vessel as
well as the owner was to be English; (3) specified goods, including sugar, cotton, ginger, indigo, dye woods (such as fustic
and brazilleto), and tobacco were "enumerated." These enumerated goods could be marketed only through Britain; they could
not be exported directly to the prospective buyers in other European countries.

For Virginia, the enumeration meant that its tobacco had to
be shipped to England and then re-exported to France, Germany,
the Low Countries, or any other nation serving as a market for
colonial tobacco. Although the colonials were rewarded with a
monopoly of the English tobacco market, the results of the Act
from the point of view of the colonials were distressing because

England could not begin to absorb the total tobacco production of Virginia and Maryland. Moreover, costs to re-export tobacco, as generally estimated, reached as high as 40 per cent of the wholesale market price in England.

Drawbacks—that its, rebates on enumerated commodities that were re-exported—eased the hardship of this cost but by no means eliminated the handling and storage charges. Enumeration consistently irritated the colonials; the heaviest burden lay on the Chesapeake colonies, and enumeration has been blamed for such far-reaching results as the long-term economic depression in Virginia and Maryland during the latter half of the seventeenth century. This depression led to concentration of land ownership because, presumably, only the large-scale producer could meet the disadvantages of the market.

The Navigation Act of 1660 did not prevent the colonials from carrying commodities other than the enumerated commodities where they wished, so long as these goods were transported in English vessels, that is, ships built in the colonies as well as ships built in England. Most of the Atlantic trade, thus the international commerce, was carried by vessels made in England, whereas those made in the colonies were largely used for intercolonial, coastal commerce.

After 1660 each Navigation Act passed was designed to make the imperial commercial regulations more effective. In 1663 the Staple Act was adopted. Under its provisions, European goods imported into the colonies were required to pass through England, with a few exceptions, mainly salt, servants, and wine. Occasionally colonials circumvented the intent of the Navigation Laws by shipping enumerated commodities from colony to colony, a coastwise trade which did not fall under the terms of the law; neglecting to unload at the colonial destination, or after making a pretense of unloading, the vessel made straightway for the European market. To close this loophole, the Navigation Act of 1673 required that whenever a vessel carried enumerated commodities, a plantation duty—that is, a bond—be paid before

a ship cleared from a colonial port. A final trade enactment of
the seventeenth century, the Act of 1696, was adopted to enforce
the entire body of Navigation Laws more effectively. It provided
for the creation of vice-admiralty courts in America, the first of
which was established the following year. In addition, writs of
assistance could be obtained to search warehouses to check possible evasion of the Navigation Acts.

By using the ingenious technique of accounting for the total
English shipping tonnage, Lawrence Harper proves that at the
turn of the century the Navigation Laws were enforced. Moreover, he estimates that the economic burden of the Navigation
Laws per capita was greater at the conclusion of the seventeenth
century than at any time during the colonial period. Perhaps this
helps to explain in part—but only in part—the great number of
rebellions sweeping the colonies in the late seventeenth century,
from Cary's Rebellion in North Carolina to Leisler's in New
York (Chapter 6). Although the aims of these uprisings had
little to do with the commercial system of the British Empire,
the burden of the system, unrealized even by the participants,
perhaps intensified the conflicts. Lashing out at each other took
the place of lashing out at a system whose grip they could not
remove and, indeed, did not think of removing even in their
most lucid or prophetic moments.

Among the significant changes brought about by the Restoration of the Stuarts in 1660 was the establishment of proprietary
colonies—New York, New Jersey, Pennsylvania, North Carolina,
and South Carolina. The increase in the number of English
colonies using the proprietary form from 1660 to 1690 was scarcely
accidental, this type embracing almost one half of the English
colonies planted in North America in the seventeenth century.
Popular attention has so often been focused on the Chesapeake
and Puritan experiments that the phenomenon of the proprietors
suffers in comparison.

Maryland served as a successful precedent, but proprietary

grants were progressively less sweeping as the century advanced and as the English policy makers became increasingly suspicious of limitless power delegated to a single man or a group of men. Late in the seventeenth and early in the eighteenth centuries, a substantial number, if not the majority, of Crown officials besieged the highest authorities to reduce the proprietaries, which, in their judgment, failed to enforce parliamentary regulations and which compromised the paramount authority of the mother country. In view of this growing opposition the irony of successful proprietary establishments is obvious. Perhaps their very success is something of a key to the outspokenness of those who opposed the creation of proprietary colonies.

Why then were so many proprietary colonies established in the period of 1660-90, in sharp contrast to the establishment of colonies by joint-stock companies in the early decades of English colonization? Before 1660, Maryland as a proprietary stood in isolation; after 1660, no colony was founded on a joint-stock basis. The answer lies in America and in England.

In America, the conditions of settlement had changed. In the first stage of settlement proprietors failed because of their limited resources. Joint-stock companies enabled enterprisers to share the risk and to multiply the reservoir of resources. It is something of a paradox that proprietaries, utilizing outmoded techniques based on the experience of fifteenth-century feudal England, failed in the late sixteenth and early seventeenth centuries but succeeded in the late seventeenth century precisely because the capitalist-oriented joint-stock company, and the advanced technique of settlement it made possible, paved the way. To sustain a colony when neighboring colonies were already thriving was much easier than to plant the first colony in a new and hostile environment. Even so, it is enlightening to remember that the only colonies that were still proprietary on the eve of the Revolution were Maryland and Pennsylvania, interior colonies flanked and protected by strong neighbors, whereas the Carolina proprietary, an example in contrast, had long since yielded to royal authority. A determining factor which made Carolina a royal province was the inability of the proprietors to defend a frontier area and still to maintain a prospering populace. Although not a proprietary, Georgia, too, required special defense assistance from the Crown, a concession that other colonies were never to receive from England on a permanent basis until 1763 when, as mature American provinces, they greeted such assistance with cynical reservation.

In England, conditions had also changed. No additional English settlements of consequence were planted in America between 1640 and 1660. Investors had found more attractive economic opportunities in enterprises elsewhere, so that corporate companies had become disinterested. Moreover, the turmoil of domestic developments curtailed the founding of colonies. With the Restoration bringing a measure of tranquillity, pent-up demands could be fulfilled, and Charles II could repay the debts, political and economic, he had incurred in the struggle to regain the throne. What easier way to compensate the favor of favorites than to grant extensive lands in the New World? Such a course would not make any demands upon the royal exchequer; it would not demand sacrifices from the Crown; and successful settlements would glorify and strengthen the royal authority and the nation. In 1660 the land most readily available in English America lay in the Middle and South Atlantic regions, and the proprietary grants were made in these areas.

The first proprietary colony created in the Middle Atlantic, New York, was made possible by conquest, not by enterprising founders. In perspective, the assimilation by the English of the Dutch settlement of New Netherland in North America appears inevitable, but the vigorous competition between the English and the Dutch in Europe during the early decades of the seventeenth century did not foreordain English superiority. The story of the Dutch settlement, fascinating as it is, cannot be elaborated upon in this account. New Netherland, although neglected, was not frail, as the durability of Dutch culture in the

form of church, language, education, and local institutions
proved throughout the colonial period. Unfortunately for New
Netherland, it faced English competition from the most aggressive and growing group of colonies, New England, where heavy
migration was reinforced by stern wills. The New England
Confederation of 1643, formed for defense, was one of the results
of New England–New Netherland competition for fertile land
and Indian trade, especially in Connecticut. If New Netherland
had faced its first English competition from the more loosely
organized and diffusely settled Chesapeake colonies, doubtless
the fall of New Netherland would have been deferred.

The final initiative to subdue New Netherland came from the
King's Council for Foreign Plantations, which, in 1664, reported
that the presence of the Dutch colony was an encroachment
upon English territory and English trade. In view of its meager
defenses and the discontent of its inhabitants, New Netherland,
so the policy makers rationalized, needed the blessing of English
rule. The King forthwith granted the territory between the
Connecticut and Delaware rivers, which included New Netherland, to his brother James, the Duke of York, to be ruled as a
proprietary province. Given four ships and four hundred soldiers,
James's deputy, Richard Nicholls, sailed to New Netherland by
way of Boston, obtained the surrender of the Dutch governor,
Peter Stuyvesant, in September 1664, and the colony was re-
named New York. Except for a brief period (1673–74) when the
Dutch recaptured the colony, New York remained an English
colony and was integrated into the English colonial system.

The process of integration was made relatively easy because
the Dutch practices and customs, including religion, were accepted under the proprietary regime of the Duke of York. Moreover, English commercial restrictions did not affect New York
adversely because its principal staple, fur, found a ready market
within England. Although a long struggle ensued after 1664
between the settlers and proprietor on the issue of representative
government, this conflict did not seem to alienate the colonials

of Dutch extraction, for they had fared no better, indeed a bit worse, under Dutch rule. Local government achieved limited goals under the Duke of York, but the central issue, the struggle for representative government, was delayed, thus furnishing a chapter in the story of the transition of English colonies to American provinces.

Part of the territory granted to the Duke of York by the Crown included the land that was to become New Jersey, and the Duke, with suitable largesse, granted this portion of his domain to his friends Lord John Berkeley and Sir George Carteret, two stout defenders of the Stuarts during the period of Puritan supremacy in England. These proprietors laid claim to political authority as well as to ownership of the land, and in 1665 a government was established under their supervision, including a proprietary governor, a council, and an assembly selected by freemen. However, this move produced a clash of interests with New York. That colony, as a proprietary and later as a royal province (1685), insisted that politically Jersey was linked to New York, that in forming a separate government the Jersey proprietors had exceeded their authority.

At the time that Carteret and Berkeley made their move to create a separate government, only scattered settlements were in evidence, the Finns and Swedes along the Delaware River and a few Dutchmen along the west bank of the Hudson. Then migration to Jersey increased, a stream fed primarily by New England Puritans who were searching either for better land than New England offered or for a place to practice Presbyterian rather than Congregational polity. The story of New Jersey next took a disputatious, tangled, but significant turn in 1674 when Lord Berkeley sold his half interest to two Quakers, John Fenwick and Edward Byllynge. Becoming heavily obligated, Fenwick and Byllynge were forced to entrust the management of their affairs to three trustees, among them William Penn.

The entrance of the Quakers into the development of New Jersey was eventually to lead to the founding of Pennsylvania,

but for the moment it led only to the division in 1676 of New
Jersey into East Jersey, retained by Carteret, and West Jersey,
owned by the Quakers. East and West Jersey gained in population, and temporarily the character of each was fixed, West
Jersey settled by English Quakers, usually on small farms, and
East Jersey settled more frequently by Puritans in town settlements. East Jersey underwent several serious crises as the inhabitants protested vigorously against the collection of quitrents
and proprietary land policy. Political friction in East Jersey, already much in evidence, was intensified when in 1682 twelve
Quakers, including Penn, bought the colony. The complex interrelationship of these numerous proprietors—twelve were added
to the original twelve soon after the purchase—produced economic uncertainty and political paralysis. Colonists probably felt
relief in 1702 when New Jersey was united into a single province
and made a royal colony.

By the time the Quakers lost control of the Jersey colonies,
William Penn had initiated his celebrated experiment, the founding of the Quaker colony of Pennsylvania. William Penn's father,
Admiral Sir William Penn, had managed to retain a close tie
with the Stuarts, even though he had fought for a time for the
Puritans during the Civil War, and his son inherited a large
financial claim against Charles II. In lieu of the £16,000 sterling
debt, land was granted to him in the New World. The precise
boundaries of Pennsylvania were in dispute for decades, but they
were eventually settled.

From the point of view of the Anglicans and the Puritans, the
Quakers were a menace to their political-religious establishments,
and, as a consequence, the Quakers were ill-treated both by the
New England Puritans and the English Anglicans. Dedicated
Quakers believed that each individual could experience an immediate and direct revelation from God, commonly called the
"inner light," a concept which conflicted with the theological
theories of Anglicans and Puritans. Neither faith condoned immediate revelation; the practice was as distasteful to the one as

to the other, for it offended their premise of a rational religion. The Quaker belief in direct revelation brought about a radically changed church organization, particularly the elimination of a trained ministry. From the point of view of both Anglicans and Puritans, this would lead eventually to a religion of ignorance and mysticism. Indeed, what might be called the "excesses" exercised by a fringe of Quakers—who pursued nonconformity to the point of nakedness—represented to Anglican and Puritan alike mysticism in the extreme.

In enforcing Quaker practices among their membership, the Quakers were actually just as strict and orthodox in their own way as the most devout Puritan or Anglican. Monthly meetings controlled the conduct of the local Quakers. Quarterly and yearly meetings were substitutes for the conventional hierarchy of other faiths; the policies determined at these meetings were enforced with a persistency that even the New England Puritans might have envied.

Much like the separatists of the early seventeenth century, the Quakers by following their religious practices became a political threat in the later seventeenth century because their acts undermined the political establishment. They refused to acknowledge superior authority; they refused to pay taxes; they refused to participate in militia exercises; and, of course, they refused to support the Anglican Establishment.

The Quakers' stubborn devotion to principle has won the admiration of later generations, and the persecution of the Quakers for their religious beliefs, often with incredible brutality, has quite naturally attracted the attention of the liberal historian. As a result, historians are inclined to depict the Quakers in highly favorable terms and to suggest that the poor (literally), persecuted Quakers succeeded despite all opposition in bringing light and enlightenment to America. Moreover, except among specialists, the history of the colony of Pennsylvania is portrayed as the triumph of sweet reasonableness, the capstone of religious and political foresight.

Some reservations must be made about this view. First, Quakers found hospitality in Rhode Island, North Carolina, New York, and New Jersey prior to their settlement in Pennsylvania. Second, the Quaker migration to the English colonies was not composed primarily of the indigent. Third, the Quakers, where they were able to control a single colony, in this case Pennsylvania, administered it primarily for their own advantage; political and economic power remained with the Quaker elite. Fourth, by the time the Quaker colony was founded in 1681, religious toleration had made such an advance in England that a newly established colony could not expect to enforce strict religious conformity; religious toleration in Pennsylvania was less of an achievement, in comparative terms, than a preliminary investigation would lead one to conclude.

Penn received his grant in 1681; he arrived in America in October 1682 and founded Philadelphia. Settlements in the territory by Swedes, Dutch, and a few English Quakers had preceded the grant to Penn, and these colonials were incorporated into Pennsylvania. Penn quieted Indian claims by purchasing the land from them, a custom that eased the conscience of Englishmen who, unlike the Indians, thought of land as property. He drafted a frame of representative government, modifying it almost immediately to meet the demands of his colonists, and within a decade the colony became sufficiently prosperous to export foodstuffs.

In the South, a proprietary grant of the Carolinas had been made as early as 1629. But the first serious effort to colonize did not begin until 1663, when eight proprietors received a grant of the land between 31° and 36° north latitude (revised in 1665, specifying a northern boundary of 36° 30' north to a line approximately one hundred miles south of the present boundary between Georgia and Florida), a princely domain by any standard. The proprietors—the Earl of Clarendon, the Duke of Albermarle, Sir John Berkeley, Sir George Carteret, the Earl of Craven, John Colleton, Sir Anthony Ashley Cooper (later Earl

I

of Shaftesbury), and Sir William Berkeley—were, as their titles
suggest, powerful figures, so powerful indeed that the King,
though reluctant to part with the territory, did so only because
he could not deny the strength of this coalition. Moreover, the
group was powerful in that most of them, in one way or another, were active in other English settlements in the New
World. Colleton had experience in the English colony of Barbados; Sir William Berkeley was famous, or infamous, depending
upon the point of view, as Governor of Virginia; Carteret and
John Berkeley were soon to become the New Jersey proprietors.

Among the attractions of the Carolinas were the possibilities it
opened up for baronial estates and, because of the warmer climate, for the production of commodities that could not be produced in England, particularly silk. The first possibility, at least
in the first half century of settlement, did not materialize, though
extensive estates became rather common in the eighteenth century; the second objective was not fulfilled as it was originally
conceived. Mulberry trees were planted and experts in the production of silk were imported at times, but all efforts to establish
the silk industry failed, an experience that was to be duplicated
a half-century later in Georgia.

Migration to the Carolinas was relatively slow. Success was, for
an extended period, in doubt, and assurance of a thriving establishment was not confirmed until the Carolinas survived the
Yamassee War (1715-18). Several attempts were made to establish colonies in northern Carolina relatively early—the attempt of
Sir John Yeamans in 1665 being the best known—but what was
to become North Carolina was first settled along the Albemarle
Sound by expatriate Virginians and around Cape Fear by migrations from South Carolina.

Hopes were high that other English colonies would see in the
Carolinas great opportunities for advancement. At this time,
New Englanders were moving to Jersey, and on occasion, to the
English Caribbean colonies, but any substantial migration of
New Englanders to Carolina never materialized. A greater num-

ber of immigrants came from Barbados. Barbados and Jamaica had undergone a social and economic transformation. By concentration on a money crop, sugar, and by the intensive importation of a slave labor force, the English Caribbean colonies were engaged in a highly specialized capitalistic agriculture, characterized by large landholdings for more efficient production and the gradual reduction in numbers of small landholders. It is ironic that the immigrants from Barbados, fleeing from a system in which they could not successfully compete, eventually transposed to Carolina a specialized plantation agriculture which encouraged extensive landholdings, promoted slave labor, and reduced the flexibility of the social system.

In the history of early Carolina, the Fundamental Constitutions, the articles of Carolina government drawn up by Ashley Cooper with the aid of John Locke, have attracted unusual attention. The customary point of departure is that the Fundamental Constitutions consisted of archaic, medieval ideas, outmoded in England itself but which the proprietors, ignorant of New World conditions, attempted to transplant to Carolina. Superficially this diagnosis appears accurate—in the distribution of lands, to cite an example—but an analysis of the disputes between the proprietors and the settlers during the last few decades of the seventeenth century and early eighteenth century shows that the Carolina colonials were repeatedly distressed that the "rights" conferred upon them as individuals and as Englishmen by the Fundamental Constitutions were disregarded by the proprietors, who through unilateral and arbitrary action altered the frame of government without regard to the requirements or wishes of the colonials.

Certain parts of the Fundamental Constitutions did operate, although usually in modified fashion: the Palatine Court, composed of the eight proprietors, did exercise its power as the supreme authority of government in the colonies; landgraves—the title was given to men awarded 48,000 acres of land—who held a place among the nobility, were appointed in a few instances;

representatives, proprietors as designated in the Fundamental Constitutions, were appointed for the colony.

The failure of Carolina as a proprietary cannot be blamed primarily on the unwieldiness of the Fundamental Constitutions (abandoned in 1693), but rather on the location of the Carolinas, which served as the southern frontier of the English colonies. The proprietors simply could not provide the defense necessary for such an exposed territory.

Finally, of course, Carolina did not develop as a whole, but in parts. North Carolina, because of its remoteness from avenues of transatlantic trade, the result of its inhospitable coast line, developed into a small-plantation, somewhat self-contained economy, whereas South Carolina, stimulated by its ready access to transatlantic commerce, concentrated more often on production for export and a commercial agriculture. Until the 1730s North Carolina was torn between the poles of South Carolina and Virginia; not until the 1740s did North Carolina show an internal unity which truly set it apart from its neighbors.

One important result of the proprietary movement, often underestimated, is the diversification it produced. Each proprietary colony brought about a distinctive migration. The Carolinas, except for the modest migration from southern Virginia to northern North Carolina, were not planted as an offshoot of established colonies but were settled by peoples from the West Indies and by non-English group migrations, notably the Huguenots. Except for its connection with East and West Jersey, Pennsylvania was a distinct enterprise, unrelated to New York or Maryland, attracting settlers from Scotland and Ireland and from the European continent. This diversification within the new proprietaries gave them a cosmopolitan character in contrast to the sectional character of New England.

In theory, the place of the colonies within the English imperial system was fixed, but the agencies set up to administer day-to-day policy on the basis of this fixed concept were under constant revision. In the first two decades of settlement, the King had consulted with advisors on specific questions relating to colonial administration, but this method fell into disuse until Charles II, in 1634, appointed a standing committee of the Privy Council, styled the "Lord Commissioners for Plantations." During the struggle between Parliament and the monarchy, many adjustments took place in colonial administration, too numerous to relate, but with the Restoration of the Stuarts in 1660 two groups were appointed by the Crown to advise the King on colonial questions: a Council for Trade, and a Council for Foreign Plantations, the member of each appointed from the Privy Council and from men outside the government. These two groups had the power to recommend, not to fashion or to enforce, policy. Apathy, inefficiency, and lack of authority produced unsatisfactory results and prompted a revision of the administrative machinery. After several experiments, a new agency, the Lords of Trade, was formed in 1675.

The Lords of Trade, in contrast to previous groups, advocated and attempted to implement a vigorous colonial policy. The disposition of the Crown to award large proprietary grants aroused opposition from the Lords of Trade, and when the later grants were made, notably to Penn, the powers given the proprietor were much less sweeping than those given to Lord Baltimore. Indeed, the Lords of Trade agitated, though without success, for the abolition of proprietary colonies, advocating that proprietary charters should be revoked and the colonies brought under direct royal supervision.

The Lords of Trade were unable to curtail the most flagrant violation of the mercantilist spirit and policy—the semi-independence of the corporate colonies of New England from England. Prodded particularly by the reports of Edward Randolph, adding to the ample evidence already available, the Lords of Trade recommended and obtained the annulment of the Massachusetts Bay Charter in 1684 and the substitution of the Dominion of New England in 1686.

The Dominion, in a sense, was a super-colony, including within its jurisdiction Massachusetts, New Hampshire, Connecticut, Rhode Island, New York, and New Jersey; Pennsylvania was eventually expected to be incorporated within this framework. The Crown, acting upon the recommendation of the Lords of Trade, appointed a governor, Sir Edmund Andros, but no immediate provision was made for an assembly, although a council of advisors was stipulated. Andros, with his limited intellect and petty, arrogant spirit, was a frail reed to entrust with such a dramatic, far-reaching, colonial experiment. The intense resentment on the part of the colonials, fostered by the lack of a representative assembly, the arbitrary dismissal of individual charters, and the appointment of Andros, caused them to cast about for some solution to their dilemma.

The Glorious Revolution of 1688, which deposed the Stuart monarchy, created an opportunity for the colonials that they quickly seized. Acting on the premise that Andros represented a discarded regime, the colonials imprisoned that unfortunate gentleman as a symbol of their allegiance to the new government set up by William and Mary. Each colony included within the Dominion hastily returned to the paths of colonial self-government practiced before the Dominion was created. The Dominion was treated as an unpleasant but fortunately brief interruption. The Glorious Revolution, therefore, marked the end of the Dominion, for political demands and domestic preoccupations did not permit King William to fashion a long-range colonial policy.

In many ways, the experiment of the Dominion of New England was a turning point in colonial political affairs. Although the colonials opposed the creation of the Dominion, they were not yet sufficiently strong to defeat or even to offset seriously the royal will. The success of the Dominion could have led to unification of the colonies under a single head and the reduction of colonial self-government. Moreover, if England had been successful in achieving a consolidated colonial government, an American revolution would not have produced a federal system of government because individual colonies would not have existed. Therefore, colonies could not have become states. A consolidated national government rather than a federal system would have resulted. But the fall of the Dominion gave the colonies a breathing spell, a respite which allowed the newly planted colonies to get their bearings and the older colonies to acquire strength.

The Revolution of 1688, by bringing to an end the experiment of dictated government in the colonies as a substitute for self-government, undermined the strength of the central authority within the Empire. But the Glorious Revolution also raised questions: Which group, or groups, within a particular colony was to wield power? Where did the power of the King and Parliament end and that of the colonials, as expressed through colonial self-government, begin?* At no time during the formative years were these issues finally resolved.

Of the continental colonies, the Chesapeake colonies were the most prized by the mother country. The statistics of trade in 1700 amply document the story. New England imported £91,000 sterling of goods from England but only supplied England with goods valued at £41,000 sterling. Although the earliest New England fur trade found a ready market in England, fisheries and shipping developing after 1640 were enterprises that rivaled those of the mother country. In practice, New England trade was ill suited to the theoretic schemes of mercantilism. In contrast, Virginia and Maryland by 1700 furnished large quantities of marketable commodities, chiefly tobacco, though naval stores and furs were included, thus fulfilling their prescribed colonial role as suppliers. Commodities valued at £317,000 sterling were exported from the Chesapeake colonies to England; goods estimated at £173,000 sterling were exported from England to Virginia and Maryland.

Because the balance appears heavily weighted in favor of Vir-

* The development of self-government as a force in the transition of English colonials to American provincials will be discussed in Chapters 6 and 9.

ginia and Maryland, the presumption is that the Chesapeake colonies could easily accumulate credit in England; yet the complaint
recorded with almost monotonous regularity is that the Virginia
and Maryland planters, although generally prospering, were in
debt. The presumption is that the planters either lived beyond
their means, which occasionally was true, or that they overex-
tended their capital investment. More rarely, the Chesapeake
planters are depicted as lovers of leisure, wastrels in contrast to
the thrifty New Englanders.

The characterization is unjust because the statistics of trade are
misleading. The statistics reflect the value of the commodities
when they enter or leave British customs. Therefore, the value of
a commodity like tobacco when imported from the colonies represents, in terms of British customs, the price of the commodity in
America plus the carrying and shipping charges which accrued in
transporting that commodity to England. In contrast, a commodity exported to the colony is valued in terms of its price in
England before the necessary shipping and handling charges are
added. From the perspective of the colonists, therefore, the statistics on the trade between the mother country and the colonies
inflate the value of the commodities exported by the colonies and
deflate the value of the English goods imported.

In this perspective, the true cash value of the commodities
shipped to England by the Chesapeake planters should be assessed
more realistically at £80,000 to £100,000 sterling, an appraisal
which tends to be confirmed by the average export during these
years (around 1700) of 35,000,000 pounds of tobacco. When this
export figure is set beside the £173,000 sterling of goods brought
to the Chesapeake colonies, the indebtedness of the Chesapeake
planters is more comprehensible.

The re-evaluations made with regard to the trade statistics of the
Chesapeake colonies do not have equal validity when applied to
New England. First, none of that region's exports were subjected
to heavy import duties when shipped to England, and, second,
New England frequently furnished its own carriers, so that those

services brought, in some measure, a balance of payments between exports and imports.

The direction of trade for the English continental colonies was, in many ways, predetermined. Only two possible markets presented themselves for New England commodities—southern Europe and the West Indies. The Chesapeake colonies, with tobacco the chief staple, found their markets in England and Europe, although the artificial device of enumeration directed the trade exclusively through England, to be re-exported to the European markets. These lines of trade in the early colonial period were generally straight lines forming various geometric patterns. The so-called triangular trade, for example—slaves from Africa to the West Indies, molasses from the West Indies to New England to be made into rum, and rum shipped to Africa to buy slaves—was rare, if not nonexistent. Until the late seventeenth century the slave trade was monopolized by the Royal African Company, although the monopoly seldom operated effectively. Dutch and English free traders poached upon it, but their operations did not become lucrative until the end of the seventeenth and the beginning of the eighteenth centuries. Not until the eighteenth century did the triangular trade develop.

The trade of the colonials created problems as well as solved them. Specie was drained out of the colonies to pay for the goods imported, and lack of currency was a chronic complaint. New England's inability to furnish goods for the English market, and thus its inability to establish a credit directly in England to pay for English goods forced its mercantile community to use a more indirect method. Credit was built up in the West Indies. By using the English agents doing business in the Caribbean as part of a pattern of mercantile correspondents, New Englanders transferred credit accumulated in the West Indies to England—in effect a bookkeeping and service operation—where it was used to secure finished goods for importation. Excessive carrying and service charges plagued the Chesapeake colonies and they responded to the problem this created in securing credit merely by producing more tobacco, causing serious marketing problems brought on by overproduction. Neither in New England nor in the Chesapeake colonies did responses keep pace with the problem, so that the issue of money and credit persisted. In modern terms, the colonies were an economically backward area which was hard pressed to find money to invest in capital expenditures and to pay for imports.

Trade should not be considered merely in terms of merchants or seaports. In a commercial capitalistic economy where production was for market, an early characteristic of the English Empire, the small farmer producing crops to sell was dependent upon the stream of trade in the same way that an established merchant was. His individual stake in trade was not, of course, as high, but in relationship to his income and livelihood his interest could equal that of a merchant.

As outposts of empire, the colonies were valued according to their contribution to the mercantile life of the mother country. From the colonial perspective and from the perspective of posterity, this standard of value is too constricting as transplanted Englishmen became provincial Americans.

6

From Colonies to Provinces

IN THE LATE seventeenth and early eighteenth centuries a metamorphosis occurred as English colonies became American provinces. This transition did not move at the same pace in every colony, for each colony had not achieved an identical level of maturity, but the Glorious Revolution in England (1688), which overthrew King James II, served in many instances as a catalyst. The final form evolving in each American province differed, for each province was the product of a diversity of forces.

Underlying the transition was a common denominator—social instability. In the early years of colonization, English social patterns, or at least the image of what those patterns should be, were transplanted to the New World. Each man recognized his place within that pattern. The perquisites and obligations of each rank in the society—the nobleman with title, the gentleman, the yeoman, the servant—were established and accepted. Although the rigorous life demanded in a wilderness environment prevented a precise reproduction of the pattern, the adjustments came about out of convenience and were presumed to be temporary. If few men of title came to America, the image of what constituted a proper social structure remained unchanged. Sooner or later, it was assumed, the colonial society would once again correspond to the familiar English image, a place for every man and every man in his place.

As second- and third-generation colonials were born who had no firsthand knowledge of the English society of the early seventeenth century, as new wealth was created and old wealth was dissipated, in short, as men and conditions changed, the familiar image of the social structure in the minds of the first Englishmen who came to settle in America became blurred. Almost unknowingly, men maturing in the American environment were searching for a substitute to replace a social system no longer immediate or pertinent with a new system in which the place of an individual would be accepted and assured. It was, in its own way, a colonial quest for identity.

As it searched for its own definitions, its own identification, in the late seventeenth and early eighteenth centuries, colonial society was affected by two outstanding considerations: social mobility and, even more important, the downright anxiety of all colonials, regardless of the social and economic position they had attained, as they faced an unsettled present and a thoroughly unpredictable future.

The amount of social mobility during the transition from colonies to provinces is, as yet, undetermined. The common assumption is that throughout the formative period (1607–1763) anyone with talent, regardless of background and origin, could attain a position of influence and power. Enough individual cases can be cited to give substance to this generalization: Sir William Phips in Massachusetts, a ship's carpenter who became Governor of Massachusetts and upon whom a title was conferred by the Crown; Benjamin Franklin in Pennsylvania, who rose from an apprentice printer to an affluent publisher-statesman-intellectual; the Manigault family in South Carolina, who, in a generation, rose from poverty to a position of economic, political, and social influence the equal of any family in the southern colonies. Moreover, these examples were probably sufficient to encourage all provincials to believe that their individual futures were promising.

However, the ready presumption of exceptional social mobility throughout the colonial period seems unwarranted, although the probability of high social mobility during the period of transition to provincial status appears logically sound but as yet unprovable. In colonies settled early—Massachusetts and Virginia—an abrupt slowdown in mobility probably occurred by the 1720s or 1730s. In colonies settled late—Pennsylvania and South Carolina—the slowdown probably came later, in the 1740s or 1750s. Factors such as the influx of indentured servants, the accessibility and distribution of fertile land, and the relative growth of seaport towns must be related to a precise investigation of individual communities in order to arrive at reliable approximations, a task historians have yet to tackle on a comprehensive scale.*

Even crude estimates, however, allow for some generalizations. In New England, for example, the rise of the new merchant class during the late seventeenth century, the reduction in the power of the Puritan oligarchy, and a modification in the system of distributing lands, enabling individuals to obtain extensive land grants, produced a new elite. Whereas the elite of the seventeenth century had been determined by a combination of religion and birth, Puritanism plus the status of gentleman, the elite of the eighteenth century was determined primarily by wealth gained either in land or trade, plus, on occasion, the legacy of being a member of an old New England family. Because the non-English migration in the eighteenth century was directed to areas other than New England, the most impoverished immigrants, who in the middle colonies comprised the lower strata of society, did not appear. A modest number of lower-class men and women did come as servants, but New England was made up primarily of a middle-class population largely devoid of the unskilled worker, who went elsewhere, and the aristocrat, who never came.

An even more significant factor than social mobility, however, in

* Professor Oscar Handlin of Harvard University, as Director of the Center for the Study of the History of Liberty in America, is supervising a significant scholarly investigation of social mobility in early America, using the roster of Harvard graduates as a point of departure.

the period of transition from colonies to provinces, involves the anxiety experienced by all colonials regardless of status, an anxiety perhaps heightened among the emerging provincial elite because they had the most to lose. Control of political power was by no means won; indeed, the outlook, in many instances, was at best obscure. The limits of England's power in the individual colonies had not been determined. The Dominion of New England had demonstrated how extensive the authority of the mother country could be when exercised with determination. Who was to say the Dominion experiment would not be repeated—and on a more comprehensive scale? Of course, in theory the limits of England's power were never determined, but in practice those limits were gradually defined during the early decades of the eighteenth century. Political and economic power were directly related. Whoever controlled the colonial government could control the distribution of land or could determine internal economic regulation, whether it be tobacco inspection laws in Virginia, regulation of wages in Massachusetts, or port legislation in Pennsylvania.

Therefore, evidence of unrest during the transition period did not reflect primarily a conflict between rich and poor, haves and have-nots, gentlemen and yeomen, seaboard and back country, merchant and farmer. Instead, the unrest reflected the insecurity of every man. No one, irrespective of his success, was assured of his present status, much less of his future status.

To cite an example, the large landholder in Virginia in the 1670s and 1680s was insecure; he was uncertain of his access to authority. In the operation of colonial government, he acted indecisively because the boundaries of power were, as yet, ill-defined. Tumbling prices brought about by legislation in England seriously jeopardized his economic position. To protect his future, even a large landholder needed more land, a bank upon which to draw as his older lands wore out. Yet the power to distribute land in the late seventeenth century remained for all practical purposes in England, where the King or one of the King's favorites could obtain a grant to a part or all of the vacant lands in Virginia. By the 1720s and 1730s, in contrast, the large landholder in Virginia had secured political power; he was a part of the system that controlled the distribution of land. Whereas his position in Virginia society in the 1670s and 1680s was shaky, by the 1720s and 1730s it was relatively fixed. Correspondingly, a merchant of New York or Boston in the 1670s and 1680s, new to wealth, experienced a period of uneasy transition until he achieved an assured social position and gained dominant political authority.

By the 1730s, generally, the structure of eighteenth-century provincial society was essentially defined, so much so that historians have written with assurance, and often with overconfidence, about the precise levels. Social mobility still permitted persons to move from one level to another within that structure, but by the mid-eighteenth century, individuals could determine within reason when they had achieved a new status.

As early as 1915 Charles M. Andrews, in editing the *Narratives of the Insurrections, 1675–1690,* emphasized the instability of colonial society during the two decades on either side of the turn of the century, but until recently these insurrections, though interesting and important in themselves, have not been considered within the context of the entire period, as a part of the formation of a provincial society. Seen in a larger framework, these evidences of instability become at once more comprehensible and more significant. Bacon's Rebellion in Virginia, Leisler's Rebellion in New York, the Protestant "revolt" in Maryland, and even the Salem witch trials and the change of charter in Massachusetts reflect in varying degrees certain underlying trends.

Bacon's Rebellion in Virginia in 1676 is too often discussed only in terms of the immediate details, or it is alluded to as a forerunner of the American Revolution. Instead, Bacon's Rebellion can be best understood as one phase in the development between the 1670s and the 1720s of a relatively fixed social structure within the province of Virginia, and with this, the development of a corresponding stability in the exercise of power and responsibility. In the 1670s the Virginians of Louis Wright's *First Gentlemen of Virginia*—William Fitzhugh, Richard Lee, the Carters, and the Byrds—began to acquire position and power, but the consequence was not assured, much less fixed, until the early decades of the eighteenth century. In addition, the relatively fluid social structure of late seventeenth-century Virginia became largely immobile by 1730. Indentured servants, aspiring to yeomanry, characterized the 1670s; slaves, confined to perpetual bondage, characterized the 1720s. Small planters held a reasonable hope of becoming large planters in the 1670s; by the 1720s this hope was fast diminishing.

Bacon's Rebellion, historians agree, was triggered by the Indian problem, with all the side issues that such a problem inevitably entailed: encroachment of settlers upon Indian territory; the struggle between settlers for Indian trade; the presence of a possible Indian trade monopoly by those holding political power, in this case Governor William Berkeley and his associates; the conflict between those colonials who wished to settle and those who wished to trade; and the struggle among Indian tribes for access to the white man's trading goods.

In 1675–76 Virginia's outlying settlements were harassed by Indian attacks, and in 1676 a substantial group of Virginia planters, perhaps a majority, wished to launch a powerful counterblow. Governor Berkeley, who had earlier won the affection of Virginia planters but who now found himself in disagreement, opposed such an operation and advocated limited defensive action. The Virginia governor's motivation is not clear; the position he took has been ascribed variously to his genuine desire to find a peaceful settlement of the dispute, to his crass self-interest, especially his investment in the Indian trade, and to his shrewd assessment that several thousand Virginians under arms might constitute a threat to the royal authority he represented.

A young member of the colonial council, Nathaniel Bacon, Junior, who had been in Virginia less than two years, became the popular leader around whom those wishing to take action rallied. Bacon eventually assumed policy-making powers, drove the governor from the capital, and led his supporters on several swift and successful missions to chastise the Indians. But the struggle against the constituted authority, represented by Governor Berkeley, proved abortive. Bacon, worn out from his intensive campaign, became ill and died. His supporters, no longer able to maintain unity, could not withstand the reassertion of authority by Governor Berkeley and the rebellion collapsed less than eighteen months after its eruption, enabling the governor to take revenge upon his opponents—at least until the King's Commissioners arrived to stay his hand and to force his withdrawal as governor.

The accounts of Bacon's Rebellion give inordinate space to the Indian provocations, the campaigns responding to these provocations, and the crisis of Bacon's assumption of authority, largely because the evidence on these points is overwhelming. However, the subtle nuances as to why the rebellion occurred and where this action fits into the pattern of colonial provincial development has not been fully explored, nor is it readily resolved. Robert Beverley, a contemporary who sided with Berkeley in this crisis, recognized in his *History and Present State of Virginia* that deeper issues obviously must be at stake to provoke men to "hazard their Necks by Rebellions," particularly to choose "a Leader they hardly knew, to oppose a Gentleman, that had been so long, and so deservedly the Darling of the People." Beverley suggested four ingredients of the internal conflict: the low price of tobacco and the depressed conditions which resulted; "the splitting the Colony in to Proprieties, contrary to the original charters"; the Acts of Trade, which were beginning to bear heavily upon the Virginia colonials; and, finally, the Indian provocations.

Each of these ingredients suggested by Beverley intensified the feeling or instability. With tobacco prices falling and depressed conditions affecting even the largest planters, the future looked

K

uncertain. Could a man retain his economic position? Could he advance his position? The Acts of Trade, which fell more heavily upon Virginia than upon other English continental colonies because of the enumeration of tobacco, constituted a threat to the Virginia economy and thus to the evolving structure of society.

Beverley's second cause is seldom given sufficient attention by modern historians. A proprietary grant in Virginia, embracing the region eventually known as the Northern Neck—and romanticized by the story of George Washington's survey of the Fairfax estates—contributed significantly to the uncertainty of the 1670s. Including the rich territory between the Potomac and Rappahannock rivers, this grant, given to favorites of the restored Stuarts while the King was in exile in 1649 and later renewed in 1669, removed choice land with easy access to sea routes from the possibility of acquisition and exploitation by native Virginians. Prominent Virginia planters, and small planters or yeoman farmers who wished to imitate the success of the larger planters, could agree that opportunities for growth in the colony were dramatically reduced by a decision in England beyond the control of the colonials. If one grant were given, could not additional grants follow? The Crown's abortive attempt in 1673 and at later intervals to make Lord Arlington and Lord Culpeper, two English aristocrats in particular favor, landlords for the whole of Virginia for a period of thirty-one years lent substance to these fears.

In addition, the grant of the Northern Neck lands to proprietors affected the Indian problem. With the natural expansion of Virginia north along the accessible waterways in doubt, the Indian barrier toward the northwest became especially important; the area occupied by the Indians automatically became the best land available for westward expansion. Disruption of the traditional Indian trade with New York and spirited rivalry among the tribes congregating along the Virginia frontier—the congestion had been growing in part because of a recent Indian migration from Maryland—aggravated the issues raised by the proprietary grant.

The Northern Neck grant, therefore, caused instability in Virginia in two ways: by raising doubts in the minds of Virginians about their economic future and by complicating the Indian problem. No wonder, then, that the colony sent a delegation to England to ask that the grant be reconsidered; ironically, the expenses of the delegation placed an additional tax burden on the Virginia colonials, a factor contributing to the general discontent.

Between the 1670s and the 1720s, colonial instability in Virginia was transformed into provincial stability. The details of this evolution cannot be crowded into a book of this length, but the outlines can be delineated. In this period, for instance, *desire* for colonial political power was transformed into the *triumph* of provincial political power, exercised in most cases with responsibility. With this transfer, the fruits of power, most significantly the distribution of land—the basis of wealth and station in Virginia —passed for all practical purposes into the hands of Virginians, in contrast to the seventeenth century when royal authority in the distribution of lands remained decisive. The social structure became clearly defined, frozen at the bottom by the influx of slaves and frozen at the top by the emergence of a provincial elite who were not easily persuaded to accept new members into their exclusive circle. It was still possible for small planters to become large planters by acquiring new lands in the West or by making an advantageous marriage, as George Washington proved in his lifetime, but those who already were large planters took advantage of their position to maintain and expand their sources of wealth—and power. By the 1730s, the pattern of provincial society in Virginia had been set.

The principal instrument in achieving provincial superiority was not, as is so often assumed, the people speaking through the House of Burgesses, but rather the actions of the elite council, whose membership was made up of select planters, who championed the cause of provincial control against the royal authority as exercised by the governor. Struggle for control arose over central issues—appointments, land grants, and the church, to mention a few—in which a determined council, made up of the most affluent provincials, clipped the governor's power in its everyday exercise. Although this trend was evident throughout the period, the years between 1706 and 1710 witnessed a surge upward of provincial prerogative; at this time, in the absence of an appointed governor, the council ruled unhampered by royal restraint. Lieutenant-Governor Alexander Spotswood (1710–22), an able official, attempted to recapture the full prerogatives of the governor's office, but he was consistently checked by the provincial leaders; at the conclusion of his service, provincial control was never again seriously challenged. From this date forward, American provincials shaped the destiny of Virginia.

During the provincial period (1720–76), the balance of power was to shift once again as the House of Burgesses gradually expanded their power, often at the expense of the council, becoming in fact the most articulate voice of the colony. The stand-up fight against arbitrary imperial authority had been won, or so it was assumed, until a new crisis occurred in the restless 1760s when imperial authority attempted to reassert itself.

Three additional insurrections, quite different in form, which occurred in New York, in Maryland, and in Massachusetts, illustrate the widespread social instability present in English America in the late seventeenth and early eighteenth centuries.

In New York in the late seventeenth and early eighteenth centuries, the transition from Dutch to English domination, the agitation for political representation, and the instability within the colony created a hospitable climate for the aggressive and ambitious. During this period, for instance, Robert Livingston gained the power and position—often by questionable means—to establish the Livingston dynasty, which extended into the nineteenth century.

The rapidity of events affecting New York in the late seventeenth century is frequently overlooked: the English capture of New Netherland (1664); the precarious English rule over a population overwhelmingly Dutch; the recapture (1673), though brief, of New York by the Dutch in the trade wars; and the change, when the Duke of York became James II, from a proprietary to a royal colony (1685). At the same time, Englishmen moved into the province in increasing numbers; competition with the French for the valuable fur trade intensified; the full force of English trade regulations were first experienced; and New England threatened to dominate the mercantile activity of New York City. As if these numerous external pressures were not enough, the internal discontent between the merchants of New York City and the outlying areas, between the English settlers on Long Island and the Dutch settlers in other parts of New York, between the artisans and the merchants, made a serious condition worse. The sense of anxiety in New York had a firm basis in fact.

Consider briefly a number of principal problems. Were the Dutch sufficiently loyal to the English so that they could be trusted in the militia? Were lands on Long Island, granted by the Dutch to English settlers without restrictions, properly subject to quitrents after the English conquest, as the representatives of the Duke of York contended? By forcing the English and Dutch settlers to "renew" their patents, many settlers, particularly those on Long Island, asserted that their property rights were being infringed. Taxes laid by the governor—without legislative consent, for no colonial assembly existed—provoked protests from the New York colonials in petitions to England that they lacked the essential "liberties of english men," a cry best articulated by the provincial elite, who complained "a yearly Revenue is Exacted from us . . . without our consents."

Internal frictions were perennial. On occasion, for instance, on the theory that foodstuffs were in short supply, prohibitions were placed upon the export of grain, thereby reducing the farmers' market. Beginning in 1679, New York City gained a monopoly in milling and packaging flour for export, a measure promoted by New York merchants that obviously irritated the landholders, large and small. In 1683 Governor Thomas Dongan finally received instructions to call an assembly, but this concession meant little because the creation of the Dominion of New England in 1686 eliminated the assembly and placed New York within the administrative structure of its more powerful neighbors.

To the English policy makers the inclusion of New York in the Dominion made good sense. It strengthened the defenses of the English settlements in America, particularly in a province so predominantly non-English. Even New Englanders had been unhappy with the attitude of New York during King Philip's War (1675–76), when the Indians had struck against the New England settlements with such vengeance. For their part, New York colonials looked upon the Dominion with dismay, not only because of the lack of representative government, which so annoyed the New England colonies, but because New Yorkers feared that the growing trade of New York City and the Hudson River Valley would become dominated by New England enterprisers. New York colonials, who had grasped a measure of power and influence and who wished to strengthen their position in any opportunistic fashion that presented itself, had no stomach for external competition.

The collapse of the Dominion of New England with the overthrow of the Stuarts in 1688 triggered a revolt in New York, commonly referred to as Leisler's Rebellion. In 1660 twenty-year-old Jacob Leisler migrated from the German Palatinate to New Amsterdam, where, in 1663, he married a rich widow whose fortune and connections enabled him to become a prosperous New York merchant. When word reached New York that New England had jailed Sir Edmund Andros, governor of the Dominion, making uncertain the tenure of Francis Nicholson, Andros' deputy in New York, the militia captains of the colony, six in number, seized the fort at New York. To judge from the evidence, Leisler, a militia captain, was not the leader in this decision, nor did he seek to be commander of the fort or, three months later, commander-in-chief. He was chosen by his peers.

From 1689 to 1691, Leisler, with widespread support from merchants, artisans, the Long Island towns, and some upcountry landholders, controlled the government. Upon the arrival of Governor Henry Sloughter, representing the new sovereigns, William and Mary, Leisler surrendered the government, but only after unnecessary delay and an imprudent display of belligerance. Leisler found himself charged with treason and in May 1691 he was hanged. The merits of this harsh verdict continue to be disputed by historians.

In terms of the social tensions within the colony, Leisler has been described by some historians as the champion of the impoverished against the privileged. This version has enough validity to become a half-truth. No doubt the Bayards, the Van Cortlandts, and the Philipses, those mighty families whose influence was sharply reduced by the action of Leisler and his followers, resented this upstart. On the other hand, powerful merchants and landholders were parties to Leisler's coup. Leisler's Rebellion brought about a slight shift of power, not a pronounced social upheaval. Most significantly, it reflected the anxiety permeating all classes and groups in society. The sequence of events had moved so swiftly and taken such an irregular course since the 1660s that no one could be assured of the outcome.

One motive for the support of Leisler, aside from the backlog of colonial grievances, was the fear of French Catholicism. In retrospect, this fear on the part of New Yorkers and Leisler appears absurd; but in the eyes of contemporaries the fear was real—and blinding. Was not King James II a Catholic? Did not Nicholson represent the King? Were not the French Catholics the great competitors for the hinterland? Had not the Dutch, who composed the great majority of the inhabitants, felt the imposition of the Spanish Catholics in their native land? Was it not, therefore, prudent, and indeed necessary, to assure the colony of protection against the possibility of a Catholic domination? Of course, the fear, in realistic terms, was baseless; but in and of itself, it was demoralizing.

That these fears could gain such headway is an indication of the powerful transition taking place in the colony of New York. The class structure was not settled, political rights were in the process of definition, and the avenues to economic advancement were undergoing a serious modification that catered to the aggressive opportunists. During the provincial eighteenth century, some of these issues were resolved—at least until a new crisis in the 1760s and 1770s reopened the inquiry as to the source of power and its exercise.

Maryland also reflected the transition from English colonies to American provinces. Despite the good intentions of the proprietor, grievances had accumulated in late seventeenth-century Maryland. To the majority of the inhabitants of Maryland, self-government had been subverted. The proprietor, so his opponents claimed, had filled the important colonial offices with members of his family, suffrage requirements had been arbitrarily altered, and, in summoning an assembly, the proprietor was able, by indirect means, to keep out those who opposed his policies. These claims, though exaggerated, had some basis of fact. When the Stuarts were overthrown in 1688, the dissident elements used the accumulated colonial dissatisfaction to alter radically the political position of the colonials. The coincidence between the objectives of the Maryland colonials and those of English imperial officials, who advocated the elimination of all proprietary colonies and a closer integration between individual colonies and imperial regulation, worked to the advantage of the colonials when Maryland was made a royal colony in 1689.

Since the general populace, uncertain what the future held, vacillated, those colonials willing to take decisive action came to the fore. "An Association in Arms for the Defense of Protestant Religion and For Asserting the Right of King William and

Queen Mary," originally led by John Coode, was the political force that overturned the proprietary assembly without bloodshed. The association issued a declaration July 27, 1689, stating the purpose for resorting to arms, together with "the reasons and motives inducing us thereunto," in a format not entirely unlike the Declaration of 1776. A new government was established, an election of delegates was held, and an assembly was called.

Throughout these proceedings, as the title of the association suggests, there ran a strong anti-Catholic bias. False rumors suggesting a tie between the French Catholics and the Maryland Catholics, properly labeled a "sleeveless [that is, empty] fear" by one prominent Maryland Protestant, effectively aroused opposition against the proprietary government. When the new government was established, it promptly eliminated all Catholics from public office, and during the first decades of the eighteenth century, severe anti-Catholic measures were enacted which forbade Catholic church schools, public religious services, and the like.

Yet it is interesting that the group which led the "revolt" in Maryland relinquished its power to the newly elected assembly and advocated greater emphasis upon local—that is, county—government. As matters developed, the widespread desire throughout Maryland for greater self-government became apparent.

With the issuance of a governor's commission in 1692 to Lionel Copley, Maryland began a period of expanding self-government which ended, in chronological terms, in 1715, but which endured, in terms of influence, up to and into the Revolution. Legislative enactment, not an ordinance from the proprietor, determined the election of delegates. For the first time in the history of the colony, the entire election process fell under the control of the Maryland provincials. New counties, the base units of political representation, were created by acts of the assembly, not by proprietary order. Even the power to create new offices was gradually assumed by the legislature, a departure from previous practice, and the machinery to administer justice came increasingly under the jurisdiction of the assembly. In sum, the power of the assembly was greatly broadened and the basis for the authority of the assembly, the consent of the governed, was strengthened. Maryland, despite the anti-Catholic repercussions of the "revolt," was transformed politically, and to an extent economically and socially, from colonial to provincial status in the final decade of the seventeenth century and the early decades of the eighteenth century.

The anti-Catholic excesses in Maryland paralleled in a sense the witch hunts in New England and Bacon's Rebellion in Virginia. For a society in transition, uncertain of its aims and precepts, scapegoats become a substitute for purpose. A society that is confident of itself, its ends and its future, does not read into the views or practices of minority segments threats of dissolution.

The witch trials in Massachusetts (1692–94) have been examined from almost every perspective except that which makes the most sense. This unfortunate episode has been used to denigrate the Puritan faith and to expose the fanaticism of the Massachusetts religious leaders; or the episode has been rationalized by comparing it with outbreaks of witch trials at other times and in other places. But the essential question remains: Why did the witch mania gain fervent support in Massachusetts during the final decade of the seventeenth century? Many factors together produced this result, but the underlying explanation lies in the transition taking place in Massachusetts society as accepted standards of value and conduct were challenged, as a new elite, uncertain of its place or purpose, began to exercise greater power, as the political certainties of the past gave way, with the issuance of the new colonial charter in 1691, to the political uncertainties of the future.

Consider, as a single example, the rapid series of political events crowded into the last two decades of the seventeenth century, all requiring serious adjustments on the part of the populace. In 1684 the Massachusetts charter was revoked. In 1686 the Domin-

ion of New England eliminated the traditional institutions of
self-government, including the colonial assembly and the right
of a franchise, and cast doubt upon the practice of local government and even upon the validity of land titles. In 1689, with the
accession of William and Mary to the throne, this threat evap-
orated only to be replaced by a new fear: What type of government would replace that of the Dominion? Meanwhile, in 1690
a Massachusetts expedition sent out to challenge the French
stronghold at Quebec ended in confusion, disappointment, and
almost disaster. Finally, after several years of indecision, a new
charter was granted to Massachusetts in 1691. The charter not
only specifically modified earlier patterns of government—for
example, it based the franchise upon property requirements
rather than upon church membership—but it also raised questions of interpretation, as do all written documents, that could
only be determined by everyday practice and experience. Until
practice and experience could resolve these issues, an air of indecision, of tentativeness, surrounded political affairs.

Thus, the Massachusetts witch mania was significant not for
its impact upon events but as a symbol of profound changes in
the structure and evolution of Massachusetts society. Former
institutions could not be depended on, either the church or
school, or the judicial or political systems. Even the protection
of individual liberties as experienced in earlier decades was uncertain. Samuel Williard spoke for many a Massachusetts provincial when he prayed, "Lord, lead me through this Labyrinth."

The list of actors involved in the witchcraft trials is extensive,
but the initial frenzy was set off by the affectations of young-
sters who, by their antics, found themselves the center of attention and, what is more, invested with rare authority when they
were urged by their elders to confess the names of their tor-
mentors. Although eruptions of the witchcraft hysteria occurred
in other New England towns, Salem was the headquarters. Before the fever subsided, more than one hundred men and women
were imprisoned and twenty were executed. A mass pardon by

Sir William Phips, the newly appointed governor who had originally approved the trials, probably saved the lives of others, although the virulence of the movement had by May 1693 largely spent itself. The witchcraft episode also became linked to leading clerics, notably Cotton Mather, whose *Wonders of the Invisible World* appeared during the height of the mania and no doubt added to it. Cotton Mather and his father, Increase Mather, by employing too literally a technique of laying on of hands upon the body of a young devil-tormented female named Margaret Rule of Boston, brought contemporary criticism upon themselves; because of this and other incidents, these two divines became wrongly identified in the popular mind as the foremost among the witch-hunters.

Increase Mather was probably the foremost Puritan cleric of his age; he was pastor of the Second Church in Boston (1664–1723) and president of Harvard College (1685–1701). In 1688 he was sent to England by the Massachusetts churches to represent them in their struggle against the Dominion of New England with the objective of securing a restoration of the original charter. After the Glorious Revolution, Mather was one of four Massachusetts agents to obtain a new charter. Increase Mather's influence can be evaluated in part by a courtesy extended to him by the new King: the privilege of nominating the first governor under the new charter.

Upon returning to Massachusetts in 1692, Mather encountered two sets of enemies with two widely separated points of view. He was opposed by the so-called conservatives within the church, who blamed him for the charter's provision altering the terms of the franchise from church membership to property qualifications; his firm support of the new charter scarcely quieted this enmity. On the other hand, the so-called liberals represented by William Brattle and John Leverett, two Harvard tutors, opposed Mather as the symbol of the unenlightened old guard of the church. The liberals advocated fixed prayers, particularly the Lord's Prayer, the abandonment of a public display of religious conversion as a qualification for full communion, baptism for all children presented by professing Christians, and the right of all who contributed to the church to have a voice in the selection of the minister.

Under these conditions, any restatement of the church's position was bound to provoke opposition. In 1705 the *Massachusetts Proposals* were advanced in favor of centralizing ecclesiastical control of the Massachusetts churches as a partial substitute for the modified church-state relationship under the new charter. Under the old charter, the civil authority had been obligated to enforce religious conformity, punishing those who offended the canons of the church. Under the new charter, this particular relationship was disrupted, and the *Proposals* were introduced to fill the power vacuum. They instituted two requirements: (1) mandatory formation of ministerial associations and (2) the creation of standing committees within the associations to supervise strict conformity within the churches. The second requirement produced the most vigorous opposition, the most celebrated being that of Reverend John Wise, who issued two explicit documents, *The Churches' Quarrel Espoused* (1713) and *Vindication of the Government of New England Churches* (1717).

John Wise of Ipswich, whose reputation as an athlete gained him almost as much contemporary respect as his sermons, was destined to be remembered for his words rather than his deeds. During the period of the Dominion of New England, Governor Andros attempted to collect taxes in Ipswich, but a number of citizens including Wise refused to pay on the premise that the Dominion, by eliminating the assembly, was taxing without the consent of people. Parenthetically, it might be added that Wise eventually bent before the power of Andros and petitioned for a pardon. After 1705, confronted by an attempt to strengthen ecclesiastical supervision of individual congregations within Massachusetts, Wise fought the proposition on the premise that each congregation was independent: "I shall . . . inferr that these Churches . . . are fairly Established in their present Order by the Law of Nature." Mather's challenge and Wise's response were part of a larger pattern as the province of Massachusetts, in its ecclesiastical-civil relationship, attempted to determine an acceptable path in the transition from the old to the new.

As in ecclesiastical matters, so in the structure of political and judicial institutions Massachusetts experienced change in the transition from colony to province. Under the terms of the former Massachusetts charter, the legislative and the ultimate judicial authority of the colony were held by the General Court; it had the power to make laws, to raise money, to levy taxes, to dispose of lands, and to receive appeals from inferior courts. The General Court could not be dissolved or adjourned without the consent of a majority of its members. Although the governor could vote, he did not possess a veto. The governor and his assistants executed the laws, and they also exercised important judicial power.

Under the charter of 1691, the governor instead of being elected was appointed by the King, as was the lieutenant-governor and the secretary of the province. The governor could veto acts of the assembly, and, as was customary in royal colonies, the King could disallow an enactment within three years of its passage. Although the governor could not use funds without the consent of the legislature, no money could be issued from the treasury without the governor's warrant. The secular base of the government under the new charter, in which the franchise was determined by property qualifications rather than church membership, had far-reaching implications, even though at the outset the modification of the electorate appears to have been much less significant than historians have usually assumed. Yet the charter of 1691 confirmed practices established in the first half century of colonial life, the right to tax and to establish towns and town governments, rights which had been withdrawn during the period of the Dominion. In addition, religious toleration was extended by charter, to conform to the evolution of toleration in England.

Among the early enactments under the new charter were four separate acts to establish courts of justice; three of the four acts were eventually disallowed by the King. These acts show how Massachusetts legislators tried unsuccessfully to confirm all the former laws passed under the original charter. This attempt to establish under the new charter a judicial structure that would be like the structure that had existed before was an attempt to forestall change.

As long as definite lines of authority remained in doubt, whether they involved the relationship between the Crown and the colony or between elements within the colony—ecclesiastical, political, or judicial—the colonists were subject to uncertainty, to anxiety, to tension, and sometimes to extremism.*

The transition from English colonies to American provinces placed a serious strain upon peoples and institutions. On occasion the strain was great enough to bring about rebellions—in most cases short-lived—and nonviolent but dramatic changes that bordered on revolution. One of the principal bulwarks which minimized violence and enabled the American provincials to adjust to rapid change was the uninterrupted vitality of local government, a factor so obvious that it is frequently neglected.

The institutions of local government (discussed in Chapter 3, but deserving a brief recapitulation here) had originally been brought from England—the township in New England, the county in the South and later in the Middle Colonies. The local officials, such as the justices of the peace and the sheriff, were among the administrative officials with counterparts in England

---

* Some of the uncertainty and fear, as it turned out, was without foundation. For example, I have observed elsewhere (Chapter 4) that the "Fall of the Puritan Oligarchy" has been exaggerated in terms of a shift of power in Massachusetts Bay—a generalization that can be readily substantiated by data on the personnel and operation of local government and, with a bit less conviction, by similar evidence at the level of colonial government. This fact, however, does not invalidate the thesis expressed in this chapter. The historian looking back can detect important elements of continuity, but contemporaries were impressed with the pulsations of change.

whose functions and offices were established in the colonial settlements. The duties and the status of each office did not, however, in every instance parallel those of the corresponding office in England. Local government in America, especially in its exercise of coercive power, played a far different role in America. It reinforced the power of the individual colonies, thereby contributing to the decentralization of British authority, whereas in England it reinforced the authority of the King and Parliament, thereby enhancing the tie between the people and the central government.

The increasing authority and self-confidence exercised by local government during the seventeenth century acted as a stabilizing element during the transition from colonies to provinces. The necessity for vigorous local government was generally recognized by the American provincials, although the practice within colonies differed. In New York local government was not generally practiced during the proprietary period, but the urgency of vital self-government encouraged agitation for and establishment of local government in the final decades of the seventeenth century and its enlargement in the eighteenth century. South Carolina did not follow the practice of establishing new counties as its population increased. Therefore, all of South Carolina was a single county, a circumstance producing a pronounced and enduring political weakness in that colony. In certain colonies local civil authority was administered through an ecclesiastical unit, the parish, whereas in some colonies county courts occasionally administered ecclesiastical as well as civil affairs on a local level.

The significance and vitality of local government during the transition period can be measured by its uninterrupted vigor in Massachusetts and Virginia despite the crises in the late seventeenth and early eighteenth centuries. It can also be measured by the determination of Maryland to enlarge local government and that of New York to develop it. Without the stable base of experience in local government, the transition from colony to province might have been far more difficult to achieve, and the character of the Revolutionary crises beginning in 1776 and extending after 1800 no doubt would have been dramatically altered.

Whether democratization was a significant factor in the upheavals which characterized the transition or whether democratization was directly related to local government is a question disputed by historians. Studies have indicated that more people had the right to vote than is often conceded, although many did not consistently take advantage of this right. Having the right to vote, of course, cannot be equated with possessing power.

In perspective, the transition generally represented a transfer of control from the sovereign to a provincial elite, although in some colonies the transfer was from a colonial group whose power had been dissipated to a newly evolved provincial elite. In almost every colony, the few, not the many, enjoyed the perquisites of power: the appointment to choice offices, the manipulation of legislation, the large-scale acquisition of land. The rise of the people, therefore, does not appear to dominate the period of transition from colonies to provinces; rather, the period was marked by the resurgence of colonial self-government and the establishment of a provincial society in which the strata were relatively well defined and understood. By 1730 the social structure transplanted from England had been replaced by an indigenous provincial social construct.

The American provinces in the first half of the eighteenth century experienced an unprecedented expansion. At the same time, as the chapters to follow will elucidate, an expanding economy provided a sound base for political, social, and cultural maturity. The English colonies in America were no longer merely appendages of the Empire; they were being transformed into self-sufficient provinces, individual in character but with underlying elements of unity that permeated thought and practice.

L

7

Provincial Expansion

A SURGE of expansion swept over the American provinces in the eighteenth century, affecting every colony and penetrating almost all aspects of provincial life. In Virginia and in North Carolina the number of counties rose sharply as people migrated to the interior. In western Massachusetts, where the frontier had been badly dislocated during the swift and vengeful King Philip's War (1675-76), the march of expansion after 1700, symbolized by the founding of Great Barrington in 1730, was pointed toward the Berkshires. Similar developments in Connecticut and New Hampshire invited larger landed interests into the interior country, making choice opportunities available to speculators and land companies. Whereas the founding of Georgia, the thirteenth colony, in 1733 marked the extension of the southern frontier, the spectacular growth of the principal seaports—Charleston, Philadelphia, New York City, Newport, and Boston—reflected the rise and influence of the cosmopolitan urban complex, a frontier second to none in importance.

Some 250,000 people lived in the North American colonies in 1700; by the 1760s the population approached 2,000,000. Moreover, the composition of the population, particularly in the middle colonies but also in the southern colonies, changed dramatically because of the substantial migration of non-English people. In terms of informal census figures, the German migration alone, between 1700 and 1770, was approximately equal to the total population of the English continental colonies in 1700. Provincial expansion exerted a profound influence on the evolution of a provincial society, not the least being the introduction of a multi-national people.

The early eighteenth-century frontier, considered either as a geographical region or as "a form of society rather than an area," a phrase of Frederick Jackson Turner's, was an important component of provincial expansion. The area involved is the "Old West," a designation used by Turner in 1908 to indicate the territory between the Fall Line and the Appalachians, to which provincials migrated in the first half of the eighteenth century. In part, the Old West resembled earlier and later American frontiers; in part, the Old West was a distinctive frontier, notably in terms of mobility and perhaps in terms of democratization. The eighteenth century frontier came much closer to the ideal of the Turner hypothesis than did either the earlier or later frontiers.*

Many of the criticisms of the Turner hypothesis—that the impoverished did not have the means to travel to the frontier and to establish homesteads and the implied correlative thesis that the frontier did not operate as a social and political safety value, to suggest the most obvious—are valid in terms of the seventeenth-century continental colonies, when they served as one of several English frontiers. The long, hazardous, and relatively expensive voyage, to cite a lone illustration, acted as a barrier to screen off the poverty-ridden and the English aristocracy, thus introducing a limited range of classes in the colonies, which resulted in a strong, articulate, and energetic middling class.

* For those unacquainted with the Turner thesis, its theme was the powerful force the frontier exercised upon American society, that the frontier promoted democratic practices, that it provided opportunities for advancement for those of little or no means but willing to work, that it produced characteristics peculiarly American such as inventiveness, unbounded energy, a pragmatic outlook, a process which indeed changed accepted institutions.

Except for the absence of forested areas in parts of the nineteenth-century frontier, the many elements of the frontiers of the eighteenth and nineteenth centuries were similar. The abundance of wild game, the extensive herds of buffalo, especially in the middle and southern colonies, and the Indian trade, furs in the northern colonies and deerskins in the Carolinas and in Georgia —these considerations are little changed in the course of the westward movement. But the Indian barrier was a more formidable deterrent in the eighteenth century than in the nineteenth. The strategic position of the most powerful Indian nations, from the Cherokees and Chickasaws in the South to the Iroquois along the New England–New York frontier, blocked English access to the interior of the continent. Controlling the interior trade by their defensive position along the Appalachian range and strengthened by their ability to play off the European rivals, France and England, these Indians held the balance of power in America for almost a century (1660–1760). Not until the French had been eliminated as a major participant in colonizing the North American continent were the English finally able to penetrate the Appalachian barrier in any great numbers. The provincial expansion in the first half of the eighteenth century, therefore, was destined to wash up against the Appalachian ridge, to be contained within the environment of the Atlantic seaboard.

Ironically, by forcing the American provincials to adhere principally to the coastal areas, the Indians contributed to their own destruction. Prevented from moving westward, the provincials established a mature, vigorous, developed society, a massive build-up, in a sense, from which to launch an assault to conquer the inland wilderness. If the Englishmen had been able to penetrate deeply into the interior of America soon after settlement, the strength gained from cohesive, highly developed colonies would have been lost. And if deep penetration had been possible, the tie with England would unquestionably have been much less influential and the political experience of the settlements would have been less sophisticated, and therefore less valuable, for only a relatively stable community could provide it. The formidable Indian barrier contributed to the creation of a vigorous and structured provincial society, and in so doing, contributed to the development of political, economic, and intellectual institutions. These institutions, in turn, became so deeprooted that the sweeping westward movement of the nineteenth century failed to alter them in any fundamental way.

Although less influential than the Indian barrier, Indian trade represented one of the most important contacts between the whites and the Indians. Many of the first modest provincial fortunes were founded on Indian trade. In South Carolina, for example, the early road to riches, as the case of Samuel Eveleigh demonstrates, was not gained by raising rice but by trading in deerskins, one of the most valuable exports from the Carolinas until well into the eighteenth century. In Pennsylvania James Logan's emergence as the first citizen of that colony was made possible through what he called the "stinking" fur trade, and in New York the Indian trade brought a fortune and a title to Sir William Johnson.

During the eighteenth century, the locus of Indian trade shifted. By 1730 New England's share of the Indian trade was limited, if not negligible, and the middle colonies, the area of greatest expansion, had become the center of the fur trade, with New York and Pennsylvania well in the lead. In the South, Virginia controlled the principal trade with the Cherokees and the Chickasaws in the late seventeenth century, but early in the eighteenth century South Carolina developed into a serious rival. Because of its location, South Carolina gradually began to dominate the trade until the founding of Georgia (1733). Although South Carolina originally greeted the establishment of Georgia with enthusiasm because Georgia would serve as a buffer against the Spanish, Carolinians became increasingly hostile as Georgia's favorable position interfered with the lucrative Indian trade. By the mid-eighteenth century, New York and Georgia were perhaps the two colonies most deeply engaged in the Indian trade.

For the Indians, the extension of trade increased their dependency: for cooking utensils, for tools, axes, and knives, and even for apparel. Dependency bred trouble since the two societies, the white and the Indian, frequently misunderstood each other's bargaining terms. Each soci ty betrayed the other's confidence. Each society lived by rules of conduct that were alien to the other.

Examples to illustrate the last point could be introduced in almost infinite variations, but two will suffice. Indian hospitality was abused by many whites, particularly by the traders. As an act of friendship, many tribes made available to visiting whites unattached female companions, although Indians considered an act of intimacy with the wife of a brave a particularly grave offense. White traders too often stepped over this carefully drawn line. When the Indians sought similar favors when visiting the whites and were refused, they were baffled by the strange mores of the white society. In addition, the Indians seldom understood some of the complexities of the economic world in which the whites operated, especially the use of credit. Previous to the outbreak of a war with the Yamassees in the Carolinas in 1715, for example, the Indians were heavily obligated to the white traders for goods on credit. When the traders tried to collect deerskins in payment, the Indians reacted vigorously and, eventually, violently.

Trade disputes, conflict over territory, and Indian apprehension of the swelling tide of white settlers caused violent clashes between the Indians and the advancing settlements. In New England the climax of Indian-white friction came earlier than in other sections, and the result was the bitter King Philip's War (1675–76). King Philip's War represented the last desperate effort on the part of the Indians of New England to restrain the westward flow of migration in that region. The war was successful in wiping out the outer ring of white settlement, but the white settler, though checked, was not defeated and the Indians in the

New England area were never again able to mount an attack of similar magnitude. Their fate was epitomized by the decapitated body of the Indian king Philip, whose name became identified with a conflict in which he was but one of several defeated leaders. Although the frontier had been temporarily pushed back, although the white casualties had been high, although the cost had been burdensome and the economy had suffered, the New England provincials recovered to win new successes.

The most savage conflict between Indians and whites in the southern colonies was unquestionably the Yamassee War (1715–18). The conflict was provoked by the customary trio of troubles —trade, land, and credit. A skirmish between the Yamassees and the whites eventually involved all the powerful southern tribes except for the Cherokees. The Indian warriors greatly outnumbered the white defenders, and the war in its early stages favored the Indians; the evacuation of Carolina was not outside the realm of possibility. The crisis was so serious that every white adult male served on the fighting line. Only successful negotiations with the Cherokees, persuading them to remain neutral, saved the settlement. The Cherokees made their decision in part because of their distrust of other tribes, particularly the Chickasaws, but the most powerful argument was the promise of almost exclusive rights to the English trade. The division among the Indians enabled South Carolina to withstand the powerful Indian offensive, but the destruction caused by the war delayed colonial expansion for a decade. Moreover, the destruction of great herds of livestock forced the South Carolina economy to shift from cattle production to naval stores such as pitch, tar, and turpentine (after all, the Indians did not destroy the trees), and later to intensive rice production.

Friction was commonplace along the outreaches of the frontier, particularly along the western boundaries of the rapidly expanding middle and southern colonies. As the strategic position of the Indians was buttressed by the growing power of the French in North America, these Indian wars inevitably became involved with the contest in Europe to maintain a balance of power. The Indian wars, in their own way, became sectors in European wars (Chapter 12).

The Indian Appalachian barrier directly affected frontier migration. The stream of migration heading westward in Pennsylvania, composed primarily of Germans and Scotch-Irish, was shunted southward between the western fringes of the Blue Ridge Mountains and the eastern edge of the Appalachians to penetrate the valley of Virginia in the 1730s. This migration gradually moved southward to enter the Carolinas in the 1740s and 1750s and Georgia in the 1760s. The migration to the frontier was no longer from east to west, but from north to south. This migration eventually made many western counties of Virginia and of North Carolina, and the western territories of South Carolina and of Georgia somewhat distinctive from the seaboard areas, not so much because these people lived on the frontier but because they did not derive directly from the seaboard, and as a result, differed in their economic life, their speech, their religion, and in many of their social values.

A characteristic of the eighteenth-century southern frontier, frequently overlooked, was group settlement. In South Carolina, as Robert L. Meriwether's studies substantiate, the middle country was frequently settled in townships—the Swiss at Purrysburg, the Irish at Williamsburg, and the Germans near Saxe Gotha, to cite only a few examples. In part, the similarity of language and familiar patterns of experience kept them together, but a decision to settle in a group was based upon other factors as well—religious cohesion, kinship groups, or the like. Thus, the eighteenth-century frontier cannot be conceived of as a unit; rather, it represented a mosaic.

The provincial frontier was more complex than is usually thought. It did not fit the simple stereotype of the poor, primitive frontier as opposed to the seaboard regions, or the isolated, ignorant back country as opposed to the cosmopolitan, confident seaboard. Many regions of the frontier were in continuous communication with the eastern seaboard and sometimes with England itself. William Johnson, operating on the fringes of the New York frontier, was often in closer communication with England than the provincial leaders in New York City. In many ways the eighteenth-century frontiersman was less limited in outlook than his eastern counterpart, for during his lifetime he frequently lived in several colonies rather than in one. His allegiance, if he gave allegiance, was intercolonial.

During much of the eighteenth century, a close contact was maintained between the seaboard and the frontier. Merchants on the seaboard, more often than not, served as the distributors for the Indian trade. Charleston's concern with the Indian trade was fully as vital as that of the upcountryman, and leading citizens of Philadelphia like James Logan were just as involved in frontier trade as the lowliest frontiersman. This could be said of the large landholders in general—in New York, Connecticut, Pennsylvania, Virginia, and the Carolinas. To George Washington the frontier was not remote. His early career—his western travels, his western surveys, and his western military missions—reflects the intense concentration of a man caught up in the opportunities provided by the West. In his own way, Washington was a speculator in much the same fashion as William Byrd II, who late in the seventeenth century gained valuable land near the fall line of the James River and who early in the eighteenth century brought in Frenchmen to settle and to cultivate the land. Historians have indiscriminately cursed the land speculators, but their activities were not perforce immoral or illiberal.

Historians of the nineteenth-century frontier have properly emphasized that migration entailed an expenditure of money and effort which kept the indigent in the East, just as costs of the Atlantic voyage, in the seventeenth century, had kept the truly indigent in England. The costs of making a journey of fifteen hundred miles from the East Coast to the Middle West, the problems of transportation, acquiring land, purchasing implements and seed, militated against the West as a safety valve for the East in the nineteenth century.

But in the eighteenth century a day or two of travel, a journey of perhaps a hundred miles, took a man from the seaboard to the frontier. Moreover, land was acquired with relative ease—by squatter's rights (as the Pennsylvania proprietors discovered), by fifty-acre free grants, and the like. With little or no cost involved in travel or in the acquisition of land, the only cost remaining was an outlay for seed and for maintenance until the first crops could be harvested. This cost was exceedingly small in the South, where a crop could be harvested early, and only slightly larger in the middle colonies—the two areas where the greatest expansion occurred. In addition, in a colony like Pennsylvania, where it is estimated that as much as 50 per cent of the population had served as indentured servants, a man who completed his indenture received automatically what the terms of the contract specified: tools, some seed, and frequently a few head of livestock. To such provincials the frontier represented an opportunity that could be immediately and readily grasped. Because of easy accessibility and the insignificant cost of settlement, the eighteenth-century frontier served as a safety valve and provided the opportunities classically associated with the frontier. In this respect, the eighteenth-century frontier differed from that of the nineteenth century.

The eighteenth-century frontier was relatively stable. During the eighteenth century, the frontier advanced slowly, perhaps a hundred miles in seventy years, whereas in the first half of the nineteenth century the frontier jumped from the Appalachian ridge to the Pacific Ocean, a distance of more than three thousand miles, even though the improvements in communication and transportation were limited. In the eighteenth century, the frontier ties to the established centers, economic and political, promoted stability. The compactness of the colonial society, its attachment to the Atlantic seaboard, its channeled, almost leisurely development, made the eighteenth-century frontier distinctive.

In the seventeenth century, the colonies were a frontier of Europe and this frontier was intracolonial in character; the frontier of the eighteenth century became increasingly intercolonial. As a consequence, the problem of westward expansion became a problem for imperial concern because no one colony was capable of coping with the array of issues affecting not one but many colonies. Obviously, the relationship of the West to British politics and diplomacy was far more important in the 1750s than it had been in the 1680s.

The founding of Georgia in 1733, the last colony to be established by the English in North America, was a phase within the story of provincial expansion. A group of distinguished, upper-class Englishmen, designated as trustees of the colony, was given a charter by the King which was to terminate in twenty-one years, at which time the colony was to become a royal province. All power resided in the trustees, who issued instructions from England, but they were not in any way to profit personally from the enterprise.

Diverse motives promoted the establishment of Georgia. The founding of Georgia has received extravagant attention as a humanitarian project creating a haven for debtors. But the accepted mercantilist principle that idle hands did not contribute to the welfare of the nation, and thus that people in indigent circumstances should be transported where they could contribute to the national good, should be kept in mind. James Oglethorpe, the head of the colony, probably conceived of the plan to transport imprisoned debtors to Georgia not so much as a philanthropic enterprise but as an application of this economic theory. A second motive for founding Georgia and one which should, to judge from the contemporary records, be given first place, was the usefulness of the colony as a barrier against the Spanish. Oglethorpe made it unmistakably clear in his words and in his actions that the principal task was to extend the British Empire against possible Spanish pretensions. In addition, a permanent English military garrison was stationed near the Spanish border, making Georgia the first continental colony to receive such special military protection. This act, quite naturally, awakened Spanish hostility, for in their view the English had encroached upon Spanish territory.

The population of Georgia reflected the diversity of motivation in its establishment. Included among the early settlers were freemen and even gentlemen who expected to exploit those opportunities available in a virgin land and to create a plantation economy equal to that of Virginia and Carolina. These men thought of the colony neither as a buffer against the Spanish nor as a haven for debtors; their minds were on landholding, on financial success. Georgia was also the focus of a utopian movement, a general plan to mold the colony into a preconceived structure in which landholding was restricted—a grant was not to exceed five hundred acres and was to be bequeathed only to male heirs—slavery prohibited, and the drinking of rum forbidden. In this utopian spirit, the Salzburghers, a zealous group of Protestants, were brought to Georgia by the trustees and, after their arrival, were encouraged by subsidies from the stores of the Georgia trustees.

The first two decades of settlement were racked with discontent. The essential difficulty was that the objectives of the various groups of settlers differed so profoundly that conflict was inevitable. The planters who wished to make their fortunes found that the method of distributing land—particularly when they were assigned their five hundred acres in some outpost where the soil was barren and sterile—hampered their ambitions, and they began to agitate for a change in the distribution of land and for the limited introduction of slavery, which they mistakenly believed would automatically alleviate their problems. The debtors transported to the colonies were always in a minority, and their purpose was not directed toward the creation of a colony that could serve as an outpost of empire against Spain, while Oglethorpe, increasingly preoccupied by the "threat" of Spanish Florida, neglected to address himself to the serious deficiencies of the settlement. Even the Salzburghers, intent on living an isolated and godly life, could not have survived without the sustained aid made available from the trustees' store in Savannah.

Other conditions caused the colonials to despair. Much of the land originally assigned the settlers was incapable of producing marketable commodities, notably mulberry trees as a basis for a silk industry that the trustees wished to encourage. Agricultural experimentation failed to produce a profitable crop, or even a subsistence crop. Of greater significance, Georgia became the only English colony in North America where self-government was unknown. Certain local officials, a storekeeper, bailiffs, and the like, were appointed directly by the Georgia trustees, who met in England, but self-government was denied.

As conditions became worse in the late 1730s, the conflict between the trustees and the settlers became increasingly tense. The issues centered principally on land policy and the introduction of slavery. The prohibition of rum, based on the premise that rum was a hazard to health in a warm climate, was not honored; almost from the outset of the settlement, this restriction was ignored. Petitions complaining of the prohibition of slavery and the restricted land policy began to circulate as early as 1735, but it was not until the latter half of the decade that the conflict reached a climax. Whereas the original petitions were addressed to specific grievances, the crisis as it developed raised an issue of principle, the right of self-government. Eventually, the dispute produced the strange spectacle of men pleading for the privilege of self-government so that they could introduce slavery. One man's liberty could lead to another man's enslavement.

The population of Georgia during the provincial period was relatively insignificant compared with expansion elsewhere. The population decreased from about 1735 to 1748, and as late as 1760 it did not exceed six thousand. Yet the settlement represented an interesting interlocking of international, national, and local factors which make the founding of Georgia unique.

Georgia reflected one of the principal features of the period of provincial expansion in that its colonizers included many men and women of non-English birth. During the transition from colonies to provinces, the composition of society slowly changed so that during the eighteenth century, in contrast to the seventeenth, migration to the English colonies was frequently non-English in origin. The result produced a cosmopolitan society that the Frenchman Jean de Crèvecoeur, commented upon in his widely quoted essay written at the time of the American Revolution: "What, then, is the American, this new man?" Since this period, America has been regarded as a nation made up of a wide variety of peoples. The groundwork for diversity had been laid in the seventeenth century with the English conquest of New Netherland and with the acquisition of the Swedish settlements along the Delaware River, but this diversity was accidental. The cosmopolitan character of the eighteenth century was the product of a conscious British policy, the tone of which was set by the passage of the English Toleration Act of 1689, an enactment that discouraged discrimination among migrants on the basis of religious belief.*

Why did the character of immigration to the English colonies change? Considerations on both sides of the Atlantic account for the growing numbers of non-English migrants to provincial America. Wars had made certain regions of Europe almost uninhabitable. It has been estimated, for example, that during the Thirty Years' War (1618–48) a single county, Henneberg, lost 75 per cent of its inhabitants, 66 per cent of its houses, 85 per cent of its horses, and 82 per cent of its cattle. During the next century of conflicts, the Rhineland became a battleground, crisscrossed by

---

* The observation is commonly made that by 1776 one third of the provincial population was non-English in origin. This estimate appears excessive unless slaves are included within that calculation.

belligerents attempting to gain control of Europe. Religious conflicts, economic disadvantages, and the uncertainty of the future prepared Germans living in the Rhineland region for the overtures from the New World.

These overtures, beginning late in the seventeenth century, were more reassuring and attractive than those offered earlier. The story of extreme religious intolerance, of hardships encountered by the first colonizers, and of the hostility of the wilderness environment was supplanted by more precise information regarding the ready accessibility of land and the toleration of religious dissent. Moreover, the fear of the unknown was reduced as Atlantic voyages became more commonplace and information about New World conditions became more reliable. Those colonies which presented the most attractive opportunities for accessible land and freedom of faith—Pennsylvania and Carolina—expanded most rapidly during the eighteenth century, the result in part of the non-English migration.

At the same time that the non-English migration increased, the English migration, for perfectly accountable reasons, was reduced. Political economists and policy makers reversed their seventeenth-century position that England was overpopulated, and accepted the doctrine that the skills with which Englishmen were endowed were urgently required in the rapidly developing commercial-industrial complex at home. Accordingly, Englishmen should be encouraged to remain where they would be most useful to the nation. Minor exceptions were made to this general policy, notably the founding of Georgia, but not so as to jeopardize the principal purpose. With Englishmen needed at home and willing to remain in England because of attractive opportunities, other migrants were officially welcomed, ranging from the German Palatinates to Scotch-Irish and Irish peoples subject to British rule. The productive capacity of these people, if transferred to the New World colonies, would strengthen the power and resourcefulness of the British nation, and the economic theories embodied in mercantilist thought would once again be served.

Why should the English rather than the French, Spanish, or even Dutch colonies become the refuge for the non-English migration? All of the parent countries subscribed to mercantilist theory. Furthermore, those forces prodding people to move from their native land—disruption, war, dissatisfaction among lower classes—could have operated precisely as they did, and yet the discontented might have migrated to colonies other than those of England if conditions had been favorable. Obviously, the English colonies offered a more hospitable haven than the colonial systems of other nations. In most English colonies in the eighteenth century differences of faith were tolerated, though in most colonies an established church was maintained. In Pennsylvania, religious freedom encouraged dissident religious groups, although it is interesting that the French Huguenots settled principally in South Carolina and New York rather than in Pennsylvania, perhaps because they were interested in political activity, which Quaker-controlled Pennsylvania discouraged. The momentum of expansion also provided ample opportunities in farming, in trade, in land speculation, in artisanship, and a growing, vigorous economy offered an almost unlimited demand for labor. These twin elements, religious toleration and economic advantage, were present in the English colonies to a degree unmatched in any other colonial system.

Historians have tended to give too much credit to the American provincials for a receptive and liberal environment absent in England or in selected areas of western Europe. In almost every case in which non-English migration was involved, ranging from the affluent French Huguenots to the impecunious Salzburghers, the stream of migration to the English colonies represented but a minor segment of the total migration of a particular non-English group. It has been estimated that more than one million Huguenots left France, yet only a small fraction of that number turned up in the English colonies. The vast majority went to other parts of Europe and to England. The Salzburghers who came to Georgia constituted only a fragment of the migration of this staunchly Protestant group, many of whom settled in England. The liberal policy in the colonies was not exclusive; a more precise assessment must give England its due.

The German migration to provincial America admirably demonstrates the dimension and character of the overall non-English migration. Francis Daniel Pastorius, a man of unusual gifts and a lawyer of exceptional intellect, led the first German settlers to Pennsylvania in 1683, founding Germantown, north of Philadelphia. Pastorius had known William Penn when the latter toured the Palatinate to win converts to Quakerism, and Penn's ambition to establish a colony in the New World offered Pastorius an opportunity to realize his goal, to live in a society free of religious oppression.

The principal migration of Germans, however, did not begin until after 1710, when a combination of reports from satisfied New World settlers and renewed difficulties in the Palatinate brought a stream of people, an aggregate of 225,000 to 250,000 Germans by 1770. When this figure is compared with the total population of the colonies at about the 1690s, estimated at from 200,000 to 250,000, the significance of the movement becomes obvious. Of the 225,000 German immigrants, approximately 160,000, or more than 70 per cent, migrated to the middle colonies—New York, Pennsylvania, and New Jersey. Of this 160,000, 110,000 settled in Pennsylvania, or almost 50 per cent of the total migration. More than twenty per cent settled in the Southern colonies, Maryland through Georgia—whereas less than one per cent settled in New England.

The reasons for this distribution become evident upon close examination. Pennsylvania afforded religious toleration, a generous land policy, and soil which lent itself to the type of farming to which the Germans were accustomed. A similar combination of inducements also explains their migration to certain parts of

M

the South, notably the Carolinas. In contrast, Rhode Island afforded religious toleration, but, by the eighteenth century, the
opportunity to acquire choice land at modest prices was seriously
limited. Moreover, the land did not lend itself to the type of
farming in which the Germans were skilled. The paucity of
migration to New England in general was caused by the New
Englanders' hostility toward the freethinking pietistic religious
sects the Germans represented, the limited choice of land, and
the fact that New England life was better suited to skilled artisans, whereas the peasant farmers from Germany were land-
oriented.

The pattern of migration for the Scotch-Irish, the Irish, and the
Scots resembled that of the Germans. In the case of the Irish,
British trade restrictions, first against foodstuffs and later against
manufacturing, had depressed the Irish economy to such an extent that survival itself was at stake. Men and women migrated to
America to find opportunities denied them at home, and they
were attracted principally to the middle and southern colonies, in
somewhat the same proportions as the German migration. "It
looks as if Ireland is to send all its inhabitants hither . . ." observed James Logan of Pennsylvania. "The common fact is that
if they thus continue to come they will make themselves the proprietors of the Province." Perhaps a slightly larger proportion of
Irish and Scotch-Irish migrated to New England, but the difference was inconsequential. Like the Germans, the Irish and
Scotch-Irish were generally impecunious and unskilled, inclined
to seek areas rich in land. Individual exceptions can readily be
found—several affluent Scotch-Irish landholders settled in Au-
gusta County, Virginia—but the general body of immigrants
was made up of the lower classes.

The French Huguenots who came to the American provinces
were largely composed of upper middle-class groups, often merchants and lawyers. They were urban in their outlook and experience, and frequently settled in colonial cities, in Charleston,
South Carolina, and in New Rochelle near New York City. Be-

cause of their economic and social position, the Huguenots achieved importance in colonial life far beyond their numbers. These Frenchmen were accustomed to exercising leadership, and it comes as no surprise that, in proportion to their numbers, they produced many more colonial leaders than the Germans, who, as they demonstrated in Pennsylvania, were often content to avoid politics in favor of devoting their efforts to gaining improved economic status.

The consequences of the non-English migration, though familiar, should be underlined. First, the population of provincial America, of course, was increased. Second, the composition of the population in the English colonies was dramatically changed, introducing Old World patterns and ideas that affected English America, an example being the religious thought and practice of the German pietists. Third, in those colonies where the migration was most in evidence the social structure was affected. The social structure of New England was scarcely touched by the migration; Pennsylvania's was profoundly influenced. Fourth, the migration provided a supply of labor for the colonies at a time when the expansion of the economy was most in need of it (Chapter 8). Labor continued to be scarce even with the migration, but without it the growth of the American provinces in the eighteenth century could well have been retarded. Fifth, the non-English migration altered the character of the English colonies, making them more cosmopolitan, more elastic, and more supple in 1760 than in 1690.

The assimilation of these alien peoples was not axiomatic. Several of the colonies, including "liberal" Pennsylvania, feared that the newcomers would become "a distinct people from his majesty's subjects." Because the newcomers to Pennsylvania were inclined to become squatters, frequent problems arose with respect to land claims. A Naturalization Act, passed by Parliament in 1709, provided the foreign-born immigrant with the rights of British subjects, but this enactment was repealed after three years. Each colony was entitled to set its definition of a citizen and the privileges it embodied, until an act of Parliament in 1740 made citizenship in one colony the equivalent of citizenship in all the British colonies after a residency of seven years and due allegiance to the Anglican Church, although this final reservation was later modified. In those areas where the migration was largest, the middle colonies, assimilation was particularly slow, but the influence was more enduring.

The non-English influence was primarily cultural, not political. English political practices, or to be more correct English political institutions modified by American colonial usage, continued to be followed. That non-English political practices failed to take root can be attributed to a number of significant considerations. Except for the Huguenots, and a limited number of Scotch-Irish and Irish, the migrants had never participated in politics in their native lands. Inexperienced in the structure of power or its exercise, the non-English peoples had no experience to counter that of the English colonials. In addition, many of the non-English settlers found the respective colonial governments the most enlightened they had known, and consequently they were not easily moved to alter them. On the other hand, cultural life, as distinguished from political life, was profoundly influenced by the non-English migration. Religious beliefs and organizations, social thought, farm practices, architecture, to cite the most obvious, reflected these cosmopolitan currents.

Although the expansion of provincial cities did not equal the expansion of the provincial frontier—in 1720, 8 per cent of the total population lived in urban areas whereas in 1740 the figure was only about 5.5 per cent—the influence of these urban communities, as the studies of Carl Bridenbaugh have demonstrated, greatly exceeded the number of their inhabitants. Moreover, no calculation has been made to account for those Americans who lived in villages and towns which, though oriented toward the rural community, did take on some of the characteristics of urban centers. Four of the five major cities—Philadelphia, New York,

Newport, and Charleston—more than tripled their population between 1690 and 1742. Boston, the largest city, more than doubled its population during the same period, although it failed to grow in the succeeding twenty-five years. Only in very recent times has urban population exceeded rural population, but even in the provincial period the urban community generally became the center of commerce and culture.

The rise of urban communities caused adjustments equal in importance to those on the frontier. Experiments in municipal government were introduced. Just as the frontier presented the problem of erecting a primitive dwelling, so urban expansion presented the problem of city construction, particularly in those cities like South Boston where space was at a premium. Just as the natural disasters meant destruction and death on the frontier, so epidemics, crime, hurricanes, and uncontrolled fires caused heartbreak and failure in the cities. Just as the agrarian areas differed in crops, climate, and scenery, so each of the major cities possessed distinctive qualities. In Charleston the architecture showed a West Indian influence; in New York, the Dutch left their imprint. Philadelphia built with bricks; Newport built with wood. Fuel, which presented such a problem in the Great Plains frontier of the nineteenth century, became a problem for the eighteenth-century urban centers as the forest retreated before the concentration of city residents.

In the same way that Indian trade routes and trails westward influenced the expanding frontier, so the extension of streets, improvement of roads, and the construction of waterfront facilities influenced the provincial city. Nor does this exhaust the list of problems. Delinquency and crime are not solely the product of modern times; the mugger of the twentieth-century city has his counterpart in the "footpads" of the eighteenth-century city. Public health and disease became a matter of common concern when an epidemic of yellow fever or small pox swiftly reduced the population. Preserving an ample fresh-water supply, encouraging cleanliness in congested areas, offering fire protection and police protection, were activities necessary for the expanding urban community.

Urban development brought its opportunities as well as its problems. A skilled artisan found a market for his talents, and he was often protected from outside competition, although he was also required to abide by the regulations of a just price. Small retailers became affluent entrepreneurs by eighteenth-century provincial standards. And the arts, education, and learning were encouraged on a public as well as private basis. So energetic and vital were the colonial cities that they compared favorably with those in England (aside from London) in population and planning and as centers of commerce and culture. In fact, by 1776 Philadelphia rated as the second city within the British nation.

The extraordinary expansion of provincial America reflected and ran parallel to the rising provincial economy. Measured in people, trade, capital investment, or any other standard, the Americans were developing their own brand of commercial capitalism. Supported by this substantial economic structure, the American provinces could and did flourish.

8

The Structure of the
Provincial Economy

AN ANALYSIS of the structure of the provincial economy
—the changing land systems, the modification in the production
and marketing of agricultural staples, the expansion of trade and
the increased complexity of trade relationships, and the changing
labor base—clearly reveals the emergence of an indigenous
American capitalism, characterized by such manifestations as production for market, specialization, and accelerated accumulation
of capital. Without this economic structure political maturity
might very well have been impossible to achieve. The evolution
and strength of the provincial economy required an adjustment
in the relationship between Great Britain and its colonies, an
adaptation of the imperial system to these new economic realities,
but such an adjustment never materialized.

The land system in provincial America became increasingly
related to economic enterprise rather than to individual or group
needs. Land rather than being primarily an instrument of settlement became an investment and, in some instances, an instrument of speculation. In some cases, the acreage of obtainable
land grants was so great that only speculators could afford to
invest in them. One impecunious individual did not have the

means to survey such amounts of land or to obtain a patent. At times, small grants of fifty acres, a manageable farm for an individual without equipment or capital, were not economically feasible. The practice of William Byrd II, who received a large land grant early in the eighteenth century and who then encouraged Frenchmen to come to America and settle on the land, purchasing smaller grants as they were able, benefitted both parties to the contract. But when, as in New York, huge grants, obtained by dubious or even false means, were controlled so as to prohibit outright purchase of smaller plots by rank-and-file migrants, the speculator became a curse.

In New England, the land system was modified in two ways, the first affecting the towns and the second affecting the expanding frontier. Property owners of a town in the eighteenth century seldom lived in the town, a distinct contrast to the seventeenth century, when the town proprietors were also residents. The interests of the seventeenth-century proprietors and those of the town generally coincided, whereas the interests of the absentee proprietors of the eighteenth century were at times in direct conflict with those of the town residents.

A number of developments explain this change. First, the second- and third-generation Puritans were frequently forced to migrate elsewhere to find new and better opportunities. Town property, originally distributed on the basis of need—according to the size of a family, for example—tended to be purchased eventually by people who had accumulated money. Second, the hold of the church, although it continued to be strong, was no longer exclusively allied with political authority so that the seventeenth-century objective of establishing towns to preserve a precisely defined social-religious community was replaced by a new objective, to establish towns which could serve the economic needs of a given area. Third, capital accumulation in New England enabled successful enterprisers to purchase land either around the settled communities or on the frontier, in either case a dramatic modification of the town system effectively used in the original settlements.

The distribution of frontier land in eighteenth-century New England also followed a different pattern than in earlier years. Large grants were awarded to individual entrepreneurs who divided the land into smaller parcels which were resold to individuals rather than to groups. The aim, of course, was to make a profit, not to create a particular type of community. As a result, the towns founded in the frontier territory frequently differed in general purpose and tone from the towns founded in the seventeenth century.

The land system in some of the middle and most of the southern colonies was substantially modified. In the middle colonies, the price of land near the urban communities increased rather markedly. The original settlers who held these grants profited from the price rise, and new arrivals or second-generation provincials attracted to the land were compelled to seek opportunities in the less settled areas where land values were better suited to their means.

In New York speculation in large land patents, some of which originated in the seventeenth century, got out of hand. A contemporary observer remarked:

> an unaccountable thirst for large Tracts of Land without the design of cultivation, hath prevailed over the inhabitants of this and the neighboring Provinces with a singular rage. Patents have been lavishly granted (to give it no worse term) upon the pretence of fair Indian purchases, some of which the Indians have alleged were never made but forged. . . .They say that the Surveyors have frequently run Patents vastly beyond even the pretended conditions or limits of sale.

Robert Livingston, founder of the eighteenth-century Livingston dynasty of New York, was able to piece together a manor of several hundred thousand acres by marrying into the Van Rensselaer family, by artful cultivation of the King's officials in the colony, but, most significantly, by taking two separated patents, one of 2,000 acres and the second of 600 acres, and obtaining a title for all the intervening land, amounting to 160,000 acres. Captain Lewis Evans, whose political connections proved highly advantageous, accumulated an excess of 300,000 acres of land within a few years of his arrival in New York. These large patents reflected an almost unchecked entrepreneurial spirit applied to accumulating the most accessible source of wealth, land. The unscrupulous agrarian enterprisers of the eighteenth century were not unlike their industrial counterparts in the nineteenth century, the major difference being that a monopoly over land was more difficult to establish than a monopoly over an industry.

It should be noted that the land policy of the Pennsylvania proprietors was, on the whole, more just. James Logan, who was closely connected with the Penn family, was able to secure some especially desirable grants, but such cases were exceptional. Thirty thousand German Palatinates, for example, who originally attempted to find agreeable opportunities in New York, eventually abandoned that colony in favor of Pennsylvania. Not only was land in Pennsylvania cheaper but a clear title was easy to obtain. Moreover, the new arrivals frequently settled on the frontier land owned by the Penn family, on the presumption that possession was nine tenths of the law.

In the seventeenth century, the distribution of land in the southern colonies had not been free from abuses, but in the 1690s and particularly after 1710, those families with position and influence within the colonies gained extensive new grants, bolstering their favorable economic position. Whereas in the seventeenth century the Northern Neck had been granted to a family outside the colony (thus arousing the antagonism of the Virginia planters), eighteenth-century grants were given to residents within the colony. Planter capitalism, which organized land resources and labor to produce a commodity for market, emerged triumphant.

Several results can be directly attributed to the modified land system. In certain colonies the engrossers of extensive holdings —the Livingstons in New York and the Carters in Virginia, to cite examples—were able to establish a landed aristocracy. Moreover, with social prestige and political position dependent upon land, a relatively rigid social system resulted, not so much in terms of who had the right to vote, but in terms of who had the power. In provincial America, perhaps more than in any other period of American history, those considered the social and economic elite were also those who exercised the most political power. Political contests were frequently a clash between giants, each seeking an advantage in the division of the land resources.

The friction between the large landed proprietor and the rank-and-file provincial, in the settled regions as well as on the frontier, was heightened during the eighteenth century as choice land became scarcer. If the territory beyond the Appalachians had not been opened by the American Revolution, the restrictive land system which favored the established few in certain colonies would undoubtedly have created more intense friction than it did. Although the issue became increasingly important, in no colony had it become decisive by 1763. Either sufficient land was still available or the hope of land beyond the Appalachian ridge allayed fears of the future.

Colonial agriculture also reflected a maturing provincial rather than a primitive colonial economy. The self-sufficient farm, characteristic of the seventeenth century, persisted, particularly in certain areas within New England and to an extent within the middle colonies, but farming turned increasingly to the production of a cash crop and to those techniques of farming which could increase production. Equally important, each group of colonies began to specialize, to produce commodities which best suited its soil, climate, labor force, and capital assets.

New England, for example, turned to grazing and the production of meat products for export. Wheat, which had generally been the staple for New England during the latter half of the seventeenth century, was now imported, for New England could not profitably compete with the new regions, just as the new regions could not, at the outset, compete with New England in grazing. Specialization reached such a point that Boston established a public granary in 1728 to guard against the possible shortage of cereals.

The middle colonies specialized in producing grains. The transfer of wheat production from New England to the middle colonies foreshadowed the march of wheat westward, a half pace behind the frontier. The statistics on the expansion of wheat production are spectacular. To illustrate, Philadelphia exported a limited quantity of wheat in 1700, but by 1765 it exported more than 350,000 bushels of wheat and more than 18,000 tons of flour. The port of New York exported approximately one third the amount exported by Philadelphia. The eighteenth-century farmer of New England and the middle colonies was as interested in markets and trade as was the merchant. The interrelation between agricultural production and overseas markets, characteristic of a flourishing commercial capitalism, suggests, in addition, that any restrictive trade provision affected the agrarians fully as much as the merchants.

The southern colonies not only increased their production of the first staple, tobacco, but to it were added additional staples, notably rice, indigo, and naval stores. In each case, the accelerating rate of export, which reflected the increase in production, was phenomenal. In rice alone, exports increased more than fourteen times between 1715 and the 1760s. More than half a million pounds of indigo were exported in the 1760s, even though indigo was not marketed until the 1740s. Naval stores had been profitably produced in South Carolina in the early decades of the eighteenth century, but North Carolina became the pre-eminent supplier among the southern colonies after the 1720s. New England, of course, shared in the production of naval stores.

In animal husbandry, the application of capital to farming was evident. Cattle breeding, the breeding of horses in the middle and southern colonies for export to New England, and the breeding of horses for domestic use in the South, not to mention some sheep farming, unknown and impractical in the seventeenth century, illustrate the change in animal husbandry.

Moreover, the use of land in provincial America, although regarded as somewhat improvident in terms of the best European standards, as the anonymous author of *American Husbandry* (1775) consistently emphasized, was less wasteful than in the seventeenth century. Rotation of crops or permitting a particular piece of land to lie fallow were practices frequently followed. The use of fertilizers was restricted, because the scarcity of labor did not make extensive fertilizing feasible. A New York farmer, in one case, found it easier to move his barn than to spread the accumulated manure in the fields. Planters like Washington and Jefferson were vitally concerned with the improvement of agricultural techniques, and they read the works of Jethro Tull, Arthur Young, and Robert Bakewell, English agriculturists who advocated a more scientific approach to agriculture.

In summary, certain general trends influenced the development of agriculture during the eighteenth century, each reflecting a growing early American capitalism. First, capital was applied on a major scale to agricultural production. Although southern planter capitalism is the most obvious example, this generalization is also applicable to much of the agricultural production of the middle colonies and New England. Second, specialization became an identifying trait in American agriculture, with each region producing those staples for which it was best suited. Third, this specialization greatly encouraged intercolonial trade, for as each region concentrated increasingly on a marketable staple, important requirements as well as attention to markets increased. The southern colonies imported meat products from New England; New England and the middle colonies imported tobacco from the southern colonies. The middle colonies exported wheat to the West Indies; the West Indies dispatched molasses to New England; and the southern colonies frequently imported slaves from the West Indies. The velocity of trade between various parts of the Empire cannot be measured statistically because duties within the Empire were not uniformly applied, but the interaction produced by specialization in agriculture was intensified.

The point could validly be made that the application of capital to agricultural production was greater in the West Indies than in the continental colonies, which raises the question, Why did an indigenous commercial capitalism grow up in the North American provinces but not in the British West Indies? The most plausible explanation seems to be that in the West Indies the large number of absentee landholders not only drained the profits from the islands, but also prevented the establishment of an indigenous institutional-economic structure. Coupled with self-government, this could have created a sphere of authority apart from that of Britain. The West Indies, dependent on the protected British sugar market, always remained an economic and colonial appendage of the mother country.

Agricultural produce figured extensively in the Atlantic trade of American provinces. England could absorb part of the tobacco production, most of the naval stores, indigo, furs, and lumber, and some of the rice, but many prominent exports, meat products, fishery products, wheat, flour, and the like, had to seek markets outside the imperial framework. Because northern Europe produced its own meat products and because its animal husbandry was often in advance of that of the colonies, provincial meat products found markets in southern Europe and the West Indies. The sugar islands in the West Indies served as a principal market for colonial fishery products, wheat and flour, and other foodstuffs. Thus, the export trade of the middle colonies and New England was primarily connected with the West Indies and southern Europe, whereas that of the southern colonies was related primarily to Britain.

Colonial imports included manufactured goods—furniture, clothing, glass, and luxury items—most of it from England, and such necessities as salt from southern Europe and sugar and molasses from the West Indies. Because of the dearness of labor, it too became a "commodity" for import, the indentures as well as the slaves. These requirements created financial problems, for the colonials did not have sufficient cash to pay for these imports.

As with all rapidly expanding economies, the capital accumulation within the colonies was not equal to the investment requirements, and outside money, therefore, was needed. Because money did not flow in as rapidly as the maturing economy required, the provincials resorted to other means, principally the issuance of paper currency and the creation of land banks. Paper currency was first adopted extensively in the 1690s, just as the indigenous commercial capitalism was emerging, and it became a favorite method to meet the shortage of money. Land banks, in which land was used to back the issue of banknotes, were, unfortunately, ill suited to the needs of the economy because of their inflexibility in extending credit when it was most in demand. With land in such abundance as a resource, however, it was natural that the provincials should look to it to solve the problem of a limited supply of money. Both expedients, the issuance of money and the creation of land banks, were finally prohibited by imperial legislation.

According to the available statistics, during the decade 1700–10 approximately £265,000 sterling of goods were exported annually to Great Britain from the colonies, and approximately £267,000 sterling of goods were imported annually into the colonies from Great Britain. During the decade 1760–70 more than £1,000,000 sterling of goods were exported annually to Great Britain from the colonies, and approximately £1,760,000 sterling of goods were imported annually into the colonies from Great Britain. Estimates have been made that the colonial trade represented one third of the English trade in 1770, whereas it constituted only one sixth of the English trade in 1700.

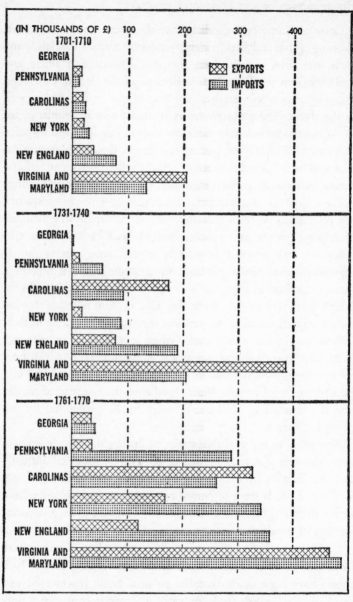

Colonial Trade with England (in £ Sterling)

These figures, first of all, dramatize the growth of trade between the colonies and the Empire during the first half of the eighteenth century. Second, the total trade of the American provinces, conventionally estimated as twice the amount of the trade with the mother country, as shown by these statistics, reveals a vigorous, growing commercial capitalism. Third, these statistics emphasize the pronounced change in the balance between imports and exports. Whereas in the decade 1700–10 the colonies, valued as suppliers of goods for the mother country, were equally valuable as markets, by 1770 the colonies were almost twice as valuable as markets for English goods as they were as suppliers. In fact, the statistics, convincing as they are, tend to underplay the role of the American provinces as a market for English goods because once again the figure given is that of the English customs. The export figure does not include the transportation and shipping charges incurred in carrying the goods to America. The import figure generally does include these costs. Therefore, the figure of £1,000,000 tends to be inflated; the figure of £1,760,000 tends to be deflated. As a result, the value of the British exports to America, in relationship to the imports, is even greater than the statistics indicate. Finally, it is axiomatic that finished goods find a market in a relatively sophisticated economy as opposed to one that is primitive, which re-emphasizes the maturity of the American provincial economy.

Although the trend which made the American provinces a flourishing English market became increasingly obvious by the middle of the eighteenth century, the British imperial policy failed to alter either its theory or practice to accommodate to the new economic realities. Consequently, the American provincials struggled to search for ways to pay for English goods: by accumulating a credit balance in the British West Indies which could be transferred to England; by using payment for services in the intercolonial and Atlantic trade to offset the obligations incurred in England; and by trading illegally outside the British colonial system, with the French West Indies and occasionally the Span-

N

ish, in order to obtain goods and specie that could be used for remittances. Certain historians have suggested that Britain eventually acknowledged the vitality of the market in the continental colonies, but contemporary letters, pamphlets, instructions, and legislation do not sustain this thesis.

The spectacular increase in trade, emerging during the eighteenth century as the mainstream of commercial capitalism itself, produced the provincial merchant-capitalist. Each colony possessed a mercantile group, although in some colonies the group was much more powerful than in others. A network of mercantile connections was centered in Boston and reached into the shipping centers of Beverley, Marblehead, Providence, Newport, and other New England ports. The Belchers, the Wentworths, the Bowdoins, the Browns, and the Hopkinses, to name only a representative sample, became identified with the mercantile elite. Merchant groups in New York City gained an economic advantage which eventually affected its politics, and the Philadelphia mercantile community, essentially nonexistent in 1700, was by the 1760s one of the most energetic entrepreneurial communities within the British nation, the equal of Boston and of most outports within England itself. Charleston, secure in its strategic location where the Ashley and Cooper Rivers converge, had ready access to the interior and, as a result, it became a thriving center for great merchants ranging from the Wraggs to the Manigaults to the Laurenses.

Virginia's mercantile development was rather distinct. The early eighteenth century was characterized by the planter-merchant. As a planter his main preoccupation was administering extensive plantation holdings, but his location on the principal rivers made him into a merchant as well, an intermediary between the London, Bristol, or Glasgow merchant and the planter whose holdings were located in the interior. Robert "King" Carter, a prototype, managed his plantations, but he also ran a store to supply other, and frequently lesser, planters, and he imported slaves for resale. As the eighteenth century advanced, a full time mercantile community developed in Norfolk, which, because of its location, could service an extensive hinterland. Merchants began to congregate at other centers, near the headwaters of navigable rivers, and after 1760 a lively trade in the upcountry was pursued by individuals, most notably the Allasons, whose livelihood depended solely upon it. The evolution of the trading community, therefore, proceeded through three phases: the planter (to the late seventeenth century); the planter-merchant (to the 1740s); and, finally, the full-fledged merchant.

The trade statistics of provincial America suggest that the vitality of the provincial economy was intimately dependent upon the prosperity of the general Atlantic community. Moreover, the commercial, market-oriented economy of the American provinces made them less rather than more self-sufficient. In contrast to nineteenth-century industrial capitalism in the United States, when the major market for finished goods was almost exclusively internal, the eighteenth-century economy was dependent on external markets for finished goods. Economic fluctuations in Britain and Europe, therefore, were a potent factor in the economic welfare of the colonies. Indeed, an entire history is yet to be written on the significance and interrelation of this community of interests among the peoples bordering both sides of the Atlantic. The inability of the United States to remain isolated immediately after the American Revolution was merely a projection of the experience of the provincial period.

A reduction in trade, either because markets failed or because war severed conventional trade channels, affected prosperity. During periods of depression, the American provincial did not starve, because sufficient foodstuffs and similar necessities (except salt) were readily obtained, but economic growth and economic vitality suffered. This generalization applies not only to the merchant but to the producer, the wheat farmer in Pennsylvania, the cattle producer of New England, the tobacco planter in Virginia, the rice planter in Carolina. The rise of commercial capitalism resulted in an intimate interweaving of the interests of provincial America with those of the Atlantic community.

The maturing provincial economy was also reflected in the rise of manufacturing. Although other commodities could be cited (the annual output of shipbuilders increased from four thousand tons in 1700 to thirty-five thousand tons in 1770), a sophisticated index is the production of iron. More pig iron was produced in the colonies around the mid-eighteenth century than was produced in England, because of the easy access of the ore and, more important, because of an abundant supply of wood for converting the ore into pig iron. Even the restrictive Iron Act, passed by Parliament in 1750, encouraged the production of pig and bar iron by permitting these products to enter England duty-free. Slitting mills, used to convert pig or bar iron into finished products, were, under the terms of the same Act, prohibited, as were plating forges and steel furnaces. Equally significant, in the present context, was the development of glassworks, flour mills, sawmills, and the like.

A discussion of the provincial economic structure would be incomplete without an examination of the skill and productivity of the labor force. In a rapidly expanding economy, labor is scarce and thus expensive. In the formative years expensive labor was a constant factor, alleviated in part by the influx of immigrants and by the accelerated population levels in the provincial period.

Reliable statistics on the labor force, not to mention a breakdown of figures within the labor force, are almost impossible to secure, but the general trend is well known. In the seventeenth century, the labor force in the southern colonies was composed principally of indentured servants; New England attracted free labor, although many families employed servants. In the eighteenth century, the indentured servant was principally drawn to the middle colonies, while the southern colonies became increasingly dependent on Negro slaves. New England, although it retained some indentured servants and continued to maintain a tradition of hiring servants, was still characterized by the family as a laboring force and the artisan plying his particular skill.

The demand for labor in each group of colonies depended largely upon its economic base. In the southern colonies, for example, where capitalism was applied to agriculture on a major scale, a large number of relatively unskilled laborers was in heavy demand. In the middle colonies, where small farming predominated, the labor needs varied, but characteristically a small farm required semiskilled labor and the towns required skilled artisans. In New England, skilled artisans found a ready market for their labor, though the semiskilled worker also was in demand.

With the growth of urban communities in the middle colonies —New York City and Philadelphia—and with the rise of Charleston as a port, the skilled laborer in the eighteenth century had a wider choice than he had had in the seventeenth century. The craftsmen became an important citizen in the community, the backbone of a relatively prosperous, important labor group. A silversmith like Paul Revere not only made history but created works of such quality that they have become artifacts reflecting the life of his generation.

Because skilled workers found the southern colonies generally unattractive, the southern provincials trained their own skilled workers. In the seventeenth century, indentured servants were trained as craftsmen; in the eighteenth century, with the rise of slavery, slaves were taught to be carpenters, joiners, planers, and bricklayers. A slave, having acquired a skill, was especially valuable. He frequently was hired out by his owner to neighboring planters, bringing added income to his owner. The skilled slave was resented by the free artisan, as complaints of the Charleston shipwrights in 1744 plainly demonstrate, and regulations in colonial cities attempted to eliminate the possible competition between these two groups. One of the reasons for the excessive tariff placed on slave importation in 1712 in Pennsylvania was the competition between the highly skilled slave and the free crafts-man.

The white unskilled and semiskilled eighteenth-century immi-grant were usually servants at first. It has been estimated that as many as two thirds of the people coming to Pennsylvania in the eighteenth century arrived under some form of servitude, and the transportation of indentured servants often figured ex-tensively in the colonial trade to the middle colonies. Another historian claims that one half of the total white immigration to the thirteen colonies arrived as bound laborers. The most com-mon form of servitude was the indenture, but involuntary servi-tude was practiced when persons kidnapped in England or else-where were brought to the New World and sold as indentured servants.

Occasionally, English convicts were given a choice of a severe prison penalty or transportation to the colonies; faced with these alternatives, the convicts usually chose an adventure in the New World, which meant that convicts sold into servitude became a part of the migratory stream and a part of the labor force. Al-though many colonies were forced to absorb convict labor, Mary-land was asked to receive far more than its proper proportion. Convict labor is often passed off lightly with the explanation that laws in England were so strict that petty crime was treated with unjustifiably severe penalties, but recent studies conclude that the convicts coming to America were often serious offenders. Certainly the American provinces fought vigorously against the introduction of convicts, and a number of violent crimes involved convicts sold into servitude. A Pennsylvania newspaper, intend-ing to satirize, reflected, in fact, the resentment and bitterness:

Our mother [England] knows what is best for us. What is a little House-breaking, Shoplifting, or Highway-robbing: what is a son now and then corrupted & hanged, a Daughter debauched, and Pox'd, a wife stabbed, a Husband's throat cut, or a child's brains beat out with an Axe, compared with this "Improvement and Well peopling of the Colonies."

In the seventeenth century, the indentured servant had migrated principally to the southern colonies, although no colony was without some. It has been estimated, for example, that between 1664 and 1671, 1,500 indentured servants came to Virginia each year, a total of 10,500. Moreover, Governor Berkeley estimated in 1671 the composition of the population as follows: 82 per cent free white, 13 per cent indentured servants, and 5 per cent Negro slaves. Although Berkeley may have underestimated the number of the indentured, the significant figure is the relatively limited number of slaves in Virginia as late as 1670. White servitude furnished the supply of labor in seventeenth-century Virginia, and no less than one fourth of the population had at one time or another been indentured. What was true of Virginia was also true of Maryland, where as late as 1700 the number of indentured servants equaled the number of slaves, in contrast to the 1750s when Maryland had over forty thousand slaves and only seven thousand indentured servants.

In the seventeenth century, particularly after the plantation system began to expand, labor was in great demand. Virginia was the only colony in which a large labor force was required for a large-scale capitalistic enterprise, producing for market. The middle colonies, speaking generally, were as yet not settled, and what labor New England required was either skilled or labor that could be supplied by the family. Therefore, the great demand in Virginia was supplied by the only labor force available, the indentured servant. As long as this system proved satisfactory, and as long as the indentured servant did not have a better place to go, conditions remained relatively stable.

In the last part of the seventeenth century and the beginning of the eighteenth century, these factors changed. Although indentured servants continued to go to the southern colonies, an increasing number were attracted to the middle colonies.

A number of conditions account for this change. First, the middle colonies were expanding rapidly, making inexpensive land available, a prize for the servant who finished his period of service. Second, the indentured servants of the eighteenth century were often non-English; the Germans, as has been noted, were attracted to Pennsylvania where they could practice patterns of farming familiar to them and practice their faith free from the burden of paying for an established church to which they did not belong. Third, as slavery increased in the South, relatively inexpensive labor, the slave, drove out more expensive labor, the indentured servant; free labor, or even bound labor, did not wish to compete with slave labor. Finally, inconclusive evidence indicates that a reduction in the flow of indentured servants at the end of the seventeenth century encouraged the importation of slaves as a substitute.

Many assumptions have been made about the practice of slavery in provincial America, but the evidence has been so limited that almost all conclusions about slavery must be regarded as tentative. Two questions merit precedence: Why did slavery gain such a strong hold in the last few decades of the seventeenth century and dominate certain geographical areas in the eighteenth century? Why did slavery develop at such an accelerated pace in the southern colonies?

Slavery was not confined to the southern colonies in the seventeenth century. Even if Governor Berkeley's estimate in 1671 that slaves constituted only 5 per cent of the population in Virginia is conservative, comparison with other colonies indicates that the potential slaveholding in those colonies was equal to that of Maryland or Virginia. In the 1690s New York City had as many slaves per capita as did any part of Virginia, a condition that found its parallel in certain New England port towns.

In the early eighteenth century, the ratio between whites and slaves in the southern colonies changed dramatically. By the second decade, slaves outnumbered the whites in South Carolina. By 1712, slaves constituted 30 per cent of the population in the southern colonies. In Virginia between 1720 and 1750, the percentage of slaves to total population rose from 25 per cent to 41 per cent.

Two considerations made this marked increase in slavery in the southern colonies possible. The first was intellectual and moral. The late seventeenth and early eighteenth centuries did not condemn slavery. In fact, in political and social thought, the discussion of liberty omitted reference to Negro slavery. Liberty as a social or political concept emphasized the protection of property, and slaves, of course, were considered property. Only by thinking in this way was it possible for a generation of Americans to raise aloft the principles of liberty on the one hand and concurrently fasten upon American society the institution of slavery. Slavery simply could not have existed, much less been expanded, if the intellectual, social, and political climate had been opposed to it.

During the provincial period, then, the question of slavery was essentially economic. Slavery for that generation was not a moral but an economic issue. It only remained to be proved, therefore, that slavery was profitable, which became obvious in the late seventeenth century. Figures become misleading, but reliable estimates indicate that slaves cost about five to six pounds sterling more than indentured servants. The indentured servant frequently required better clothes and better food, and he received an allowance once his period of indenture had been completed. A slave, whose diet was meager and whose clothes were primitive, who reproduced himself and who gave life service, was obviously a better investment, even if, in some cases, he did not always possess as much skill initially as the white bond servant.* Slavery became highly profitable, particularly in those areas in which a large supply of relatively unskilled labor was required. The economic advantage, then, became the second pre-eminent consideration that made the acceleration of slavery possible.

* Many Negro slaves came to the continental colonies equipped with a high degree of agricultural skills.

A number of factors more limited in scope help to explain the immense profits to be obtained from the enslavement of the Negro—profits for those who transported the slaves, for those who owned the slaves, and for the British, who consistently opposed all attempts to limit slave importation on the grounds that such restrictions were inconsistent with the economic goals and policies of the Empire, which thrived on the production of staples such as tobacco, rice, naval stores, and indigo.* The Royal African Company, which held a monopoly of the British slave trade, lost its favored position early in the eighteenth century, thus encouraging a wave of free traders eager to explore New World slave markets. Demand for labor rose as southern plantation agriculture expanded; the free traders supplied this demand. As the supply of slaves was stepped up, the price of slave labor went down—depending upon the vagaries of the trade—in comparison with other labor.

Slavery expanded rapidly with the accelerated pace in the securing of large land grants among the elite in the southern colonies. The first William Byrd possessed 25,000 acres of land, but his son possessed 175,000 acres. Many other families greatly multiplied their acreage, among them the Beverleys, the Fitzhughs, and especially the Carters. Land, in itself, was of little or no value until cultivated; to make cultivation possible, labor was needed, and the exploitation of slaves became the accepted answer.

The ownership of slaves as well as land began to determine position and status within the society. In Massachusetts, wealth gained by trade gave men status; in Virginia, where trade was merely a midwife, status depended on land cultivated by slaves. Slavery inevitably became involved with personal prestige, and this, in itself, offered an incentive to extend slavery.

Although the records are incomplete, the pattern of slaveholding by 1750 resembled that of the ante-bellum South, except

* Britain repeatedly invalidated all legislation passed by the provincial assemblies which attempted to limit the importation of slaves.

that the upper limits of slaveholding, that is, the number of slaves owned by a single planter or planter family, were more restricted. In Essex County, Virginia, for example, about 45 per cent of the inventories of estates did not include slaves, about 30 per cent of such inventories show an ownership of two to five slaves, and only one estate reported between twenty-five and fifty slaves. As one would expect, the density of slavery was greatest in the Virginia and Maryland Tidewater and in the Carolina river basins.

Historians do not agree whether slaves were legally recognized as slaves in the seventeenth century. It has been suggested that as late as the end of the seventeenth century, no definite distinction was made between servitude and slavery, despite such statutes as that of 1662 in Virginia, which declared that children of a slave mother were committed to bondage. Certainly, no codification of enactments relating to the slave was made until the late seventeenth century, but it is not clear whether the codification merely confirmed conduct long practiced, a consummation, or whether it marked a departure. Historians do agree that the status of the slave was defined by the early eighteenth century. He had no resort to the courts; his offspring were subjected to perpetual bondage; his mobility was restricted to the general jurisdiction of his master; runaways were severely punished; and even minor crimes by slaves were dealt with harshly. Punishments were often administered by the planter, so that court records do not provide a reliable picture of the suffering of the slaves.

No one can question the hazards, the grave injustices, and, by today's standards, the unquestioned immorality of slavery. Conditions on slave ships were notorious. Chained together and lashed to the lower decks, the slaves lived in foul quarters, to be brought up on deck for brief intervals for the light and air necessary to maintain life. When slaves were brought from the West Indies rather than directly from Africa, the voyage was shorter but the treatment was similar. Upon arrival, the slaves were placed on auction at the slave markets in a town or near the residence of a planter-merchant. Here they were examined for soundness of limb and for disease, not unlike a parade of stock animals.

The large plantation system provided the preponderance of exportable commodities in the southern colonies. The plantation became a rather complex institution. Slaves were assigned tasks according to their skills; skilled slave labor replaced skilled free labor. Slaves who became craftsmen were frequently lent to a neighboring planter when his skill was required, and the slaveowner received a fee for the services performed by the slave. Slaveowners, although profiting from slave labor, seldom escaped its problems: the training of slaves, the care of slaves, and overseeing production. A planter was both a product and prisoner of the system. As the overhead costs of slavery rose with an increase in the numbers of unproductive older slaves and young children who had not yet become useful laborers, the slave system became somewhat more oppressive to the slaveowner. The southern colonial planters complained, but, as a group, they were unwilling to forego the comforts provided by the slavery system in order to throw off its burdens.

Planters, of course, bequeathed their slaves, together with other property, to their children. Slaves constituted an investment to be passed down from generation to generation. In some cases, dependents were bequeathed slaves with the idea that the slave would be hired out, and the dependent would be maintained by means of the income secured. This process occurred often in the nineteenth century, but it was already operating by the middle of the eighteenth century.

Although the evidence indicates that by the 1750s the larger plantations in Virginia were not producing the returns enjoyed earlier in the century, one conclusion appears beyond challenge: While the land was new to cultivation and before a plantation produced its overhead of older and more dependent Negroes, while planter agriculture was growing in response to a generally strong market for the staples produced in the southern colonies, the plantation economy prospered. Aside from the issue of morality, the economic shortcomings of the system began to appear shortly before the American Revolution (the 1750s in Virginia) and persisted until rescued by the upsurge of cotton and sugar production in the early nineteenth century.

Government involvement in economic life was commonplace during the formative years (1607–1763). The notion of nonintervention on the part of the government was never at issue, only the question of which level of government was to exercise regulatory authority. It should be noted, in context, that business relationships were frequently regulated—the price, for instance, that could be charged for a particular commodity or product. Monopoly of any kind was feared by merchants, laborers, and planters; and the government, sometimes local and sometimes provincial (imperial regulation is not under scrutiny here), acted to maintain a set of economic conditions favorable to the general welfare of the provincial community, usually as expressed by the more powerful members within that community.

Free labor in colonial America was frequently hampered by more restrictions than is popularly imagined. A laborer could seldom charge as much as he pleased. Labor was so scarce that if a laborer charged what the traffic would bear, he would inflict hardship upon that community, or at least so the community reasoned. Therefore, colonies at times enacted laws, enforced by the community, specifying the fee a laborer could charge, the conditions of labor, and the criteria and specifications for apprenticeship. Moreover, laborers were subjected to social pressure as well as legal authority.

Apprenticeship was a common condition throughout the formative years; it became more common in the eighteenth century with the increase in population and in the number of craftsmen. Orphans, children of indigent parents, and children born out of wedlock were often bound out, customarily until the age of twenty-one. In this way, the children, whose ages varied at the time they were apprenticed, would not be a financial burden to society; presumably they would be learning skills that would enable them to make a living when they attained maturity.

Apprenticeship was not confined to aiding the poor and the orphans; increasingly parents of modest means turned to apprenticeship as a way of providing their children with training that would lead to the acquisition of skill in a trade. Sons frequently served as apprentices to successful merchants or to craftsmen—silversmiths, cabinetmakers, and the like. Daughters in families of modest means were sometimes apprenticed and sometimes hired out to neighbors.

Neither in Massachusetts nor in the middle colonies were extensive colony-wide regulatory codes for free labor passed during the eighteenth century, although specific localities at times invoked regulations to apply to a particular trade. Tradesmen also began to organize for their individual protection. In New York, for instance, workers in the building trade in 1747 resembled a modern union in acting against "interlopers" from New Jersey; in 1741 the bakers of New York refused to bake because of high wheat prices; in eighteenth-century Charleston, carpenters agreed to a schedule of prices for their labor.

As the eighteenth century advanced, few restrictions were applied to the free laborer, and business as well as labor began to anticipate its future "liberty" to exercise its will in getting what it wanted, when it wanted it, and at a price it wished to pay. Some of the concepts of supply and demand and a free market, which were to be stated eventually in Adam Smith's *Wealth of Nations* (1776), were already becoming a part of the provincial experience by the mid-eighteenth century.

A provincial American economy continued to flourish despite the burdens imposed upon it by the British commercial system. The fundamentals of the system in theory and practice remained in the eighteenth century what they had been in the seventeenth:

the colonies existed to supply new commodities for the mother country; the provincial economy could be regulated in the best interests of Britain.

Because of the growing sophistication of the provincial economy just at the time Britain itself was emerging as an industrial nation—1750 is frequently cited as the magic date—the emphasis shifted from the regulation of trade, the primary concern in the seventeenth century, to the regulation of manufacturing. The threat of competition provoked the adoption of a number of enactments whose object was to curb the expansion of manufacturing in the provinces.

Three acts are customarily cited: the Woolens Act of 1699, the Hat Act of 1732, and the Iron Act of 1750. It is significant that the first restrictions applied to textiles, which symbolize the earliest stages of manufacturing, and that the later restrictions applied to iron, which symbolizes a more advanced stage. The Woolens Act prohibited the shipment of colonial wool or woolen goods outside the borders of a colony. The Act was directed more toward Ireland, where its effect was devastating, than toward the American provinces. Its impact in America was primarily preventive, halting any tendency to develop woolen manufactures rather than curtailing an industrial activity already fullgrown. Household manufacture of woolen goods was lively, but the records reveal little or no export of textiles. Moreover, raising sheep could not be carried on extensively in the provinces, largely because of the scarcity of labor.

In contrast, the Hat Act of 1732, the result of intensive lobbying on the part of London hatters, directly affected the American provinces. New England and New York had exported hats to other colonies and to southern Europe, offering competition to the hatmakers of London. To restrict this competition, the Act prohibited the colonial exportation of hats, instituted a seven-year apprenticeship for aspiring hatters, limited each manufacturer to two apprentices, and excluded Negroes from the industry, a provision to prevent cheap labor from competing with the English laborer. All these provisions seriously hampered the development of hatmaking in the American provinces, but the provision to enforce a long apprenticeship was particularly destructive because of the shortage of skilled labor. From the British point of view, the Act was exceedingly effective. Colonial competition was curtailed, and English hatters captured markets previously held by provincials. After the American Revolution, when the restrictions laid down by the Hat Act were automatically eliminated, the industry in America quickly revived, even though the advantage of having furs close at hand was less of a factor after than before the Revolution.

The Iron Act of 1750 was, in many ways, a special case. As noted earlier, the Act granted colonial bar and pig iron preferential treatment, but it prohibited the erection of additional slitting mills and forges, the manufacture of hardware in the colonies, and the export of colonial iron outside the Empire. These provisions reflected mercantilist thought, but they also reflected a division within the iron industry. Producers of bar and pig iron in England suffered because they could not compete with the provinces, whereas English owners of slitting mills prospered, in part at the expense of provincial producers of finished iron products.

Colonial assemblies, notably Pennsylvania's, defied the Act by subsidizing the development of slitting mills, but the question arises whether provincial capital that would normally have been invested in iron manufactures was employed elsewhere for fear that English authorities might confiscate slitting mills erected contrary to the law. This issue cannot be fully resolved. Perhaps the safest assumption is that the Iron Act did restrict manufactures, but that its full effect was never felt, because the Great War for Empire (1755-63) tended temporarily to set aside British restrictions and because the crises preliminary to the Revolution interfered with normal trading and manufacturing.

Britain gave preferential treatment to extractive provincial industries that contributed to the strength of the Empire. A choice example is shipbuilding. By the time of the American Revolution, one third of the British marine was colonially built. Most of these vessels were engaged in the coastal Atlantic and Caribbean trade, for 80 per cent of the transatlantic traffic immediately preceding the American Revolution was carried on in British bottoms, an indication that the Americans built the smaller vessels—sloops, schooners, and the like. Because of the specialization involved in American shipbuilding, it did not, in fact, directly compete with English shipbuilders. For this reason, the preferential treatment in shipbuilding was perhaps less beneficent than a superficial examination would make it appear.

Perhaps the most thorough evaluation of the operation of the Navigation Laws during the provincial period has been made by Lawrence Harper, but even his estimates, as he readily admits, are at best approximations. According to Harper's calculation, the per capita burden upon the colonials was greater at the end of the seventeenth century than in the provincial period. More income was obtained by the Crown through the regulatory acts than was projected under the Stamp Act or the Townshend duties, twin symbols of the American rebellion.

The Navigation Acts also were generally enforced—except for the Molasses Act of 1733. This Act was passed to aid the British West Indian colonies, but its effect was to thwart the trade of the continental colonies, New England in particular, though the Carolinas should be mentioned as well. The Act placed a prohibitory duty on sugar, molasses, rum, and spirits imported by the provincials from non-British possessions in the West Indies. If strictly enforced, the Act would have impoverished New England trade because molasses was imported in large quantities to be used in making rum, an important export. Sugar had been enumerated as early as 1660. By the provincial period, the British West Indies were almost entirely dependent upon the mother country as its preferential market, because the British West Indies could not meet the competition of the French West Indies.

o

Therefore, the British West Indies were twice blessed, while the continental provinces were placed at a decided disadvantage.

The operation of the Navigation Acts continued to burden the provincials. The Staple Act of 1663, specifying that goods imported into the colonies must be shipped via England (except for wine and salt, and provisions and servants from Scotland), continued to be a part of this burden. After the American Revolution fewer British goods proportionately were imported into the United States than before the Revolution.* Commodities grown or obtained in provincial America were added to the enumerated list: rice and naval stores (1705), skins and furs (1722), and raw silk, potash and pearlash, and lumber (1764). What is much more significant is that the enumerated commodities constituted one half the total value of exports from the provinces to England.

Although the British market could absorb such enumerated commodities as potash and pearlash (purified potash), naval stores, and much of the fur and skin trade, the market for rice and tobacco was found outside England. It has been estimated that England provided no more than 4 per cent of the market for American tobacco in the mid-eighteenth century and 20 per cent of the market for American rice; the bulk of these commodities was re-exported. Although drawbacks softened the impact, the extra costs—handling charges, storage charges, and losses in transit—fell eventually upon the producers, who already were operating on a minimum margin.

On the other hand, by the 1760s Britain spent over $300,000 annually in bounties for provincial commodities, including naval stores and indigo. Moreover, the success of indigo production was dependent upon this subsidy. After the American Revolution, indigo production collapsed, not so much because American

---

* French trade was greatly stimulated during the American Revolution but it failed to retain its position after the war. This seems to contradict the statement made in the text, but it should be remembered that credit relations, the type of British goods, and the British Atlantic carriers account in part for this shift from France.

producers could not compete on an open market but because the subsidy Britain continued to give to its other colonies, a subsidy no longer available to the Americans, gave the producers within the Empire an advantage.

Lawrence Harper has estimated that in 1773 tobacco enumeration cost the provincials from $2,000,000 to $3,500,000 annually, and that rice enumeration cost them from $200,000 to $500,000 annually. He further concludes that by 1773 British policies affecting trade cost the American provincials in excess of $3,000,000 annually. This large sum is equal to approximately one third the annual cost of the War for Independence. The question raised by these figures is simple. Was the financial burden imposed by imperial regulations balanced by the protection Britain furnished? If the Americans had had to furnish their own navy and arms to protect themselves against the aggressive claims of the French and the Spanish, would the provincial economy have been overwhelmed by the costs of defense? In this light, perhaps the British trade regulations were worth the price, for the general growth of the economy of the American provinces during the eighteenth century suggests that the imperial system, however burdensome, was not so restrictive as to choke off economic growth.

Commercial capitalism did not reach its zenith until the nineteenth century, but by the middle of the eighteenth century its characteristics were everywhere present. An American society could not have matured without the financial institutions, the extensive trade network, the accumulation of capital, the expanding and experienced labor force, and the emergence of a merchant-capitalist group. These ingredients served as a foundation upon which the later American economy was built. Equally significant, the vitality of the indigenous economy supported a special kind of political independence not developed in the English colonies in the West Indies. In the eighteenth century, the colonies in the West Indies had fully as many political grievances as the continental colonies, but, economically, they had become wholly dependent upon the mother country. When the decisive crises arose in the 1760s over the authority of Parliament as opposed to the authority of the provinces, the American provinces took a wholly different course from that of the West Indian colonies. The answer, at least in part, lies in the economic structure that developed in the British provinces in North America.

9

The Provincial Spirit:
The Clash of Faith and Reason

CONTRADICTORY CURRENTS run through the cultural and intellectual life of provincial America. Some historians find the foundations of a rich, indigenous American culture, while others find a pale replica of the English mind of the eighteenth century. To make this issue even more difficult to resolve, historians must explain another seemingly irreconcilable predicament: Why did the provincial American environment that welcomed the rationalism of the Enlightenment also respond to the emotionalism of religious revivalism? This question becomes the focus of this chapter; the degree of distinctiveness of the American mind serves as the focus for the chapter that follows.

The seeming contradiction of thought between the rationalism of the eighteenth-century Enlightenment and the exuberant emotionalism of a religious revival known as the Great Awakening is especially intriguing because these two momentous movements ran a parallel course. Each gained strength from its English connections, although the spirit of the Awakening needed less nourishment from abroad. Each gained headway in the American provinces during the 1720s; each was sustained into the early nineteenth century. Such longevity is remarkable for any movement in American history, regardless of period. Moreover, the durability of the spirit of the Awakening, though it was an emotional movement, indicates that it had a much more profound significance than a mere surface enthusiasm.

It must be conceded at the outset that the Awakening and the Enlightenment cannot be entirely reconciled, but the fact that they existed simultaneously suggests that a larger theme, a common base, underlay these two movements. Certainly each movement, in its own way, challenged accepted theories and institutions. As a result, each movement released an independence of spirit and action, the Great Awakening among the lower classes and the Enlightenment among the intellectual, social, and political elite. It is too much to expect men of little or no learning to be attracted by concepts dependent upon experiments and inquiries of which they have no knowledge; in the same way it is too much to expect men steeped in scientific learning to discard reasoned inquiry in favor of explanations dependent solely on faith.

The Enlightenment and the Awakening also possessed in common a fundamental pragmatic quality. Every American provincial generalized upon his individual experience. Benjamin Franklin abandoned metaphysical inquiry when it led him to intellectual positions that he found to be scientifically in error, although he admitted that irrefutable logic had carried him to those positions. The exalted theologian Jonathan Edwards generalized upon his sense of a mystic conversion, a spiritual rebirth, which he cultivated throughout his life, and his command of Enlightenment thought, to erect a reasoned defense of orthodox Calvinism that continues to demand respect and attention. To a preacher of the Awakening or the farmer in the field, the gateway to a perfect life and to happiness was achieved by a spiritual rebirth; to the enlightened intellect, the gateway to these identical goals was gained by a reasoned inquiry. Obviously no monolithic structure embraced the whole of the provincial spirit and mind, but a pervasive strain of pragmatism, of men elevating experience to precepts, tended to distinguish the provincial American.

As late as the early nineteenth century, even after the full impact of the Enlightenment had infused the nation, Alexis de Tocqueville observed that religion was a powerful force in American life:

> Religion in America takes no direct part in the government of society, but it must nevertheless be regarded as the foremost of the political institutions of that country; for if it does not impart a taste for freedom, it facilitates the use of free institutions. Indeed, it is in this same point of view that the inhabitants of the United States themselves look upon religious belief. I do not know whether all the Americans have a sincere faith in their religion, for who can search the human heart? But I am certain that they hold it to be indispensable to the maintenance of republican institutions. This opinion is not peculiar to a class of citizens or to a party, but it belongs to the whole nation, and to every rank of society.

Yet it is frequently and erroneously assumed that religion played a minor, even an insignificant, role in the life of the eighteenth-century American provincial. Fascinated by the complexities of the Puritan faith and theology of the seventeenth century, many mistakenly presume that with the demise of the oligarchy, or at least the disintegration of the concept of a political-social-religious community, New England of the eighteenth century no longer depended upon the church as an integral unit of society and that secularism emerged triumphant. In this context, the Great Awakening revivalism of the 1730s and the 1740s is considered an aberration, the final death spasm of ancient and archaic spiritual precepts, when in fact it should be looked upon as a natural development of a faith-oriented people. The further assumption is made that secularization in the southern colonies, mistakenly associated with their development in the seventeenth century, was writ more boldly in the eighteenth century.

The spirit of the eighteenth-century American provinces cannot be understood without some comprehension of the continuing and pervasive influence of religion. In New England the church provided much of the political and intellectual leadership; it continued to operate as a central institution in the community and in the society; it influenced, in an intimate way, everyday life and conduct. In the southern colonies, the importance of religion was almost equal to that of New England. The life of many immigrant groups who migrated to the southern colonies centered upon religion—the Germans and Swiss in South Carolina, the Quakers in North Carolina, the Scotch-Irish and Germans in the valley of Virginia. Church records reveal that in many of these groups stringent regulations governed Sunday observance, and the church community enforced a rigorous code of personal conduct. The more tolerant attitude of the Anglican churches—irregular church attendance, the Sabbath as a day of recreation and play, the absence of a distinctive Anglican-American theology—obscures the significant observation that the letters of the Provincial Virginian or Carolinian, even of men such as William Byrd II, whose lusts rivaled those of Boswell, show a surprising preoccupation with the afterlife, with the power of God, and with the nature of man in relation to God. That this concern was often deliberately subdued rather than overt reinforces the pervasiveness of faith.

The Quaker control of Pennsylvania and the conflict between Presbyterians and Anglicans in New York, where political life tended to be polarized around these two sects, illustrate the impact of religion in areas where, because of rapid expansion, influx of diverse peoples, and tumultuous opportunism, it might have been expected to languish. The issue of church-state relationships was important to the colonial eighteenth century, arousing contests not between secularists and religionists but between religious groups equally devoted in their church allegiance. Indeed, atheism was generally outside the framework of eighteenth-century provincial thought.

In discussing the religious development in the American provinces, five trends deserve primary consideration: (1) the spread of Anglicanism throughout the colonies; (2) the spread of dissenter sects including the Baptists, the pietists, and, in a somewhat different category, the Presbyterians; (3) the secularization of the society as reflected in the growth of religious toleration and, to a more limited extent, the evolution of religious freedom; (4) the religious as well as intellectual ramifications of Enlightenment thought in America, and (5) the stirrings of the Great Awakening, which affected the spread of Anglicanism, the spread of dissenter sects, and secularization.

The seeds of Anglicanism had been planted in Virginia, and in the late seventeenth and early eighteenth centuries Anglicanism spread throughout the southern colonies; in the provincial period Anglicanism not only reached into the middle colonies but also invaded New England, the citadel of Congregationalism. The extension of Anglicanism throughout the South can be traced by its establishment as the "state" church in the various colonies: Maryland in 1689, South Carolina in 1704, North Carolina in 1711, Georgia in 1750.* The Anglican Church attained a modest following in Philadelphia and became sufficiently strong in New York to create a church-state establishment in the lower counties of that colony late in the seventeenth century, despite strong opposition from within the colony.

The penetration of Anglicanism into New England represented a major departure. The origin of the movement was related to the Yale College controversy of the 1720s. Yale had been founded in 1701 as a conservative college for training the Congregational clergy of New England. Its charter date was not accidental; it coincided with the emergence of an unpopular liberalism at Harvard College, formerly the fount of clerical Congregationalism. In the 1720s a number of faculty members and students at

---

* The establishment of a state church in any colony made it the official church, which customarily involved support by public taxation and a generally favored position. Of course, a tie between church and state was a carry-over of European and English practice.

Yale were influenced by the first stirrings of Enlightenment ideas in America. The writings of Francis Bacon and Robert Boyle, of Isaac Newton, John Locke, and John Tillotson, were eagerly read; on the basis of these writings, many members of the faculty reconsidered their theological position. A visit to New England (1728-31) by George Berkeley, an Anglican prelate of extraordinary intellectual gifts and high motives, intensified the discussion.

The power of ideas, together with a favorable climate of opinion, produced an intellectual insurgency. Those faculty members who were involved were dismissed from Yale. Among them was Samuel Johnson, who traveled to England, was consecrated as an Anglican cleric, returned to minister to the first Anglican congregation in Connecticut, and eventually was attracted to New York City, where he became the first head of King's College (now Columbia University). Anglicanism apparently appealed to a number of New England intellectuals who found a hospitable home in the concept of man's perfectability without the necessity of a conversion experience.

The activities of the Society for the Propagation of the Gospel in Foreign Parts, the S.P.G.F.P., founded in 1701 by the mother church in England, also revealed the awakened energy of Anglicanism, for it functioned, in part, as the evangelical component of the church. The Society sent ministers and teachers to areas, nominally under Anglican supervision, that could not afford either. It established schools for slaves in the southern colonies and missionary outposts among the Indians.

However, the principal work of the S.P.G.F.P. in America, to judge from the expenditure of men and money, was, interestingly enough, the dispatching of missionaries and teachers into New England to assault the citadel of Congregationalism. The Puritan faith had, indeed, come upon strange times. The irony of this development sets the historian to speculating whether the Congregational Church of New England fulfilled the spiritual impulses of the provincial populace.

As Anglicanism spread, gaining power and influence, the question of an Anglican bishop in America became increasingly prominent. Too often this issue is considered exclusively in terms of the American Revolution, another factor of friction to irritate the many non-Anglicans in America. Construing the issue in such narrow terms tends to mislead. It fails to recognize the relationship of the episcopate to the structure, practice, and thought of the Anglican Church in the various American provinces.

In those areas newly converted to Anglicanism or where Anglicanism was weak, that is, in the middle colonies and New England, the plea for an Anglican bishop was much more urgent than in the established Anglican communities in the southern provinces. The reason for this—aside from the zealousness which often characterizes the newly converted, whether it be in religion, politics, or social thought—was that the Anglican Church in the southern colonies, as the reader will recall (Chapter 4), had in practice become congregational in organization, with control retained principally by the self-perpetuating vestry. A New World bishop, clothed with all his ecclesiastical authority, would undermine the ecclesiastical independence of the vestries; his very office would invite enmity. The urgent cry for an Anglican bishop, therefore, did not come from the southern provinces, where Anglicanism was in the ascendancy, but from the middle provinces and particularly New England, where Anglicanism was struggling for survival.

By implication, the question of the Anglican bishop introduced another issue, the relationship of imperial authority to church and state in America. If an American bishop were established, the British line of authority would not only extend to economic and political spheres but to religion as well. The extension of Anglicanism, therefore, automatically became an imperial question, a political as well as a religious issue.

The dissenter sects, the Baptists, the Presbyterians, and the Quakers, as well as the numerous German sects—the Mennonites, the Dunkers, the Moravians, the Reformed, and the Lutherans—gained adherents during the eighteenth century, the result in part of the influx of non-English peoples. The Baptists had roots in early seventeenth-century England, and the New World Baptists claimed Roger Williams (Chapter 2) as their patron saint. However, John Clarke, a trained physician and preacher, was known as the foremost Baptist leader of the seventeenth century, and his pamphlet *Ill Newes from New England* (1652), emphasizing the persecution of the Baptists, provoked English criticism of the New England Puritans. Not until the late seventeenth and early eighteenth centuries did the Baptists become strong enough to influence church history and, in some cases, the church-state relationship.

Early in the eighteenth century Philadelphia was the strongest Baptist center in the colonies, and a Philadelphia Association which included Baptist congregations in the vicinity was formed. The spread of the Baptists to the southern colonies in the first half of the eighteenth century was slow, but the pace accelerated rapidly after the 1750s, the center of the movement being Sandy Creek in Guilford County, in north central North Carolina. The growing strength of the Baptists in Virginia, more specifically upcountry Virginia, has often been described as phenomenal. In provinces as widely separated as Massachusetts and Virginia, the Baptists advocated not merely religious toleration but the complete separation of church and state. In the crisis preceding the American Revolution, the Baptists in Massachusetts, in formal petitions to the legislature, asserted that if Parliament did not have the power to tax the unrepresented colonies, then the established church in Massachusetts did not have the power to tax Baptists for the support of the Congregational Church.

The Presbyterian Church had a modest following late in the seventeenth century, but its development into a strong church organization with intercolonial connections was an eighteenth-century phenomenon. Rooted primarily in the Scotch-Irish migration of the eighteenth century, the Presbyterian Church eventually embraced a variety of peoples: natives of New England, English and Welsh migrants, as well as Irish and Scots. By the 1760s no American province was without a Presbyterian church.

Although the most significant growth occurred after 1710, corresponding with the Scotch-Irish migration from Ulster, preliminary and formative steps had already been taken to develop an American Presbyterian church. The lead was taken by Francis Makemie, a Scotsman born in northern Ireland, who arrived in America as a missionary in 1683. Before the century was concluded, he had labored in North Carolina, Virginia, Maryland, and Pennsylvania, and he was eventually to extend his influence northward. Makemie was responsible for the formation of the Presbytery of Philadelphia in 1706 which grew into a Presbyterian Church organization, the Synod of Philadelphia (1716).

The Synod was American in origin, character, and government, even though many of its early ministers had received their theological training in the British Isles. In 1740 alone seventeen new Presbyterian churches were organized: eight in Pennsylvania, two in Maryland, three in Virginia, three in New Jersey, and one in Delaware. When a serious shortage of ministers developed, the Reverend William Tennent, a graduate of the University of Edinburgh, responded by founding the "Log Cabin" college at Neshaminy, Pennsylvania. The life and correspondence of Samuel Davies, who became a famous preacher in Virginia in the 1750s, illustrates the scope and intercolonial character of the Presbyterian Church in particular, and of the growing group of dissenters in general.

The various religious sects transplanted to the American provinces by the German migration, the Reformed and the Lutheran groups being the strongest, greatly swelled the number of dissenters. The character of these sects—Mennonite, Dunker, Moravian, Schwenkfeldian, as well as Reformed and Lutheran—was pietistic, that is, devoted to religious practice as a way of life rather than emphasizing theological tenets. The pietistic movement has been described as the "left wing" of the Reformation, but the pietistic movement was not necessarily radical in political, economic, or social thought; rather, its radicalism was based on religious zeal, which sometimes incited pietists to practice communal living, or to preserve a simplicity of apparel, or to establish utopian communities. In the late seventeenth century the pietistic movement swept through Germany, the Low Countries, the Scandinavian countries, and even touched Britain. It drew strength from the University of Halle, in Saxony, which trained many of the pietistic clergy (in excess of six thousand in thirty years), and from the Saxon village of Herrnhut, which became the center of the Moravian Church led by Count Nikolaus von Zinzendorf.

The Mennonites were among the first Germans to migrate to America, and Lancaster County, Pennsylvania, became the principal center of this sect. The Mennonite migration was also one of the first to slacken during the provincial period. Their beliefs emphasized a return to an unsophisticated Christianity. They held that religion was an individual matter; they rejected infant baptism; they believed in separation of church and state and in nonresistance; they insisted upon marriage within their religious group and they exercised a strict discipline over their own members; they dressed simply, wore beards, and selected their leaders by lot. They were not dependent upon an educated clergy or upon outside aid or authority. The Dunkers and the Schwenkfeldians, although distinct sects, were also in this "left-wing" religious tradition, as was the Ephrata Society, which, under the guidance of John Conrad Beissel, de-emphasized sex relations (women wore veils and both men and women wore unattractive garments), encouraged celibacy, and insisted upon the seventh day as the day of rest. The economic enterprises of this religious group—a gristmill, a paper mill, a printing press, and the like— were operated on a communal basis.

Unlike the other extreme sects, the Moravians continued to maintain close ties with members of their faith in Europe. Count von Zinzendorf of Germany came to America to unite the various pietistic sects in 1742, but the final result was to promote division and discord rather than harmony. From Nazareth and Bethlehem, in Pennsylvania, the Moravians spread into other colonies, especially North Carolina. They practiced a system of "general economy," communal ownership and communal activity, including schools, which by 1755 had an enrollment of three hundred pupils and a staff of eighty teachers. The prosperity of the Moravians in the New World enabled them to send money to Moravians in Europe, who on occasion faced economic distress. The reverse was true, however, of the Moravians who settled in Georgia.

The German Reformed and Lutheran churches, like the Moravian, also maintained their ties with the Old World during the provincial period. Both denominations were originally handicapped by poverty, in part because they were dependent upon voluntary contributions of the membership (unlike established churches) and in part because the membership of the church was composed of men and women from the German Palatinate, most of whom came to the New World as indentured servants. As one of their ministers reported: "When these people have served out their time, they are just as poor as when they first arrived, and, it takes a long time until they contribute anything to the church." Yet both the Reformed and Lutheran groups opposed all attempts at unification. Although Pennsylvania remained the center for both church groups, congregations were established in the southern colonies. By the conclusion of the provincial period, some one hundred Lutheran congregations had been formed, about seventy in Pennsylvania and the middle colonies, and about thirty in Virginia, the Carolinas, and Georgia, in direct correlation to the distribution of the non-English immigrants. The Reverend Henry M. Mühlenberg, who arrived in America in 1742 as a missionary, became the foremost Lutheran clergyman. The lack of continuing leadership impaired the growth of the Reformed Church, and its dependency on the Holland Synod in the end proved to be a handicap.

Quakerism, in its own way a radical religion until it became associated with the stability of the elite group in Pennsylvania, greatly benefited from the migrations of the eighteenth century, for the population in the Quaker colony of Pennsylvania grew at a pace unparalleled in the other American provinces. The Quaker missionaries in Europe and America were largely responsible for this migration. That it was concentrated in the middle colonies is not surprising. The fierce opposition to Quakerism in New England (which resulted in the hanging of four Quakers in the seventeenth century, including the celebrated Mary Dyer), did not encourage extensive migration to that region, and the rise of slavery diverted Quakers from the southern colonies even though originally some Quakers settled there.

Jews had migrated to America in the seventeenth century, but in the eighteenth century, with the rise of provincial cities, particularly Newport, New York, Philadelphia, and Charleston, their numbers increased. Most migrants were Sephardim (Spanish-Portuguese) Jews, but there were a limited number of Germanic and East European Jews. The two groups were extremely hostile toward each other, creating internal enmity. Fortunately, except for Boston, the major provincial cities were located in colonies that exercised religious tolerance, and during the provincial period, synagogues were erected in New York and in Newport. A number of Jewish families became prominent merchants, but very few colonies enabled the Jews to participate actively in politics.

The increase in the diversity of religions during the eighteenth century had profound consequences. Religious groups, including the dissenter sects, became intercolonial in character; this relationship often extended to their communications, to their church government, and to their ideas and practices. This development was one of the components in the total stream of a growing intercolonial self-consciousness. The increasing numbers within the dissenters' ranks intensified the issue of a church-state relationship within certain colonies, and ceaselessly tested the slow evolution of religious toleration. The presence of thousands of dissenters forced the practice of toleration. Enforcement of rigorous religious conformity would have roused tensions too burdensome for a society that was now engaged primarily in exploring opportunities for material improvement, rather than in the establishment of Biblical commonwealths based upon prescribed theological doctrines.

Toleration and even religious freedom entered the intellectual and religious mainstream.* The rise of secularization in the provincial period is well illustrated by comparing Franklin's *Poor Richard's Almanack,* a best-seller of the eighteenth century, with Wigglesworth's *The Day of Doom,* of the seventeenth. Apathy toward organized religious institutions, which is what secularization entails, resulted in a more relaxed attitude toward those holding different religious convictions, whereas intense commitment frequently gives rise to intolerance. It is important to remember, in the light of this premise, that perhaps as much as one half of the provincial populace had no firm church affiliation. These people were not necessarily untouched by religion, but they formed a silent multitude who, with the dissenters, stood opposed to church establishment and to policies that called specifically for conformity.

Toleration, then, was the only practical course to be followed. It grew out of necessity and practice, not out of principle. Religious toleration was eventually elevated to the status of principle on the basis of practice, to be invoked in subsequent genera-

---

* The meaning of toleration and freedom should not be confused. Toleration means what it says: to suffer, to tolerate another religion. No assumption of freedom of religion can be made, for toleration implies some restriction or limitation. In Virginia, for example, Presbyterian ministers were allowed to preach after receiving permission from the provincial legislature, but each Presbyterian was required to provide his share of the financial support for the Anglican Church through taxes. Religious freedom implies that a complete range of choices exists, from extreme piety to atheism. Religious freedom in this sense did not exist in the provincial period, for even in Pennsylvania an officeholder was required to believe in God.

P

tions as one of the touchstones of liberty in America, which indeed it became.

An exception to the general trend of toleration was found in the treatment of Catholics, particularly in Maryland where they were most numerous. An enactment in Maryland in 1704 included the following requirements: (1) no Roman Catholic service could be held except in a private house; (2) no Roman Catholic could teach school; (3) children of Catholic parents had to take the Anglican oath of supremacy; (4) the penalty for failing to take the oath was forfeiture of inherited lands and disposal of these lands to the nearest Protestant kin; and (5) a Catholic could not purchase lands. A Maryland law of 1717 stated that those Catholics who were unwilling to take the Oath of Supremacy to the English church and its head, the King, would be disenfranchised.

Upon preliminary examination, Maryland, the colony that had passed the Toleration Act of 1649, a so-called landmark in the history of religious liberty in America, had become by the eighteenth century one of the most intolerant of colonies. This does not take into account the fact that the Toleration Act was a desperate attempt to make certain that the Protestant majority would not overwhelm the Catholic minority and that the proprietor would be able to defend his charter in the face of the Puritan supremacy in England. The fear of losing power, once having gained it after the "revolt" of 1689 (Chapter 6), made the Protestant clique in Maryland all the more desperate and determined to subordinate the Catholics without regard either to principles or preachings. Whenever a sense of insecurity gained ascendancy in the province (and the same point could be made in other colonies), most prominently revealed during the eighteenth-century wars between the French and the English, intolerance was intensified.

Of course, the Catholics fared poorly in England in the eighteenth century, for the Act of Toleration (1689) specifically excluded them on the premise that their first allegiance was to the

Pope rather than to the civil authority. Even in Rhode Island and Pennsylvania Catholics were disenfranchised, and in almost every colony Catholics were subjected to discrimination and abuse. Although the Catholic Church prospered financially, it did not grow in membership as the Protestant sects did. To survive in the New World, the Catholic Church was also forced to modify its position on a close church-state connection, and, indeed, temper its unwillingness to accept the coexistence of other faiths.

The evolution of the Enlightenment in America was intimately related to its development in England. Despite the turmoil of domestic politics and the tribulations attending foreign policy in seventeenth-century England, one determinative force rose steadily to the forefront, the genius of science. It was the supreme legacy made to future generations by the seventeenth century, a legacy which altered permanently the life and thought of mankind. Sir Isaac Newton, who issued his celebrated *Principia* (*Mathematical Principles of Natural Philosophy*) in 1687, was the central figure in the new science, but the movement permeated the countries of Europe and its impetus did not slacken as it swept into the mainstream of Western civilization. American provincials were caught up in the intellectual excitement of the times, observing eclipses, identifying plants, and even speculating on reasonable explanations for the mysteries of nature, a preserve previously reserved for God, to be revealed only so far as He should see fit.

The transition from exploring objects and patterns in nature to speculating upon man's place in the universe was an easy one, for man, in discovering some of nature's great secrets, demonstrated the undeniable power of his mind, and, in so doing, his importance and potential. Moreover, if immutable laws existed in nature which governed its harmonious relationships—it had been found, for instance, that every particle of matter was attracted to every other particle with a force proportional to the product of the masses and inversely proportional to the square of the distance—surely similar laws as yet undetected must govern human behavior. The discovery of these laws and the adjustment of human institutions to conform with them would bring happiness and eventually perfection. Discernment of such laws depended upon a reasoning and inquiring mind, the same course followed by Newton in his exploration of the elements within the new science—calculus, physics, astronomy. Nothing could be accepted as truth until observed by demonstrated experience. Only a trained mind, trained formally in schools of learning or self-trained through reading, study, and experimentation, was equipped to uncover these truths.

These enlightened ideas emerged into a schema: Man by the disciplined use of his intellect—"right reason" and "rationalism" became key phrases—discovered the determinative and immutable laws of nature; by adjusting his life and by modifying human institutions to conform with these laws, man would reduce the friction between himself and the system of cosmic relationships governing the universe. Man would be increasingly in harmony with the laws of nature and thereby become happier. By improving the environment, progress would be inevitable. Man had the opportunity, therefore, to achieve perfection. The gateway to happiness and perfection was through reason, not through a spiritual rebirth.

Within the philosophy of the Enlightenment, God's role in man's affairs was sharply reduced. God was a Prime Mover who had created a universe held together by harmonious laws, but once having created this perfectly operating universe, it was destined to exist indefinitely without further adjustment. Man, therefore, did not appeal to God, the Prime Mover, but to the immutable laws of nature, laws which governed God's creation. God and man were remote from each other, an idea that contrasted with the thinking, experience, and practice of the Great Awakening, in which spiritual commitment and dedication alone held out hope, hope for a heavenly afterlife rather than earthly perfectability. The Enlightenment concepts, which delimited the power of God and elevated that of man, and which emphasized goodness and relied exclusively upon good works rather than faith, were embraced in Deism.

Enlightenment ideas entered into American thought at approximately the same time that the first restless stirrings of the Awakening were heard. In contrast to the Awakening, as we shall note momentarily, the Enlightenment did not light on a particular geographical region and then extend its influence. It gained a following in urban centers throughout the colonies, from Boston to Charleston, wherever the social and intellectual elite were found. In fact, Enlightenment thought in provincial America has been credited with forming a self-conscious intercolonial elite, which is at best a half-truth for many institutional experiences supported the emergence of an intercolonial American awareness among this group.

Enlightenment ideas also found a warmer reception among Anglican communicants than among most of the dissenter and Congregational groups. The Anglican hierarchy in England espoused Enlightenment concepts, which, at the minimum, prevented the emergence of a clerical opposition among their co-religionists in America, and, at the maximum, encouraged the church in America to welcome enlightened ideas. Notable Anglican leaders, the Reverend Alexander Garden of Charleston and the Reverend Samuel Johnson, championed Enlightenment thought. Yet Deism, as a stated belief, had made only modest gains before the onset of the Revolutionary crisis of the 1760s. Its major growth occurred after the Revolution.

Although the official attitude of church and lay leaders explains the ready reception of Enlightenment thought among Anglicans in the American provinces, how can the adoption of these ideas by the elite groups of most colonies be explained, when, as in some cases, these groups included a Jonathan Mayhew or a Charles Chauncy, prominent clergy in the Congregational Church of Massachusetts? The answer is that the Enlightenment suited the experience of the provincial elite, although in somewhat contradictory ways.

The provincial elite, having obtained a pre-eminent place in the society, could, in terms of the Enlightenment, readily rationalize their good fortune. In the natural order of things, they belonged where they found themselves, at the focal point in the provincial structure of power and prestige. Their achievement, from their point of view, proved the significance of man's place in the universe. Moreover, the Enlightenment placed the provincial elite in an exceedingly comfortable and advantageous position; human institutions could be modified to bring about a betterment of the human condition, and they, the elite, were the select group to bring about the change. The rank and file were not equipped to accomplish so important a task, for they lacked the learning and training required for disciplined reasoning and inquiry.

In short, the Enlightenment ideas, as applied to the human condition and to human conduct, contained an undeniable degree of snobbishness which appealed to those holding the reins of power. That Enlightenment ideas took root in provincial America because they appealed to the self-interest of the elite group is a view seldom espoused by scholars. Scholars are quite naturally in rapport with the elevation of the mind to first place in the order of things and impressed by the quality of eighteenth-century American leadership. Indeed, it should be underscored that at no other time in American history has the configuration of the intellectual elite so closely followed that of the political and social elite.

The explanation of self-interest on the part of the elite groups must be tempered. The influence of toleration and secularization permeated the populace as a whole, providing a congenial environment for Enlightenment ideas that were man-centered rather than God-centered, ideas that emphasized physics rather than metaphysics. In addition, the growth in population and in prosperity, providing fresh opportunities for individuals, was congenial to the idea of the essential goodness of man and the beneficence of God.

To the provincial American, progress was self-evident. In his lifetime, he witnessed vast changes: the indentured servant in Pennsylvania who became a small farmer; the storekeeper in Boston who became an adventurous and prosperous merchant; and the immigrant in New York who acquired land sufficient for a barony. The world of the provincial American was filled with evidence of almost unbelievable successes. Why should he not believe in progress, in God's goodness, in man's greatness? In this restricted sense, Enlightenment thought "influenced" the rank-and-file provincial because it reinforced his experience.

Indeed, in the eyes of many observers, Europeans and Americans alike, America was the true laboratory of the Enlightenment because America was a new, a formative society. Free from the incrustations of centuries of institutional and intellectual baggage, society in provincial America could presumably adjust more speedily and effortlessly to nature's laws, as they were discovered, than could Europe. Some contemporary intellectuals, American and European, were confident that a perfect society was already being developed in America.

The Great Awakening, a sweeping religious revival extending over three decades, affected most aspects of religious, and to an extent secular, development. Specifically, it stimulated the atomization of religious sects and jarred church-state relationships; it provoked political disputes and affected intellectual life. The concurrent emergence in the eighteenth century of the Awakening and the Enlightenment, emotionalism as opposed to reason, presents an intriguing paradox.

The progression of the Great Awakening is easily discernible. It began in the middle colonies, the first outstanding revivalist being Theodore J. Frelinghuysen, a German educated in the pietistic tradition, who served as minister for three Dutch Reformed churches in New Jersey. His effort proved to be contagious, particularly in influencing the graduates of the "Log Cabin" college of William Tennent. The Awakening made significant inroads into New England early in the 1730s, promoted in part at least by the zeal of one of America's greatest theologians, Jonathan Edwards, and it reached a climax in 1740 with the arrival of that round-faced, engaging young revivalist George Whitefield, an Anglican clergyman from England who began his American tour in Delaware in 1739. Eventually, the Awakening reached the southern colonies, beginning in the 1740s and achieving its zenith in the 1750s and 1760s. In many respects the Awakening spirit lasted into the early nineteenth century, although its manifestation then is frequently set apart as the "second" Awakening.

Special conditions enabled the movement to gain momentum in the middle provinces. First, the pietist movement transplanted from Germany lent itself to a humanizing and more emotional evangelical religious experience, though the Awakening generally was far less dependent upon Europe than was Enlightenment thought. Second, except for a few counties in the province of New York, the absence of an established church allowed the movement to proliferate without serious institutional opposition. Third, the extremely rapid growth characteristic of the middle provinces overtaxed the regular church organizations, creating a need filled by the Awakening. Fourth, the broad and varied composition of the population induced religious instability, a breeding ground for religious experimentation.

The spread of the Great Awakening to New England and the lag in spreading to the southern colonies is also understandable. The strong religious tradition of New England, modified by almost a half century of toleration, prepared a favorable environment for the Awakening. Moreover, the urban character of the region, the towns and even provincial cities, provided an audience. In contrast, the scattered mode of settlement characteristic of the southern colonies was a disadvantage for an evangelist gifted in stirring crowds. In addition, the established Anglican

Church in the southern colonies was not only permeated with the new rationalism of the eighteenth century, but it had absolutely no tradition of revivalism. Only when the back country began to be populated with non-Anglicans did revivalism find a welcome environment in the southern colonies, but this did not happen until the 1740s, 1750s, and 1760s.

Although the progression of the Great Awakening can be explained, the timing of the movement—that is, why the movement emerged on the American scene when it did—is something of a mystery. Suggestions have been made that the frontier environment, or the rise of secularism, or the development of an individualistic spirit, or the emergence of select religious leaders, or the influence of social disorganization in traditional church institutions were responsible for the timing. Each suggestion is helpful, but certainly some are more significant than others. If a relationship existed between the Awakening and the frontier, for example, it was indirect rather than direct. The large audiences that responded to the preaching of the Awakening were found in the towns and cities, not on the frontier. Except for the Awakening in the southern colonies, the relationship with the frontier was generally remote, and even in the southern colonies revivalism was primarily the result of the people who came, the Presbyterian Scotch-Irish and the pietistic Germans, rather than the frontier environment.

Social disorganization is a more telling point. By the late seventeenth and early eighteenth centuries, the traditional religious institutions, as noted in such developments as the rise of dissenter sects and the influx of Quakerism, were being challenged. In such a period of transition, when theological tenets formerly accepted are subject to critical analysis and when religious organizations must adjust to new conditions, the new, the fresh, the experimental is more likely to find a hospitable reception. In New England, for instance, the highly rationalistic theology of the Puritan fathers had been badly battered by the second and third decades of the eighteenth century.

Two of the suggested influences, secularism and the individualistic spirit, are difficult to define. Perhaps the influence of secularism, as it applied to the Great Awakening, has been overdrawn. The Awakening did not take hold where people were irreligious but in regions noted for their religious tradition and heritage. Eighteenth-century secularism, in fact, did not necessarily imply an irreligious attitude, but rather that a speculative attitude about man and his relationship to the cosmos was articulated in secular rather than in religious terms. The rise of secularism, therefore, was no doubt more important to the rise of the Enlightenment than to the Awakening.

Individualistic spirit and egalitarianism are also vague concepts, but the general message of the Awakening that man could control his destiny appealed to the common man. "He [God] does not reject the prayer of the poor and destitute," affirmed Whitefield. In certain practical respects, not in theology or church organization, the Awakening was to the eighteenth century what Quakerism had been to the seventeenth before it became overformalized.

It has been said that the Great Awakening would have taken place without the presence of a Gilbert Tennent, a Jonathan Edwards, or a Samuel Davies, a conclusion which appears convincing. Yet these and other men who served as leaders gave the Awakening life and spirit, each man making his peculiar contribution. Tennent became identified with his sermons of damnation and his ability to awaken a physical response from his listeners which aroused scorn and cynicism from his critics. Whitefield, though not a person of exceptional intellectual ability, was obviously a young man whose personality and preaching won thousands of converts. Even the witty, rational Franklin found Whitefield attractive and persuasive.

Jonathan Edwards was a man of a different nature. Although his congregation at Northampton, Massachusetts, was one of the first to experience the wave of revivalism, Edwards himself remained the remarkable logician and theologian, perhaps the greatest ever produced in America. In seeking a rational religion, Edwards was the product of his age, but he used the instruments of the Enlightenment to fashion a defense of orthodoxy: predestination, the selection of the elect, the impotence and insignificance of man in the presence of God. Edwards manifested the peculiar theological duality of the Great Awakening, the exaltation of the individual, which implied that man is important, and, at the same time, the glorification of the unlimited power of God, which implies that man is powerless.

The Great Awakening produced certain highly tangible, as well as some unmeasurable, results. It produced division within the established church groups. It resulted in the founding of colleges. Because the Awakening was intercolonial in character, it strengthened intercolonial ties. Other claims are more controversial: that revivalism introduced many men and women to a religious experience previously denied them; that the Awakening aroused a democratic spirit which influenced the Revolutionary generation; and that the Awakening influenced provincial thought.

The first of these results, division within existing religious organizations, revealed itself in conflicts between denominations— for example, the strife between the Anglicans and the Congregationalists in Connecticut—and within denominations between the "new lights" and the "old lights." Unhappy with the power exercised by the established groups in the churches, the ministers of the Awakening, like Gilbert Tennent, often condemned the "unconverted ministers" in highly inflammatory language: "Hirelings, Catterpillars, Letter learned Pharisees, Men that have the Craft of foxes and the Cruelty of wolves, plaistered Hypocrites, Varlets, the Seed of the Serpent . . . dead dogs that cannot bark . . . Swarms of locusts." Even the more temperate Whitefield attacked ministers of the organized churches, charging that "the reason why congregations have been so dead is because they have dead men preaching to them. . . . For how can dead men beget living children?" The Reverend Charles

Chauncy of Boston, the most influential religious figure in New England, responded to one of the Awakening preachers by writing an open letter: "Suffer me, Sir to take this opportunity, to beseech you in the bowels of Christ Jesus, and as you regard your own soul, to review your conduct in this matter of *rash,* and *uncharitable* judging."

At its root, the dispute involved a contest for ecclesiastical power. The new leadership wished to gain control of the churches, or more specifically over the church organization, and those already in power were unwilling to relinquish it either in whole or in part. The conflict, therefore, was not primarily a dispute of liberal versus conservative theology, or evangelical versus nonevangelical faith, although the issues were sometimes expressed in this form; principally, it was a contest for control. These divisions touched directly upon the familiar questions of toleration and the role of the established churches. In this way, the Great Awakening, although not conceived as a movement to advance liberal causes, in fact produced liberal effects.

As a result of the Great Awakening, four colleges were founded by four separate religious denominations: The College of New Jersey, later Princeton (Presbyterian, 1746), Brown (Baptists, 1764), Rutgers (Dutch Reformed, 1766), and Dartmouth (Congregationalist, 1769). The premise, in each case, was that the existing institutions of higher learning were unsuitable for training acceptable "new light" ministers.

The intercolonial character of the Great Awakening appeared not only in its progression from the middle colonies to New England to the southern colonies but in its intercolonial impact upon the ministry, upon church organizations, and upon the intercolonial brotherhood of the laity. As an intercolonial religious movement, the Awakening corresponded with the intercolonial character of provincial trade and provincial expansion, all of which prepared the way for a nascent nationalism.

The effect of the Great Awakening in terms of personal religious conversion and in terms of a democratizing movement is difficult to evaluate. Statistics, even if they were available, would be unreliable; extravagant enthusiasm within the Awakening has perhaps been overemphasized. Yet, to view with unrelieved skepticism the human experience of conversion is to misjudge part of the results of the Great Awakening. A Connecticut farmer tells of his own response to the news that Whitefield was coming to Middletown to preach:

> i was in my field at work[.] i dropt my tool that i had in my hand and run home and run thru the house and bad my wife get ready to go[.]

He saddled his horse. Knowing that he had no more than an hour to go twelve miles, he frequently ran alongside the horse to give the animal a breathing spell. He saw a cloud rising which he mistakenly thought to be fog but which was in fact a cloud of dust raised by thousands of his neighbors who were also rushing to Middletown. After hearing the eloquent Whitefield, the Connecticut farmer concluded:

> And my hearing him preach, gave me a heart wound; By God's blessing: my old Foundation was broken up, and I saw that my righteousness would not save me.

It has been claimed that the Great Awakening was the first step toward the American Revolution because it emphasized in religious terms the importance of the individual and the necessity for throwing off outmoded forms, and that religious individualism carried over into political individualism. A fairer assessment might suggest that the Awakening, in reviewing traditional institutions, created a climate of freedom in which individualism received new emphasis.

The impact of the Great Awakening upon the prevailing thought in provincial America is contradictory and controversial. The theological assumptions which arose out of the Awakening were often conflicting. It is usually assumed that the spokesmen for the Awakening preached from the elementary text of Calvinism: predestination, the insignificance of man in God's hand, the saving of one's soul through the intercession of Christ, and justification by faith. The fact is that the Awakening preached from a variety of texts which were, at bottom, contradictory. Jonathan Edwards erected a theological system that served as a monument to Calvinism—man was reduced to impotency and entirely dependent upon God's mercy. George Whitefield represented a peculiar blend of the Enlightenment and old-fashioned Arminianism which stressed freedom of the will. Man, in Whitefield's preaching, had the power to save himself by his believing, an idea contradicting predestination and implying that man possessed a certain sovereignty over his destiny. In contrast to the position of Jonathan Edwards, some clerics engaged in the Awakening preached the doctrine of immediate revelation. In this respect, the Awakening foreshadowed the transcendentalist thought of the early nineteenth century, in which a person could divine the immutable laws by an almost intuitive instinct, a gift possessed by everyone.

These divergences re-emphasize a principal generalization about the provincial spirit: considered either in terms of the Enlightenment or the Awakening, reason or faith, the American "mind" was made up of a great number of streams of thought, many of them contradictory. Neither the Awakening nor the Enlightenment produced in America a single accepted system of thought.

Whereas in theory the positions of the Enlightenment thinkers and the Awakening preachers were poles apart, the practical goals of both movements frequently overlapped. The Enlightenment thinkers, to cite an example, were often critical of the existing churches and advocated a curtailment of their power, a goal championed by spokesmen for the Awakening for an entirely different reason, namely, that the clergy were no longer preaching the true faith. On the other hand, the Reverend Charles Chauncy bitterly opposed the Awakening, believed in a benevolent God, and championed selected Enlightenment ideas; yet, he defended the existing church structure.

What these contradictions emphasize is that the Awakening and the Enlightenment found a response in provincial America not because they espoused particular intellectual tenets but because they introduced an attitude of mind essentially compatible to provincial society. For the Enlightenment the starting point might be reason, while for the Awakening it might be an inner, somewhat indefinable spirit, but the result in each instance challenged accepted tenets and institutions. As manifested in the clash of faith and reason, individualism is the key that unlocks the character of provincial society.

10

The Provincial Mind:
Its American Characteristics

DEFINING THE DISTINCTIVENESS of the American mind has been the preoccupation of historians and literary critics for several centuries. The range of views can be briefly summarized by presenting two authors who, within the last decade or so, have reviewed the eighteenth-century provincial mind. "Yet as one . . . studies . . . he must admit that the adjective 'English American' rather than 'American' describes the dominant culture, even as late as 1765," observes Clinton Rossiter, a political scientist-historian. "The colonial mind," he concludes, "was largely derivative and often downright imitative." Not so, responds Max Savelle, who outlined at length what he conceived to be the matrix of the American mind. "In the century between 1650 and 1750 . . .," he concludes, "an intellectual revolution had taken place in the British colonies on the continent of North America. . . . They had created a new culture; they knew it, and they were proud of it."

But what was the American mind in the provincial period? And who spoke for it? The Reverend Gilbert Tennent, who declared that God was omnipotent, that man essentially was without goodness? Or Charles Chauncy, who found in man the goodness of God, and who believed that man could, by means of enlightened thought, find God's purposes? Did Benjamin Franklin, neatly balancing his amiable but undiverted pursuit of profit and his zest and curiosity about the unknown, typify the American mind? Or was an untutored German immigrant of the Ephrata Society, who shared his poverty in communal living and who satisfied himself with simple precepts, more representative?

Obviously, in the provincial period there was no one American mind but a complex of American minds, something of an American characteristic in itself. Historians are not debating what was said and practiced but what significance to place upon the expressions of a contemporary eighteenth-century witness or to attribute to a particular practice, and thus they strive to determine the measure of distinctiveness or the degree of derivation.

English intellectual and cultural patterns affected the American colonies throughout the provincial period; learned men on both sides of the Atlantic communicated scientific observations to each other, and many prospective provincial leaders were educated in England, to cite immediate examples. At the same time, the effect of the American setting—the presence of non-English peoples, the establishment of distinctive practices in church government, the individual conditions affecting education, political behavior, and the like—were gradually transformed and eventually they were reflected in the institutional forms that developed. To make a judgment, each element within the intellectual complex must be evaluated; in each case a decision must be made.

To analyze the many puzzling facets of the provincial mind requires an assessment of a broad spectrum of provincial life, scattered throughout the Atlantic seaboard. Indeed, the decentralization of cultural and intellectual activity was, in contrast with the European and English seats of Western culture, an American characteristic. Generally, the European intellectual community was a closed society concentrated in a single metropolis, where the exchange of ideas and the development of the arts benefited from intense and incessant stimulation. In provincial America there was no single hub; this condition, together with a preoccupation with activities outside the conventional intellectual sphere, a mark of a young society, affected the quality and character of intellectual and cultural life. Moreover, maturation was taking place. Approaching the intellectual and cultural life of provincial America from a variety of perspectives, most historians have concluded, either explicitly or implicitly, that a cycle occurred. A rather sophisticated level of culture was transplanted from England to America in the early seventeenth century. With the passing years, this level of sophistication and quality was compromised. Slowly an indigenous provincial culture developed. Although rooted in an earlier period, it matured after the middle of the eighteenth century, the product of New World conditions and concepts, or perhaps more correctly, an absence of concepts.* "The first drudgery of settling new colonies, which confines the attention of people to mere necessaries, is now pretty well over," said Benjamin Franklin in 1743, "and there are many in every province in Circumstances, that set them at ease, and afford leisure to cultivate the finer arts, and improve the common stock of knowledge."

The cyclical approach to colonial cultural life has merit. Whatever may be said about Roger Williams, John Winthrop, or other stimulating intellectual leaders in the first settlements, they were, first and last, Englishmen who came to America. Their training, their experience, their frame of reference was English. The intellects of the late seventeenth and early eighteenth centuries—John Wise, Jonathan Edwards, Benjamin Franklin, and others—were products of a different intellectual environment, having only their American experience and training to draw upon. Their relationship to England, at least in their formative years, was secondhand. Even after Franklin and others of his generation

* The best statement of this position is found in James T. Adams' *Provincial Society*.

traveled abroad to savor the sophistication of England and of the Continent, America was home. No one can read the pre-Revolutionary letters and intimate reflections of a young John Adams or a young Jefferson without finding this impression clearly and forcefully expressed.

Yet the character of provincial culture and intellect as it evolved in the eighteenth century is not easily described or measured. Certain familiar standards must be used—libraries and literature, science, medicine, and law, schools and colleges, music, painting, and architecture—to define more sharply the character of provincial culture, and to determine whether it was, in fact, indigenous or mainly dependent upon the cultural dynamism of the Old World, particularly England.

Even if books were acquired for no other purpose than to gain prestige, the accumulation of libraries by provincial Americans was an indirect acknowledgment that the society placed a value upon books. The mere fact that Cotton Mather of Massachusetts possessed three thousand volumes, that William Byrd II of Virginia owned four thousand volumes, and that James Logan of Pennsylvania was a book collector, indeed, a bibliophile, indicates that by the provincial period libraries had become a tangible manifestation of culture. Even in the eighteenth century, however, personal libraries in excess of one hundred books were rare. "They are more inclinable to read Men by Business and Conversation," wrote Hugh Jones of his fellow Virginians in his publication, *The Present State of Virginia,* "than to dive into Books."

Enlightenment thought, by insisting that the discovery of nature's immutable laws depended upon the application of an informed mind, placed a premium upon books and upon libraries, with a new emphasis in the eighteenth century on public libraries. The deputy of the Bishop of London, Commissary Thomas Bray, whose avid interest in founding libraries gave him a special place in the culture of provincial America, might be expected, in terms of his interest in education, to have devoted primary attention to founding schools. But the fact that Bray gave priority to libraries, and that he wished these libraries to be used extensively, indicates that he believed the great truths would be found by a learned mind, a reasoning mind, a mind stimulated by books.

Within these library collections, books on science held a prominent place, as did volumes on medicine, especially those filled with handy home remedies. Every library, regardless of whether it was in the middle colonies, the southern colonies, or New England, included a larger proportion of books on religion than on any other subject. A section was customarily devoted to history and less frequently to political economy, and a few books, particularly in libraries in the southern colonies, were devoted to scientific farming. Certain private libraries, quite naturally, reveal the special interests of their owners; one third of the library of Robert Carter, a prominent Virginia planter, consisted of books on law.

Few books were devoted to the arts—literature, music, architecture, or painting. Of the arts, literature found greatest favor, although usually there was a preference for the English classics of a previous period rather than contemporary English writings. Alexander Pope, for example, was not widely read. A library of any size appeared defective if it failed to include a sprinkling of the classics, accepted as the true mark of a cultivated mind.

Although books, for the most part, were possessed by the affluent, inventories of estates (and the law required that the estates of every deceased person be inventoried) indicate that provincials, even of modest or humble status, enjoyed a common heritage of some books: the Bible or the Book of Common Prayer, a dictionary or a historical work. The majority of estates seldom included more than two or three books, so it is fair to assume that the majority of provincials read few books and were oriented to training, knowledge, and learning gained only by experience. This is the foundation perhaps of the somewhat unfortunate American mythical tradition that book learning is inappropriate for red-blooded Americans whose achievements must be measured by their possessions and their ability to rise from the ranks by native shrewdness and experience.

Daniel Boorstin, in an important and provocative book, *The Americans: The Colonial Experience,* argues cogently that the identification of learning with the elite was shattered in colonial America, that the monopoly of learning was broken, and that the American colonial served literacy rather than literature. Advancement without learning, without book knowledge, and without a family heritage was no doubt easier in America than in England, but learning in eighteenth-century provincial America continued unmistakably to be associated with the elite. Boorstin's concept is perhaps more applicable to the nineteenth century, when the structure erected in the eighteenth century was turned topsy-turvy by the industrial revolution.

Indeed, the social, economic, and political elite, those who exercised power in provincial America, were generally the intellectual elite as well. This was especially true in the middle and southern colonies. No learned university group or clerical order had been formed, to take a pertinent example, which could train and supply an intellectual elite to influence political thought or the exercise of political power, a contrast to Europe and England. Even in New England, where the ministers had served as an influential intellectual elite in the seventeenth century, the power and influence of the clergy, though still important, had been reduced. In the Virginia of William Byrd II, Robert Beverley, and their contemporaries, and in the later Virginia of Thomas Jefferson, James Madison, and their contemporaries, few men gained intellectual prominence who were not already prominent as first families in the economic, social, and political sphere. What was true of Virginia was also true of South Carolina (the Pinckneys), of New York (the Livingstons or the Morrises), and, to a slightly lesser degree, of Pennsylvania (James Logan or later Benjamin Franklin).

If the cultural and intellectual maturity of provincial America is measured in conventional terms, the results are disappointing

—and misleading. Not a single person made his living by writing, a development that awaited the nineteenth century when a larger audience, improved communications, more leisure, and more money made a literary profession possible. Literary production was not only sparse but unconventional; writing was done not for the sake of art but for communication. Moreover, writing represented only one facet of persons whose talents were broadly diversified. William Byrd II, a Virginia planter and a leading political figure, wrote numerous pieces, among them *History of the Dividing Line,* a satirical work describing his experience as a member of a joint commission to survey the boundary between North Carolina and Virginia. Byrd's writing was an indulgence, done to amuse a few select friends in America and Europe, and limited to a private printing. Benjamin Franklin—publisher, legislator, entrepreneur, diplomat—was also a writer. The subject matter of many of his most brilliant pieces was seemingly commonplace, notably his well-known essay on the Franklin stove. Even the celebrated reports on his electrical experiments were written in a straightforward, unadorned, yet highly readable style.

Taken together, the provincial writers, although widely separated in background, in interests, in vocation, and in residence, had a common characteristic. Their subject matter related directly to their experiences and was, therefore, American. This literary output was probably as near to being indigenous as any part of American literature until the days of Whitman and Mark Twain. In terms of their varied interests—science, agriculture, writing, politics—these provincials were men of the eighteenth century, generalists rather than specialists.

The publication of the *Boston News Letter* in 1704 ushered in an era of colonial newspaper publishing. The maturing American society now required wider communication, predominately within and between colonies, but to an extent between the colonies and Europe. A printer who published a newspaper in one colony was likely to own or be associated with newspapers in other colonies as well. Often, many members of a family were involved in the business of printing, publishing, and editing. Franklin, who had gained experience in Boston on the *New England Courant* (1721), founded by his half-brother James, purchased the *Pennsylvania Gazette* in 1729. He helped to found the *South Carolina Gazette* (1732) with one of his printers, and entered a partnership with James Parker to publish the *New York Weekly Post Bay* (1743), the *Connecticut Gazette* (1755), and the *Constitutional Courant* (1765) in New Jersey. William Parks was the founder of the *Maryland Gazette* (1726) and the *Virginia Gazette* (1730), and William Bradford, publisher of the New York *Gazette* (1725), was also associated with the *American Weekly Mercury* (1719) in Philadelphia, founded by his son Andrew. Another William Bradford, Andrew's nephew, founded and edited the *Weekly Advertiser, or Pennsylvania Journal* (1742) and was later known as the "patriot printer of 1776."

Although a postal system, managed from England, had been established as early as 1691, Franklin, not surprisingly in view of his publishing activities, was appointed as one of two deputy postmasters general in 1753. Franklin used his position to increase the distribution of his newspapers, often discriminating against his competitors by failing to give them equal service, a business tactic that brought Franklin greater profits.

The content of the newspapers varied. News from England or from other colonies frequently received more space than news of local events. This was especially true in a province like Virginia, where news from the mother country directly affected the tobacco market. Diplomatic decisions that had a bearing on war or peace with Spain or France and political policies that affected the English mercantile classes, for instance, determined the relative prosperity or lack of it for the entire Virginia populace. Only when catastrophic events or highly significant developments warranted coverage were local events reported in detail. The cost of paper and printing was too great to be wasted on local gossip that readers already knew from conversations with their neighbors. Already informed on local matters, readers in provincial America wanted information on what was happening elsewhere. Even so, the advertisements and brief snatches of local news have provided the social and cultural historians of provincial America with one of their richest sources.

The observation has been made that provincial newspapers were conservative in tone because in order to succeed they required contracts from the colonial government for the printing of official reports, forms, and proceedings. This dependence upon a close tie with government to insure a substantial profit no doubt softened criticism or at least encouraged editors to be discrete, but the case can be overstated, for newspapers responded sharply to genuinely important developments. Few institutions played as significant a role as the newspapers during the series of crises, beginning in the 1760s, which led to the Revolution.

Although newspapers proliferated in the eighteenth century at a rate which probably exceeded that of England, few books were published. Daniel Boorstin suggests that the economics of publishing was largely responsible—the inferior type and its scarcity, and the limited amount of paper and ink. To tie up scarce commodities in a book whose sale was questionable discouraged publishing ventures, it is true, but these limitations did not seem to prevent an astonishing output from the Massachusetts press in the seventeenth century. Moreover, it should be particularly noted that writers in the American provinces were not writing full-length books. To write an article or a series of articles was one thing; to devote the time and energy required to write a full-length book was quite something else. In short, provincial Americans had no books to publish, and consequently, authors made no genuine demand for book-length publication.

Provincial America produced a rather full complement of historians whose writings continue to be consulted by modern scholars: Hugh Jones's *The Present State of Virginia,* William Smith's *The History of the Province of New-York,* Thomas Prince's *A Chronological History of New England in the Form of Annals,* and Thomas Hutchinson's *The History of the Colony of Massachusetts-Bay.* These historians shared common characteristics. They wrote of their particular province, their "country," often concentrating on the subject matter they knew at first hand, in no way attempting to engage in the extensive scholarship required to write a history of earlier civilizations or of other lands. A book by William Douglass, a Scottish physician who settled in Boston, reflected an awareness on the part of the American provinces of themselves as a composite; the book was entitled *Summary, Historical and Political, of . . . the British Settlements in North-America.* Because these contemporary histories were often built upon personal observation as well as upon available records, they possess a documentary quality. The thought, the practice, and the ideas of their own time, in a sense indigenous traits and provincial subject matter, are portrayed from a provincial point of view.

What is particularly startling is the absence of verse in provincial America, somewhat in contrast to the seventeenth century. The reasons for this lack are not at all clear, but it is likely that poetry, an art form transplanted from England to America, was not sufficiently suited to the provincial environment in order to flourish. Its very absence becomes a provincial characteristic of practicality.

Newtonian science stimulated the mind of American provincials in the same way that it touched intellectual life throughout the Western world, but its effect was not precisely the same. Cotton Mather, attracted by scientific inquiry, was censured by Samuel Sewall, the celebrated New England diarist, because Mather preached on scientific phenomenon in relation to the sun rather than on a strictly Biblical text. James Logan of Pennsylvania was apparently the first provincial to obtain a copy of Newton's *Principia,* and he was instrumental in disseminating scientific information throughout the middle colonies. William Byrd II, along with other American provincials, took particular pride in his membership in the Royal Society of London, and he corresponded extensively with his English friends. In science, however, a Byrd or a Logan was a colonial satellite revolving around the glories of England.

Not all of provincial scientific inquiry was derivative. To that part of science called natural history, Americans contributed knowledge—almost every specimen collected and every natural phenomenon noted added to the store of scientific information. John Bartram collected botanical specimens throughout the provinces and cultivated various species in a garden near Philadelphia. Carl Linnaeus, the foremost botanist of Europe, called Bartram the finest contemporary "natural botanist," and Linnaeus sent one of his favorite pupils, Peter Kalm, to visit Bartram. Mark Catesby, celebrated for his extraordinary *Natural History of the Carolina, Florida, and the Bahama Islands,* explored the available resources, the individual character of the topography, and the flora and the fauna of the New World. Interestingly enough, on the first page of Mark Catesby's attractive volume of drawings is the American bald eagle, a suggestive symbol of nascent American feeling.

With the exception of Benjamin Franklin, Americans did not contribute to theoretical science, which, in the eighteenth century, was called "natural philosophy," as opposed to natural history. In contrast to botany, in which mere observation was sufficient, physics required a knowledge of higher mathematics; only with a thorough background could a scientist contribute to the field. Franklin never claimed to be a master of mathematics or of elaborate scientific theories. In fact, in his letters explaining his observations, he takes some pride in speaking the language of the layman rather than that of the specialist. Franklin's experiments, therefore, which contributed to basic theories about electricity, were atypical, almost freakish, and succeeded because he entered a field of physics which was less advanced than other fields and which allowed room for the gifted amateur. In some respects, his results were determined by shrewd analysis as much as by experimentation, particularly his identification of lightning as electricity and his conclusion that electricity jumped more readily from points than from a spherical surface. His observations concerning the flow of electricity, in which he employed the now familiar plus and minus symbols, and the equalization that occurs between highly charged particles and those less highly charged were based more definitely upon experimentation. Franklin's experiments were repeated throughout Europe, including the court of the King of France, and he became famous in scientific and intellectual circles.

Although science and mathematics were taught in some of the provincial colleges, the best-known position being the Hollis Chair at Harvard, held from 1738 to 1779 by John Winthrop IV, institutions of higher learning were not necessarily the center of scientific or intellectual inquiry. More representative was the American Philosophical Society, proposed by Franklin in 1743 and founded in 1744. Obviously, a large group of provincials felt the need for an intellectual association, even though a limited number of provincials were fellows or members of the Royal Society and contributed papers to it. The membership list of the American Philosophical Society was impressive: Dr. John Mitchell of Virginia, a Fellow of the Royal Society who was interested in botany; Cadwallader Colden, a lieutenant-governor of New York whose interests ranged from Franklin's experiments to the Linnaean system of classifying plants, and who wrote an illuminating historical-anthropological study entitled *History of the Five Indian Nations;* David Rittenhouse of Pennsylvania, an astronomer and mathematician, whom Jefferson mistakenly claimed to be the equal of European astronomers.

Medicine was at once an aspect of science and an insight into the professions. Except in the willingness to inoculate more readily in America, medical practice was no more advanced in provincial America over that in England. Some physicians were also scientists of natural history. As a profession, medicine in America followed the same pattern as other professions transplanted to America; the specialist had to become a generalist. In England the physician, the surgeon, and the apothecary were specialists. In America a physician had to serve in all three capacities if he were to prosper. Generalists also characterized the legal profession. Neither profession had quite recovered from the unflattering assessment of William Byrd II, "It [America] was a Place free from those 3 great· scourges of Mankind, Priests, Lawyers, and Physicians." In the area of public health, the Americans occasionally moved forward more quickly than the English, notably by providing better facilities for fresh water and sewage disposal in towns and by providing mass inoculation for smallpox.

The educational system, as a reflection of provincial culture, provides contradictory evidence. The "public school" system that had been established in early Massachusetts, for instance, did not expand with the growth of the colony, even though the town of Boston as well as Newport, Rhode Island, as Carl Bridenbaugh has suggested, developed public education "to the highest degree of any contemporary communities in the western world." Although difficult to measure, the intellectual level of elementary and grammar school education in the eighteenth century was probably inferior to that of the mid-seventeenth century. The teachers were not as well qualified, the education laws were not effectively enforced, and the curriculum, compared with that of the early seventeenth century, was diluted. John Adams, as a youth, found school dull until he convinced his father to place him under private instruction, which he found more stimulating.

The middle colonies never established a system of public schools, and the education of the children varied greatly. The Quakers established their own schools, as did many of the Scotch-Irish immigrants. Of the German immigrants, only the Moravians founded schools, which at one time had an enrollment of three hundred pupils. Despite these private schools, most provincial Pennsylvanians were trained by experience alone. In New York all attempts to provide a system of public schools proved abortive, but selected private schools flourished. In 1762 at least fourteen private schools operated in New York City alone.

In the southern colonies, the pattern of the seventeenth century was continued in the eighteenth: maintaining a limited number of private schools; hiring a tutor to teach the children on a plantation; and sending children to England to be educated. South Carolina made several attempts to initiate a public school system but without success. Whether the intellectual content of education in the southern colonies changed is difficult to ascertain, but certainly more emphasis was placed on science and mathematics and probably less emphasis was placed on classical languages than in the early colonial period. One generalization can be made with certitude: "public schools" were not the heritage of the formative years (1607–1763) but a creation of nineteenth-century America.

During the provincial period, the number of colleges increased greatly. The College of William and Mary had been chartered in 1693, but it did not operate effectively for almost a quarter of a century. Yale College, it will be recalled, was founded in 1701, in part as an antidote to the "liberalism" of Harvard. The Great Awakening also produced a number of colleges (Chapter 9). King's College (to become Columbia University) was founded in 1754 by the Anglican Church (although men of other faiths were included on the board), with Samuel Johnson serving as its first president. Johnson had turned down an offer to become head of the College of Philadelphia chartered in 1755. In neither case was the training of ministers a leading object; a broader purpose, an enlightened and learned leadership, was to be served.

What is notable about these provincial colleges is their proliferation, again an American characteristic, and their manner of organization. Oxford and Cambridge retained a legal monopoly on higher education in England, whereas numerous colleges were chartered in America, some of them on a questionable legal basis. Moreover, those American institutions founded during the provincial period—for instance, Princeton and Yale—served as prototypes for the establishment of institutions of higher learning throughout American history. In contrast to Oxford and Cambridge, and Europe generally, where the faculty was the seat of authority, in provincial America this power was held by an out-side group of laymen, or trustees, who hired the president. The president, representing the trustees and the faculty, engaged the faculty, and thus put into effect a direct "corporate" line of authority from the head down to the faculty. This system of out-side control came about because the number and quality of learned scholars were not sufficient to command the necessary authority and because the institutions required lay support in order to thrive. As a result, the faculties of institutions of higher learning in America have never received the respect or exercised the self-government experienced by their colleagues in England and Europe.

The products of the provincial institutions were often states-men of exceptional quality: Thomas Jefferson attended the Col-lege of William and Mary, James Madison, Princeton; the Adamses attended Harvard, and Alexander Hamilton studied at King's College. However, other prominent figures in the Revolu-tion, George Washington, Benjamin Franklin, and Robert Mor-ris, were dependent entirely on a modest amount of elementary education and their native gifts, for they received no college training.

Interest in the arts developed slowly. As Franklin aptly noted, "After the first Cares for the Necessaries of Life are over we shall come to think of the Embellishments." The point to be noticed, however, is that the development of the different arts in pro-vincial America corresponded to a remarkable degree with that in England, not in quality, but in emphasis. Except for George Frederick Handel, the great German composer who migrated to England after his genius was already recognized, the English made only modest contributions to this art form. In painting, the English record, revealing shafts of brilliance, is far more en-couraging. Perhaps the most lasting contributions, however, were made by English architects.

From these observations, a number of generalizations can be

drawn. In the arts, where the American provincial was least proficient, he was more of a "borrower" of English culture and less of a contributor. Moreover, the provincial American borrowed both English strength and English weaknesses—a strength in architecture, for instance, and a weakness in music. Finally, provincial architecture and provincial gardens (and the same generalization could be made for England) mirrored the natural orderliness of Enlightenment thought as expressed by the mind of the elite.

Keeping these generalizations in mind, the evolution in the American provinces of the respective art forms is much more comprehensible. Music, especially classical music, did not appeal strongly to the American provincial, and it appears that only the Moravians carried with them from the Old World the music of great contemporary composers, in this case Mozart and Haydn. No native compositions of consequence were written, although concerts were given in almost every colony in the eighteenth century. Of course, music for balls and dancing was commonplace in the South, and forms of popular music played by a fiddle, the jew's-harp, or virginal found their place in many homes.

Though somewhat more developed than music, creative work in painting was also limited. Provincial art appreciation left something to be desired It was not unusual for an American provincial to write to England ordering a picture by measurement, to fill a prescribed area of wall space. The type of picture was carefully designated—say, a landscape or seascape—but the quality seems to have been inconsequential. Jeremiah Theus, a Swiss who came to Charleston in 1735, mirrored many of the characteristics of the contemporary artists who practiced in America. He concentrated on portraits—for portraits were in demand as the provincial elite acquired affluence—and each portrait made the subject appear aristocratic, a subtle flattery used to attract more business. John Smibert, an artist of greater ability, came to Newport, Rhode Island, in 1728, having had art training with the great painter William Hogarth in London. Smibert settled in Boston in 1729, a cultural event in the history of that provincial city.

The two artists who were to achieve lasting fame reached their maturity later in the provincial period, John Singleton Copley, born in Boston in 1738, and Benjamin West, born the same year near Philadelphia. Interestingly enough, although both had studios in America, both settled in London, West when he was only twenty-five. Despite its growing cultural maturity, provincial America probably did not provide adequate stimulation for the aesthetic talents of men such as Copley or West. Moreover, the status of artists in provincial America was unpredictable, and both men believed their talents were better appreciated in a more sophisticated society.

Drama also lagged, its performance as well as its creation. The delay cannot be blamed entirely upon the absence of an urban audience, since the most urban region, New England, was the last to enjoy dramatic productions. The first theatre of record in the colonies was built in 1716 at Williamsburg, Virginia. The Quakers as well as the Puritans found plays a frivolous waste, and a number of provinces in New England and the middle colonies enacted legislation against theatres. The intellectual and social milieu obviously affected the developments in drama. Little purpose would be served in specifying each of the recorded traveling companies and their various offerings, which, in retrospect, contained some of the best and the worst, from Shakespeare's *Hamlet* to Nicholas Rowes's *The Fair Penitent,* but it is worth noting that the performances of traveling stock companies gradually gained favor in most of the colonies, including New England. Perhaps the warmest reception to dramatic productions was given in the southern colonies, with Charleston being particularly attractive to touring companies. The vast majority of the plays and players were importations rather than developments of an indigenous art form.

Architecture as an art form attracted attention never equaled by music or painting. Jefferson, an example of a cultural Virginian, was devoted to the study and practice of architecture, took modest pleasure in music, and was almost cold to art—rather a typical response in provincial America. The explanation of the focus on architecture lies in part in the greater development of architecture in England and in part in the utilitarian quality of the provincial mind. Architecture was not only an aesthetic expression but beauty combined with utility; a house with superior appointments could be admired—and also lived in. The attention which Thomas Jefferson lavished on Monticello has become a classic example of the preoccupation of the provincial elite with architecture as a creative art form.

Of course, in the provincial period, as merchants in the port cities improved their financial position and as planters achieved a measure of affluence, these successful provincials began to demand homes reflecting their position. Although many of the buildings were derivative—copies of English construction—provincials attempted to design buildings appropriate to their particular environment. High ceilings were more suitable to southern colonies, for instance, whereas in New England heat in the winter was much too precious to squander.

Most of the architecture was designed by intelligent amateurs, in much the same way that lawyers became amateur scientists. Peter Harrison, a ship's captain who settled in Newport, can be appropriately called a semiprofessional architect. Harrison not only designed Newport's Redwood Library but the Jewish synagogue and the Freemason's Hall in Newport as well as Christ Church in Cambridge, Massachusetts.

A lesser form of art, produced by skilled craftsmen, included a variety of utensils and furniture. Benches, chairs, and cabinetwork often combined utility and beauty. Except for Charleston, more craftsmen plied their trade in the middle and New England colonies than in the southern colonies. Native woods were used, although mahogany was sometimes imported from the West Indies and from Spanish America. In modern America, collections of these antiques by private owners have become

R

status symbols undreamed of by the simple craftsmen who made them.

Practical inventiveness became an American characteristic. Franklin, responding to an everyday need, not only invented a more practical stove for heating houses but he also constructed an ingenious air intake system so that fresh air could be warmed by the heat from the fireplace and then by a simple system of ducts distributed throughout the house. Jefferson's invention of the dumbwaiter, Captain Andrew Robinson's building of the Yankee schooner to be employed principally in intercolonial trade, and the wheat drill popularized by the Reverend Jared Eliot of Connecticut were made in the spirit of practical provincial ingenuity.

A sophisticated culture manifests itself through composers of enduring music, painters of masterpieces, architects whose work is timeless. Provincial America produced no long list of aesthetic geniuses, but this accepted standard of measurement is inadequate in the case of a formative society. Provincial America was moving toward its own distinctive expression: in its pragmatism, its utilitarianism, and its absence of a uniform system of thought.

Of course, pragmatism in American thought can be misunderstood by being conceived too narrowly as an absence of ideas. Because experience preceded theory in America and because theories were, in a sense, tested by experience before being embraced as precepts, the influence of ideas in American life can be easily misread. Pragmatism in provincial America constituted a much more sophisticated process in which ideas were based upon everyday practice. Principles evolved out of experience.

In no area of provincial life was this process more clearly revealed than in American political and social philosophy. During the provincial eighteenth century, in contrast to the colonial seventeenth century, the American was seldom called upon to defend his attitude toward the social institutions of family and schools, or even toward the structure of society, but he was required to defend his attitude toward religion and toward politics. In the defense of his practices, the provincial American developed theoretical arguments to explain them; these formulations of principles were derived directly from his experience, that men can govern themselves, that they can select their own officials, that they can, given sufficient cause, alter their government.

The provincial's definition depended upon circumstances of time, place, and issues. In Georgia during the 1730s, agitation to obtain a modification of policy from the trustees in England turned, in the heat of discontent, into a question of principle: "Your honours say persons not content with Government are equally unable to Govern themselves. We are able to Govern our selves, and think you unable to chuse Governors for us, as we best know the people, and who is fittest for the Magistry."

The approach to and organization of higher learning, the proliferation of the press, the mosaic of cultures formed by non-English peoples who migrated to America, the diffusion of culture as opposed to its concentration, all illustrate the distinctive character of the provincial intellectual experience, but certainly, at no time did the English influence upon American cultural and intellectual life disappear. The influence of Sir Christopher Wren in architecture, the training of American-born children in England, the exchange of scientific observations between provincials and Europeans, reinforced this consistent and continuous communication. But in provincial America the distinctiveness was already more important than its imitativeness.

While in England receiving an education, Peter Manigault, the scion of a wealthy and distinguished South Carolina family, received a letter from his uncle admonishing him to make good use of his time because he, Peter, had an important place to fill in "his country," meaning provincial America, and more specifically in South Carolina. What the Manigaults, a family of French origin, felt about the responsibility of their progeny personalized an American attitude, which, although not precisely measurable, was unmistakable.

11

The Structure of Provincial Politics

THAT PART of provincial life universally thought to be most distinctively American, the structure and practice of provincial politics, was in many ways the part most influenced by English institutions and practice. British parliamentary procedures and powers were precisely those most desired and most imitated by the provincial legislatures. Despite a few differences that arose in practice, the exercise of local government was modeled after local government in England.

Britain and the American provinces followed a parallel course in defining rights, privileges, power, and authority in the eighteenth century, but the results of their deliberations made a clash likely, if not inevitable. By the simple act of defining their powers, the provincial legislatures, in fact, defied the theoretical legislative supremacy of Parliament; by their everyday actions, the provincial legislatures set limits upon the authority of Parliament. By institutionalizing their practices as well as strengthening the exercise of those practices, local governments in America supported the vitality and independence of the individual provinces; thus, they were supporting decentralized authority as opposed to the centralized authority of the King and Parliament. By institutionalizing the structure of political power as it developed in eighteenth-century America, the provincials inadvertently laid the groundwork for independence and ultimately for nation-hood.

The structure of provincial politics, and thus provincial political experience, had three levels: (1) imperial government, (2) colony-wide government, and (3) local government. These three levels were not mutually exclusive. Imperial policies sometimes met with universal disapproval by the provincials, but at other times provincials were divided on the wisdom of a particular imperial enactment or policy. By the same token, a local problem such as providing for the indigent, could explode out of control if the authorities in England, in implementing official policies, transported convicts to the colonies. The provincial problem of protecting an exposed frontier could and did become an imperial problem because of intercolonial implications when the frontier in a key province was endangered. Although the political structure in the colonies had assumed definite form by the provincial period, the exercise of power within this structure was under constant revision as the political experience and practice in England and in America matured.

The structure of the English colonial and commercial system was set by the end of the seventeenth century, but adjustments continued to be made in the eighteenth, not merely by the addition of new measures or the modification of previous enactments, but by a marked alteration within the internal English political structure. Also, the development of the American provinces dramatically affected their interrelationship. In the seventeenth century, for example, the American colonials had been oriented almost exclusively toward England, but in the eighteenth century the American provinces achieved a cosmopolitan character which was reflected in their economy, their people, their ideas, and, though less obvious, their political practices. At the same time, the political and economic evolution of England in the eighteenth century made it a far different country in the 1760s from what it had been in the 1690s; it experienced a silent but dynamic revolution.

English politics in the eighteenth century witnessed the fulfillment of the ideas expressed in the Glorious Revolution of 1688. The rationale of the revolution, according to the text of John Locke, that the King had failed to honor his compact with the English people and that, therefore, the people through their representatives had the right to replace him, allowed Parliament to redress the balance between the legislative and executive authority and laid the foundation for the eventual supremacy of Parliament.

A host of enactments sealed the bargain: the English Bill of Rights enacted in 1689; the Act of Toleration, passed in the same year; the Mutiny Act (1689), restricting the King in the employment of the military by requiring annual renewal of his power over the military; the Triennial Bill (1694), which insured the attendance of Parliament; and the Act of Settlement (1701), guarding against the restoration of the Stuart monarchy, protecting England from a Catholic sovereign, allowing judges to hold office for life rather than at the King's pleasure, and invalidating any law that did not have the signature of the Privy Council, a body composed of leaders of Parliament. The purpose of these enactments was to place greater power within the purview of Parliament and particularly the House of Commons. With the elevation of the House of Hanover to the throne in 1714, Parliament became more powerful still. The Hanoverians' lack of familiarity with British institutions and the English language, the result of their German derivation and training, made them dependent upon the principal leaders in Parliament, especially in the reigns of George I and George II (1714–60).

These changes within Britain affected the North American provinces profoundly. Each provincial assembly perceived itself as a miniature Parliament, or, more specifically, a replica of the House of Commons. The powers acquired by Parliament in its continual contest with the Crown were aspired to by the provincial assemblies in their contests with the governor, the representative of royal authority in America. Provincials frequently called upon the English Bill of Rights when a policy of the Crown or even of a rival faction within their colony threatened what they considered to be their English liberties. "Revolution Principles," the right of the legislature to be free from royal encroachment, became a watchword for the American provincials as well as for the parliamentary leaders in Britain.

In imitating Parliament, the assemblies trod the path that would eventually lead to an impasse between Britain and her colonies, for the provinces operated on the premise that the Crown served as the tie between Britain and themselves, whereas Parliament held the position that its authority knew no bounds, that the colonies were subject to the legislative supremacy of Parliament. A pamphleteer in New York, supporting the British position, advised that colonial assembly "to drop those parliamentary airs and style about liberty and property, and keep within their sphere." When Massachusetts, in 1733, appealed to the actions of the House of Commons as precedent for their own position, Parliament renounced the Massachusetts petition as a "high insult upon his Majesty's government."

A second trend within the domestic politics of England that affected the American provinces was the emergence of a modified two-party system, the Whigs and the Tories, during the eighteenth century. Historians of England in the past generation have devoted an enormous amount of research to prove that these parties were less unified in thought and action than was once assumed and that they represented, in fact, coalitions of widely diversified interests. But party labels, however misleading, were used, and among American provincials each British party was identified with certain actions and policies. The influence of the evolution of the English party system upon the American provincials is somewhat intangible, but the political factions developing in the American colonies, loosely constructed to be sure, looked to the English party system as the example to imitate;

in certain colonies, associating a cause with the Whigs proved to be extremely popular with the electorate.

In some cases English party policies directly affected the American provinces, or a segment thereof, and provincials informed on English affairs often associated themselves with one or the other of the parties. During the ascendancy of Robert Walpole as first prime minister (1721–42), the object of the Whig party was to preserve peace at almost any price, to refrain from fighting France and Spain, and to continue to encourage and stimulate trade and internal growth within England. This policy provoked William Byrd II to complain bitterly about the lethargy of British leadership, a point of view that was echoed by other provincials who were particularly aware that the American provinces served as the sensitive membrane between English, French, and Spanish ambitions.

The development of a cabinet form of government in eighteenth-century England had a somewhat different effect upon provincial America, for it tended to confuse the lines of communication and authority between the mother country and the provinces. Which Cabinet member was responsible for a particular policy touching upon one or all of the American provinces? If a province had a grievance, to whom should an address be directed? To the King? To the Board of Trade? To a particular Cabinet official? To the House of Commons? Where did the source of power reside in a government in which the internal balance of authority was forever shifting? The English Cabinet, although theoretically responsible to the Crown, was composed of parliamentary leaders who could command a majority in the House of Commons. They were, in fact, legislative leaders not executive functionaries. The provinces conceived of their attachment to England through the Crown; yet an official such as the Secretary of State exercised extensive power over provincial affairs, even though he was principally responsible to Parliament and enmeshed in complex questions of patronage at home and diplomacy abroad.

Confronted with the English confusion of responsibility as it applied to overseas territories, almost every colony employed an agent in England to represent its cause. It was the responsibility of the agent to follow an issue through the maze of overlapping and conflicting jurisdictions within the imperial structure. Official British policy recognized the need for this intercession. When Governor Arthur Dobbs of North Carolina, a staunch imperialist, fought to eliminate this "privilege," he was advised by the home authorities to concede—which he was eventually forced to do.

As the Cabinet system evolved, therefore, imperial policy can be said, in most cases, to have represented the position of Parliament rather than that of the Crown. The consequence of this modification in the institutional structure of the Empire obviously affected the relationship between the British provinces in North America and the mother country. To cite but one example, imperial policy tended to favor the West Indian colonies over the North American provinces, not only because they produced staples desired by Britain, but because the affluent absentee owners of West Indies property wielded a powerful influence in Parliament.

Economic developments within England also affected the American provinces. A second round of enclosures in the eighteenth century, when the larger landholder gained additional land and when the number of smaller leaseholders was reduced, this time encouraged rather than discouraged by the government, permitted a wider application of capital to agriculture, making the English market in foodstuffs even less accessible to the American provinces. Moreover, the enclosures, by promoting the production of wool, further stimulated the textile industry, the single best index of the early advance of industrialization. The year 1750 is customarily accepted as a convenient date to herald the emergence of the industrial revolution within England, and, presumably, Britain in the second half of the eighteenth century would become increasingly aware of markets. British theory seriously lagged behind reality, and the British refused to recognize the significance of the increasing market in the American provinces. As a result, the growing American provinces not only were faced with new problems, but the old problems of exchange, money, and credit were intensified.

To meet these issues, the provincials responded by attempting to create their own banks and by issuing currency. In each case, their efforts were eventually nullified by the imposition of British control: the Currency Act of 1751, which applied to Massachusetts but which was extended to all the American provinces in 1764, and the extension in 1741 to the provinces of the Bubble Act of 1720, which prohibited land banks. British merchants feared the inflationary effect of large issues of provincial currency and the instability of banks dependent solely upon land as reserve, for such banks, as the United States discovered after the American Revolution, lacked fluidity and flexibility in times of financial crisis when these qualities were most needed. An indigenous American economy required banks and other sophisticated financial instruments, but the British exercised their authority to check these obvious needs.

In 1696 King William authorized the creation of a Board of Trade. The purpose of the Board was not only to make recommendations with respect to commercial colonial policy but to include within its surveillance the entire trade of Britain, a much broader authority than is often recognized. The Board of Trade consisted of sixteen members, eight "working members," some of whom—such as William Blathwayt and John Locke—were experts. Ex officio members from the Cabinet included the Secretary of State for the Southern Department, whose jurisdiction encompassed the administration of the provinces, the Chancellor of the Exchequer, the First Lord of the Admiralty, and other key officials. These "great men" attended the Board's meetings less frequently as time elapsed. Instructions to the royal governors were customarily sent out through the Secretary of State for the

Southern Department, but many significant issues involving the colonies were referred at one stage or another to the Board of Trade for its advice. For slightly more than a quarter century, the Board of Trade worked actively; from the 1720s to 1750 the Board's activities, because of the official position taken by the Secretary of State, can generally be described as lethargic.

The ex officio members of the Board of Trade represented the various agencies which in some measure had jurisdiction over the colonies. At the head of each agency stood a member of the cabinet. Although preoccupied with diplomatic and domestic policies, the Secretary of State for the Southern Department had the authority to select the royal governors for the provinces. He also sent them instructions and, more rarely, requested reports. Some of the best information to be obtained today about the provinces is found in these reports to the Secretary, but, unfortunately, he seldom consulted the reports and rarely acted upon the information contained in them. The Admiralty had the responsibility of enforcing the Navigation Acts and of attending to convoys, guard ships, and numerous other needs requiring naval action. The Treasury was responsible for collection of revenue in the provinces. A subordinate agency of the Treasury, the Commissioners of Customs, supervised the collection of duties designated by law. Several surveyors of the customs were appointed to supervise a host of subordinates in the various American ports. Assisting in drafting charters and in making judgments with regard to the legality of provincial—and parliamentary—legislation were other officials of high rank, the Solicitor General and the Attorney General.

Bringing the colonies within a more closely supervised imperial framework was discussed by the British authorities in the eighteenth century, but it was never pursued with the same vigor which had prompted the Lords of Trade to establish the Dominion of New England late in the seventeenth century. Certain colonies originally established as proprietaries were made royal colonies. In 1729 for instance, the Carolinas were taken over officially by the Crown, not so much, however, because of an aggressive policy on the part of authorities in England, but because of the inability of the proprietors to meet the problems of colonial defense and other issues.

By the 1750s, eight of the thirteen colonies were under the direct control of the Crown. Of the exceptions—that is, Maryland (where the proprietary had been re-established in 1715), Delaware, Pennsylvania, Connecticut, and Rhode Island—only Connecticut and Rhode Island were relatively free from intensive political pressure from England. A strong effort was made by the Crown in 1712 to purchase the charter of Pennsylvania (and Delaware), but it failed. When the Hanoverians took the throne, which introduced an added uncertainty in the exercise of executive as opposed to parliamentary authority over the American provinces, the existing imperial structure remained generally undisturbed. The executive bureaucracy, notably the Board of Trade, frequently advocated a more positive policy to eliminate proprietary colonies, but George I and George II failed to act decisively. Parliament, in turn, preoccupied with a wide variety of issues, in addition to those pertaining to the provinces, and undergoing a power revolution of its own directed against the royal prerogative, could not spare the time for a major overhaul of the imperial framework or of imperial policies. Indeed, in its contest with the prerogative, Parliament found it advantageous not to make the remaining charter and proprietary colonies into royal colonies for fear of strengthening the position of the Crown in its contest with Parliament.

The strictly political relationship between Britain and the provinces in the eighteenth century was a continual choreography of movement in which the provinces attempted to enlarge their authority while Britain attempted to circumscribe and even restrict that authority. By 1750 self-governing colonies had assumed ("assumed" is precisely the right word, for the home authorities never acknowledged any inherent right of the provinces to exercise power) certain powers and generally conceded that the mother country was entitled to other specified powers. The mother country, the provinces acknowledged, possessed the power to regulate trade among the colonies, for trade was obviously intercolonial in character, and, therefore, the responsibility of the state, not its dependencies. By the same reasoning, diplomacy was also a function of the state. On the other hand, the American provinces, in exercising self-government, defined their own franchise and officeholding requirements, provided internal improvements and taxed themselves, initiated all domestic legislation, and in general dispensed justice.

There were areas, however, where the powers divided between the province and the mother country overlapped, or at least intersected, provoking a series of questions, most of which were eventually answered. Did the provincial assembly have the right to elect its own speaker? To control the civil list, that is, colonial officials appointed by the Crown but whose compensation was controlled by the assemblies? To determine the frequency of meetings? Did a province have the right to assume authority to charter banks and to issue bills of credit? Many provinces claimed jurisdiction in these areas, but British officials responded with instructions to the governor, often denying the authority of provincials. When the assemblies disregarded the instructions, which from the British point of view formed a part of the constitutional base of the British-colonial relationship, Parliament passed legislation—the Currency Act of 1751 is an apt example—defining the authority of the mother country and restricting provincial practice.

Although persistent, the clash between the authority of Britain and that of the provinces was carried on in a relatively low key, because the Spanish and French threats along the borders of the American provinces forced both sides to limit the exploitation of these issues. Evidence of friction should not be mistaken for violent factionalism; the danger to Britain and the provinces was too serious to countenance unnecessary division. The situation was not unlike periodic crises in later American history in which an external threat to the country forced the parties to minimize, at least temporarily, their differences. Whenever the external threat faded, these frictions, always present but subordinated, moved into focus.

The collision between the authority of the provinces and that of Britain usually found its primary expression in the actions of the provincial assembly on the one hand and those of the governor on the other. In most provinces, the governor was overcommitted, saddled with more duties than he could expect to fulfill competently. His duties were to represent the King, to execute colonial legislation, to serve as commander-in-chief of the militia, and to serve as chief magistrate, to list the most obvious. Any one of these would have been a sufficient occupation, but in combination they presented a governor with innumerable conflicts of loyalty. As the chief executive, his duty to enforce controversial colonial legislation tended to place the governor in a dilemma, for a colonial enactment often contradicted his instructions from England. An effective governor could reduce the differences between provincial assertions of authority and the Crown's claims of a prerogative, but no governor, however able, could eliminate the conflict altogether. Native Americans like Governor Lewis Morris of New Jersey and Thomas Hutchinson of Massachusetts fared no better than those governors who came from England. What was at stake was power, not personalities.

From the American point of view, the provincial government derived its power from the consent of the governed. From the British point of view, the provincial government derived its authority from the royal grace and favor expressed by the colonial charters, the governor's commission, and the instructions issued to the governor. From the point of view of the provincials, their rights were inviolable; from the point of view of the British, provincial government could be altered or modified or even abolished, depending solely upon the favor of the British authorities. Eventually, the provincial experience would be elevated into principle, as the provincials were forced to define their authority after 1763 when Parliament disguised as the Crown acted on the theory that the constitutional structure of provinces in the Empire could be altered by unilateral action, in short by royal grace and favor.

During the eighteenth century, the clash for control continually erupted, and assemblies generally gained power at the expense of the governor, representing the prerogative. Election of the speaker, control of the finances, including those expenses connected with the civil list, and initiation of all legislation were among those powers specifically secured by the provincial assemblies, though nowhere was this authority obtained without friction. Where other rights were at stake—for instance, the right of an assembly to enlarge its membership or to establish counties ("districts") or to enact Triennial Acts to force the Governor to call an assembly at least once every three years (New Hampshire proved to be an exception in 1728)—the royal authority successfully challenged the assemblies.

To think that the assembly stood alone in representing the provincial interest is a mistake. In many colonies, the council was the first group to contest the authority of the Crown, or more precisely the governor representing the Crown. In tracing the democratizing influences of these formative years, the story begins with the colonial councils rather than with the assemblies. Only after the 1720s, when the assemblies acquired greater power, did they supersede the council as spokesmen for colonial authority against that of the Crown and Parliament.

When the councils expanded colonial authority during the transition from colonies to provinces, they were motivated primarily by self-interest. They wished to control the distribution of land and to curtail the governor's authority; they wished to obtain control of appointments to principal colonial offices, either for themselves or for their friends. Any curtailment of royal authority would enhance the power of the people, as had happened when the nobles wrung concessions from King John in the Magna Charta.

The power of the assemblies increased markedly during the provincial period, often at the expense of the colonial council as well as the governor. With the increase in population from 250,000 to 1,500,000, and with the increase in the number of provincial elite, not necessarily in the same proportion as the total population, the few council appointments, never more than a dozen and often semihereditary in character, were insufficient to satisfy those capable of holding office or ambitious to wield power. Gradually the assemblies added to their number of substantial citizens and, modeling themselves after the gains made by the English Parliament in its contest with the Crown, enhanced their authority.

The governor and the council, then, tended to represent the *status quo,* and they were opposed by the assembly, the innovating force, which attempted to establish a new balance of power within the province. The assembly wished to have a stronger voice in the distribution of lands, in official appointments, and in the policies of the colony, many of which affected the exercise of power. The alignment of forces was not absolute. A faction in control of the assembly often had spokesmen in the council chambers, and political ties were dependent on factors subject to change—economic interests, sectional interests, and, in New York and Virginia, family ties, a provincial "establishment."

The constitutional structure within which the struggle for power took place was remarkably similar throughout the colonies. Except for the method of choosing a council, Massachusetts is a representative example for the provincial period. By the terms of the Massachusetts charter of 1691, the governor was appointed by the Crown and the council was elected by the assembly (except for the first council, which was appointed by the Crown) with the governor holding veto power over the prospective appointees. The council served as the upper house of the General Court, the provincial legislature, while the assembly, elected by the people, the "people" being defined in terms of a property requirement, served as the lower house.

This pattern was generally followed in provincial America, but exceptions did exist. In the charter colonies of Connecticut and Rhode Island, the governor as well as the members of the council and the assembly were elected by the freemen. In New York and Virginia the council was appointed by the Crown, with advice from the Board of Trade and other officials, from a list of names submitted by the governor. Seniority, social and economic position, and, to a limited extent, place of residence played a critical part in the appointment of council members. In Virginia the council members with seniority automatically exercised the authority of the governor if, for any reason, the governor was temporarily absent or was removed without a replacement. In Virginia the council was composed of an elite group.

In many ways, Pennsylvania was an exception. Originally, the structure of government in Pennsylvania gave the council special authority. It was the body that enacted legislation; the assembly could only consent to or block the action of the council. In 1701, however, a constitutional reform by the Penn family established a unicameral legislature, unknown elsewhere in the American provinces. No provision was made for a council, but the governor created an ex officio council by seeking advice from a select group who were loyal to him. The Pennsylvania assembly gained the right to choose its own speaker, to judge the qualifications of its own members, to prepare bills, and to exercise other powers of a miniature Parliament.

Although franchise qualifications varied, every colony required property ownership. In Massachusetts, for example, the requirements specified that a man must either have a freehold with an income of forty shillings or an estate valued at forty pounds sterling. In Virginia an act in 1705 required that a man possess a fifty-acre freehold in order to vote; in 1736 the requirement was expanded to a hundred acres of unoccupied land with the alterna-

s

tive of twenty-five acres of land with improvements, a house and plantation, or a house and lot in one of the towns.

The number or percentage of people who could meet these requirements has been disputed. Was it more difficult to obtain a freehold with an income of forty shillings in Massachusetts than it was to obtain a hundred-acre freehold in Virginia? The final answer has not yet been found, although it was probably easier to meet the qualifications in Virginia because of a freer land policy, but the evidence at hand indicates that more provincials were qualified to vote in Massachusetts than historians a generation ago were willing to acknowledge. It is wise to add a word of caution that having the right to vote was not the equivalent of possessing political power.

Early in the twentieth century, J. F. Jameson estimated that 16 per cent of the population of provincial Massachusetts was qualified to vote and that this percentage was slightly higher in Virginia. This estimate at first glance appears small, but considered in modern terms it exceeds expectations. Approximately 70,000,000 out of a total population of 180,000,000 voted in the 1960 presidential election. More than half of this 70,000,000 were women. Subtract women, and 30,000,000 to 35,000,000 people voted, that is, 16 to 20 per cent of the total population. A larger percentage of men, of course, were eligible to vote, but it should be remembered that because of modern public health, a much greater percentage of the nation's population is twenty-one and over. The obvious conclusion is that, properly equated, the number of men eligible to vote in provincial America was more comparable to modern times than has often been recognized. Robert E. Brown has examined the records of Massachusetts with care and estimates that J. F. Janeson's figure, if anything, was conservative. Certainly, the percentage of adult white males qualified to vote in provincial America exceeded that in England, largely because land, being much cheaper and more accessible in the New World, was not so great a barrier in the acquisition of the franchise.

To be able to vote was not necessarily to exercise power. The available evidence suggests that in many colonies an elite oligarchy, an establishment, held power, which was checked only when a highly controversial colony-wide issue aroused the rank-and-file voter, who thereupon elected a new oligarchy. Certain legislators were repeatedly elected. Within the legislatures, the leadership remained remarkably stable, with influential gentry families retaining key committee posts. Wealth was important in obtaining these assignments. Peter Manigault, son of one of the wealthiest men in South Carolina, did not need to wait out a seniority list in order to be elected Speaker of the Commons House of Assembly. He was, by virtue of his station, a legislative leader from the outset. Of course, in a modern American Congress or in a state legislature, the leadership also remains remarkably stable, indeed, at times annoyingly so.

Part of the explanation for this stability of leadership is that whereas franchise requirements were not difficult to meet, the property requirements for holding office were. In Maryland, for example, the assembly was composed of men with large estates. Out of 125 delegates, only 16 possessed fewer than five hundred acres of land. The average landholding of council members ranged from seven hundred to eight hundred acres. The persistence of the notion that an officeholder in order to be politically responsible must have an economic stake in the society in the form of land can be seen as late as 1787, when the Northwest Ordinance required officeholders to possess three hundred acres of land in the territory.

The election procedure itself at times encouraged the re-election of an established group. Candidates were often drafted by a clique of merchants or planters or a family alliance that operated as an informal caucus. Moreover, voting in provincial America was an open demonstration of loyalty to a particular candidate. In Virginia the candidates were usually present at the polling places. The official presiding over the election asked the voter to indicate his choice; the voter announced his selection before all the candidates, and the voter's name was properly recorded in the column of the candidate he selected. The social pressure was obvious. It is inconceivable that a voter who lived in the immediate vicinity of William Byrd's plantation or that of some comparable figure was not influenced by his relationship to him, particularly if the voter were dependent upon the larger planter for favors, an exchange of goods, the use of his land, or the consummation of a land deal, all common occurrences. In addition, running for office was expensive. Liquor and food were dispensed freely. No reimbursement was made for the time spent away from earning a living. Only a man of some means could afford to hold office.

Another possible explanation of the continued re-election of a select group is that the eighteenth-century American often looked to men of affluence as leaders, and therefore considered them entitled to office. Each man had his place in a well-ordered society, and the large landholder or the prominent merchant, because of his economic position, was fitted for political privilege. In short, the percentage of people who were eligible to vote, important as it is, does not answer all of the questions that must be raised with regard to the exercise of political power in provincial America.

The political issues that arose reflected the changing American society and the tensions created by these changes. On an intercolonial level, friction developed between certain colonies because of boundary disputes, rivalry in the Indian trade, and competition in specific areas of the general trade. Boundary disputes involved Connecticut and New York, Pennsylvania and Maryland, and Virginia and North Carolina, to mention the most obvious examples. In each case desirable lands were at stake, but in each case the dispute was finally settled, though Connecticut and New York held on to their grievances longer. Rivalry in the Indian trade affected New York and Pennsylvania, Virginia and the Carolinas, and South Carolina and Georgia. In trade, New

Jersey was subject to pressures from New York and Pennsylvania; North Carolina experienced much the same problem in its relationship with Virginia and South Carolina. Virginia and Maryland frequently competed in trade.

Intracolonial issues were in many ways more significant because they represented not merely the tensions within a colony but the maturity of provincial political experience and action. The list of issues is long, though it should be emphasized at the outset that every issue did not appear in each colony.

Among the more prominent issues were the following: the Indian problem, including rivalry between groups of provincials for Indian trade or Indian territory and defense measures required by settlements exposed to Indian attack; internal improvements, involving the building of roads and the like; taxation, the type and amount of tax to be levied and the mode of collection; the problem of a church establishment, an issue confined to those colonies where a particular church was supported in whole or in part by general taxation; balanced representation, an issue arising most commonly in those provinces undergoing the greatest growth, so that newly settled areas were underrepresented in proportion to the total population of the colony; nativism, an issue particularly pervasive in colonies of "new," that is, non-English, migration; money and banks, an issue arising in most provinces at one time or another and becoming especially prominent when a policy of paper currency was approved or disapproved during periods in which a shortage of capital was particularly acute; and finally, land, the procedure for procurement and distribution.

Occasionally, imperial problems were reflected in intracolonial disputes when provincials, to curry favor with the Crown, aligned themselves with an English commercial or colonial policy. Edmund Jenings of Virginia always allied himself with the governor regardless of the issue—except when the governor was absent. But this was an exception. An intracolonial dispute more often intruded upon imperial policy.

The danger of reading the intracolonial issues through the refraction of the Revolution is very real. All too often these frictions have been mistakenly interpreted as conflicts so deep as to provoke violent recourse. It is more accurate to evaluate them as issues that could be expected to arise in any healthy republican society. The emergence of these issues is, in fact, an indication of political maturity, as important questions are raised for discussion and men have the freedom to respond. The debates, the patterns involved in the struggle for power, and the compromises reveal the highest level of political practice.

Political practice in operation can be seen in Pennsylvania, where many of the intracolonial issues found expression: protection from the Indians, internal improvements, port legislation, nativism, money, and representation, to mention the most obvious. As a frontier province with a widely diversified population undergoing phenomenal expansion, Pennsylvania not only was faced with the problem of protecting the outlying western settlements, but with the militant anti-Quakerism of the Scotch-Irish settling in those areas. It was the pacific Quakers who, with the acquiescence of the large German population, possessed political power. As a result, the relationship between the Germans and the Scotch-Irish in the colony was far from harmonious.

As people migrated westward, internal improvements became an increasingly significant issue. The rivers in Pennsylvania, the most accessible means of transport, flowed from a northwest to southeasterly direction. The Susquehanna River and its tributaries, which penetrated the western territory of the province, emptied into the Chesapeake Bay, making communication and trade between the eastern and western parts of Pennsylvania largely dependent on roads. Building roads entailed an expenditure which the provincial legislature, controlled by the eastern counties and dominated by Quakers, was not always willing to support, though the issue by no means represented a clean east-west split. Certain merchants in Philadelphia who wished to sell goods in the interior were as concerned about the problem as the western farmer who wished to market his crops. The rate of population increase in Pennsylvania, which exceeded that of any other province, also increased the discrepancy between the representation of the eastern part of the province and that of the western part.

The money issue plagued Pennsylvania, as it did most of the maturing provinces, including Massachusetts, Rhode Island, and South Carolina. The division of opinion was not strictly east-west, creditor-debtor, or the poor against the rich. A merchant in need of capital often supported the issuance of currency, though he usually was more discriminating than some of his fellows so as not to deprive the currency of its effective role as a reliable medium of exchange and standard of value. The professionals, lawyers and doctors, as well as workmen sometimes opposed the issuance of currency for fear that their standard of living would suffer as prices rose more swiftly than fees or wages.

Nativism as a political issue in Pennsylvania was not a constant. At first, the Quaker elite feared that the influx of some 100,000 Germans would overwhelm them, but when the Quakers recognized that the Germans served as silent allies against the more articulate Scotch-Irish, who, with increasing stubbornness, demanded a greater voice in self-government, the Quaker elite shifted its protest to the Scotch-Irish. Indeed, the most persistent political antagonism within provincial Pennsylvania was between the Quaker elite and the Scotch-Irish; this factionalism became sufficiently intense that by the 1760s historians have frequently noted the emergence of a "Presbyterian party," in effect, a party composed mainly of Scotch-Irish, who held views on many significant issues distinct from those of the dominating Quaker politicians.

Pennsylvania provides an interesting sample of political debate, but each colony experienced problems peculiar to its circumstances. In Massachusetts, for example, at least five issues dominated the eighteenth century: the distribution of land, the consequence of trade, the type of taxation, and the problem of currency and banking. This last issue furnishes an excellent example of a recurring problem, involving many ramifications.

Paper money was first issued in Massachusetts in 1690, secured upon the faith that the provincial government would be able to meet its obligation rather than upon some tangible asset like land or precious metals. The problem became more and more complicated, not only by the issuance of additional paper money by the province, but also by the actions of special economic groups. A land bank was organized in 1740; it issued notes, with land as security. Without official authorization, a group of merchants, principally from Boston, organized their own bank, popularly called a silver bank, in opposition to the Land Bank. This Silver Bank also issued notes; acceptance of the notes was based on the ability of the organizing merchants to meet their obligations.

It is probably fair to suggest that the majority of Massachusetts provincials favored the public currency issues, but people on a fixed income (ministers and workmen) suffered from the general inflationary policy which resulted, even though an adjustment was usually made. Certainly, the political division on paper money did not take the form of the merchant versus the landholder, the east versus the west, or the poor versus the wealthy. An affluent merchant, for instance, was usually a creditor and a debtor. Careful examination of the subscribers to the Land Bank has revealed that men of substance throughout Massachusetts supported this measure, while men of equal substance opposed the Land Bank. To nullify the effectiveness of the Land Bank, the opponents not only refused to accept currency issued by the Land Bank, but a few politically important opponents appealed to the British authorities to outlaw the Bank by extending the Bubble Act of 1720. Extension of the Bubble Act did defeat the Land Bank, but Governor Shirley of Massachusetts permitted the supporters of the Bank to liquidate gradually, which reduced the shock. The political implications within Massachusetts can be measured in part by the resurgence of power of the supporters of the Land Bank concept. In Salem, the second largest city in the province, supporters of the bank gained political control at the expense of the Bank's opponents.

In 1750 a grant by Parliament enabled Massachusetts to resume specie payment. The debate in the Massachusetts legislature did not dwell upon the virtues or vices of paper money but upon the wisdom of redeeming all the paper currency at once; in a close vote, immediate redemption won out. The experience of Massachusetts in trying to adjust to an expanding economy was shared by many other provinces.

In the colony of New York, the land problem was a significant issue, though other issues—an Anglican Church establishment and the Indian policy—were also important. With favorites obtaining extensive land patents, forcing the small farmer in many areas to lease land, the politics of New York tended to be polarized around families, principally the Livingstons and De Lanceys. It was a battle of giants, with the middle- and lower-class groups serving at best as secondary allies. The Livingstons presumably were more representative of the landed elite and the De Lanceys of the mercantile elite, but both families had relatives in commerce and land. New York politics, because of its almost exclusive dependence upon elite groups, retained a different character from the politics of Massachusetts, Pennsylvania, or even Virginia.

In Maryland, taxes became an important domestic issue because they were levied, for the most part, on tobacco. Yet by the mid-eighteenth century the eastern shore of Maryland raised wheat and the western shore raised tobacco. The incidence of taxes, therefore, rested unevenly upon the Maryland provincials, which resulted in repeated attempts on the part of the tobacco growers to win an adjustment.

In Virginia, land, representation, defense against the Indians, the church, and tobacco inspections laws were among the main issues. A number of these issues might suggest a division between the east and west, the Tidewater against the Piedmont and the valley. Such an evaluation greatly oversimplifies the reality. The river and waterway system which interlaces Virginia often produced divisions between one river system as opposed to a rival river system, or between a planter possessing a landing on a river and those adjacent landholders who wished to gain access to water transportation, or between the Northern Neck and the remainder of the province. Alignments were relatively flexible, with rival political factions representing a complex of power rather than a simple east-west split. Moreover, in the first three decades of the eighteenth century, political divisions within the province were somewhat muted for fear of giving the governor a chance to exploit intraprovince divisions as a means of enhancing the prerogative.

Patronage was frequently used in attempts to mold a party. Governors attempted to use the gift of a provincial office to build a party that would support their policies, but in most cases they were not only checked by the councils or by the assemblies, who also wished to control appointments, but even at times by the authorities in England, who sometimes ignored the governors' recommendations. The operation of an underlying check and balance, the governor versus the council, the governor and council versus the assembly, faction versus faction in the council and in the assembly, prevented any single segment of government from securing overriding control.

When Governor Alexander Spotswood of Virginia deliberately set about building a governor's party, the results were a setback rather than a gain for the royal prerogative. In 1713–14 Spotswood attempted to use the Tobacco Inspection Act as a lever for appointing assembly favorites as inspectors and thus strengthen his control. He was shocked to discover in the ensuing general election that the small planters rebelled and, in almost every instance, voted out of office the incumbents who accepted his appointment. Thus, it seemed that the small planter was willing in most cases for his "betters" to represent him in the legislature so long as they did not forfeit the good faith placed in them.

On intracolonial issues many of the provinces shared similar experiences. New York, Pennsylvania, Virginia, and the Carolinas, for instance, were faced at one time or another with impressive Indian problems. The issue of a church establishment touched many colonies: Massachusetts, New York, Maryland, Virginia, and the Carolinas. Proportionate representation became an important issue in Pennsylvania, Virginia, and the Carolinas, and the issue of nativism developed in those areas that were, in fact, most cosmopolitan: Pennsylvania, New York, and the Carolinas. The Indian problem was as important to Pennsylvania as it was to the Carolinas and to Virginia. Land, as the elemental form of wealth, was important to all the colonies. Some semblance of an east-west political division was evident in Pennsylvania (and in Virginia in the 1750s and 1760s) as the Scotch-Irish and Germans migrated from the back country of Pennsylvania southward, but such a division was less common than an earlier generation of historians assumed.

The political issues that arose in provincial America resulted in factions rather than in formal parties, in temporary coalitions rather than fixed, enduring political alignments. No colony had what could be appropriately designated a party structure. Political alignments in Virginia coalesced around a nucleus of politically important families and in Pennsylvania around a dominating group of Quaker coreligionists. In New York economic and family groups, the merchants and the landed elite, formed the nucleus for political coalitions. To recognize issues and to recognize bitter grievances is not to suggest that these differences were so intense as to border upon civil disorder. Instances like the Paxton boys' march on Philadelphia in 1764 and the Regulator movements in the Carolinas from 1767 to 1771, when certain back-country settlers took the law in their own hands, are exceptions rather than the rule.

During the eighteenth century, local government in the American provinces thrived. Descriptions of the oligarchical character of county government in eighteenth-century England and provincial Virginia are remarkably similar. Basil Williams, an authority on Hanoverian England, observes: ". . . in local affairs the forms of self-government to be found in the parish, the manor, the shire [county], and the chartered boroughs . . . resulted in the main in a government of local oligarchies." Charles Sydnor, in describing the county courts of Virginia, writes: "Long before the American Revolution the county courts had become, for all practical purposes, independent, self-perpetuating bodies, beyond the control of the governor or of any other branch of provincial government."

Each scholar also observed that the justices of the peace, the chief officials of local government, exercised almost unchecked jurisdiction. "In the eighteenth century," writes Williams, "the power of these justices in urban as well as in rural districts was immense, since they combined administrative with judicial functions, thus signally refuting Montesquieu's contemporary theory of the complete separation of such powers in the British constitution." A description of the power of the Virginia justices, identical in substance, is given by Sydnor: ". . . the records of the courts . . . show very clearly that the court, despite its name, was a legislative, executive, and electoral, as well as a judicial body. Separation of powers, and checks and balances, were unknown in Virginia county government. Every variety of governmental power was vested in the single body known as the county court."

To delineate the power of local government in provincial America, Virginia can be used as a choice example. Commissions were granted to the justices of the peace by the governor from a list submitted to him by the county court, which consisted of the justices. The governor's freedom of choice was practically nil. On the list submitted to the governor, the justices' names appeared in order of seniority of service. Distribution of justices somewhat equally throughout a county, so that each area could be represented, was a common practice, especially for counties created in the eighteenth century. If the governor failed to comply with the list, the county court simply refused to meet, bringing all local business, the principal concern of the great majority of people, to a halt. The sheriff, by law, was appointed from the list of justices, and the county court, if it did not have direct appointive power over local authorities, exercised its virtual authority to get those men chosen whom it favored.

A man did not appear on the list of justices unless he was someone of repute in the county. His fortune did not need to be great, but he was required to be a responsible individual of some means. Several terms as justice of the peace qualified a man for higher office, presumably in the House of Burgesses. Not all justices, however, were ambitious for higher office. There were many cases in which a Virginia planter made a career of being the first man in local government, the prince of the oligarchy. In this capacity his personal power was something like a big-city boss of the late nineteenth and twentieth centuries. There were also members of the House of Burgesses who had not served an apprenticeship in the county court as a justice of the peace. Of course, there were many more justices of the peace—sometimes twenty or more for a county—than burgesses, so not all justices could attain the higher office.

In the eighteenth century the county court had a wide range of authority in local affairs, and the list of specific duties was long. The court supervised construction and maintenance of roads. They licensed taverns. They enforced colonial legislation. They tried civil cases. Every three months they met as a court of oyer and terminer to act in criminal cases not involving life and limb; in this capacity their jurisdiction was less restricted when dealing with slaves. In conjunction with church vestries, whose membership usually consisted of justices, they cared for the indigent. The court administered the estates of orphans and appointed guardians for them. The court, in summary, managed local affairs.

Not every province had as vigorous a local government as

Virginia, but each province except for Georgia had by 1750 a minimum of a half century of experience with some form of local government. Whether local government operated in terms of townships, as in New England, or counties, the result was to elevate a group of local gentry who became accustomed to managing local matters. The vigor of local government strengthened the ranks of leadership in many provinces, and most important, strengthened colonial rule, as opposed to imperial rule. The significance of local government was recognized during the crisis of the American Revolution when it enabled provincial society to bridge the transition from colonies to states with a minimum of disruption. This transition could never have been accomplished so competently without the institutions of local government, which remained virtually unchanged in an age of drastic upheaval. Although the machinery of local government remained the same, further investigations must determine whether a different class gained control of that machinery during and after the Revolution.

One additional consideration with regard to local government has been neglected by scholars. Local oligarchies controlled local government. Local government in practice, therefore, cannot be considered democratic when the great majority of men fell outside the oligarchic establishment. Can it be said, as expressed by the Jeffersonian partisans, that local government was closer to the people because it was under their control? Or is it more realistic to say that the only recourse open to those outside the local oligarchy, if they were to secure a redress of grievances, was to address themselves to a higher political authority?

The problem of analyzing the political system of provincial America—indeed, for all of American history for that matter—in terms of a series of oligarchical groups that are controlled by local "establishments" and that answer to more elevated oligarchical groups until the top level of power within a province is reached has not yet been examined with discrimination and penetration. But it does seem clear that despite the widespread use of the franchise and even with a rotation of men in office, counties and towns were frequently controlled, sometimes without the obvious exterior signs, by a select group in much the same way that a relatively few people do, in fact, control towns, suburban communities, cities, and states in twentieth-century America. Robert Lynd's case study of *Middletown,* in which the few, despite unrestricted adult suffrage, in practice decided what was good for the community and then exercised power in many subtle ways by controlling the machinery of political action, is not unlike the operation of the political process in the counties of Virginia or in the towns and cities of New England. Whenever a county or town was new, the situation obviously was somewhat more fluid.

The development of local government in provincial America had a lasting influence upon its own time and upon the future political tradition in America. It strengthened the provincial government as opposed to the imperial government; it established institutional machinery which resolved many local problems expeditiously and effectively; it served as an apprenticeship for political leadership; it enabled the colonies to endure the American Revolution with a minimum of disruption in their daily affairs; it established an orderliness of law and custom; it served as a link between the consolidated government of the province and the individual communities; it created machinery of government which even today continues to affect the life of every American.

Although the American provinces modeled themselves after British political institutions, the result was not, as one might assume, an imitation, but a new synthesis that was distinctively American. Like many great creations in literature, architecture, and the arts, familiar forms or materials re-structured within a different context are invested with new meaning.

In this instance, the legacy of the provincial political structure was enduring. The distribution of authority between the central government and subordinate colonies was, for the most part, worked out through eighteenth-century experience: intercolonial problems such as trade and diplomacy were met by the authority invested in the central government—in the provincial period by the British Parliament and later by the federal government—whereas issues intracolonial in character fell within the jurisdiction of the individual colonies and later of the American states. The federal system—subordinate states with definitely assigned power and jurisdiction and a central national government with a superior sphere of authority—is a product, not only in its practice but in its theory, of the colonial-provincial experience. Moreover, local government, which today maintains the offices and retains the responsibilities practiced in colonial America, has served throughout American history not merely as a record-keeping agency (probate records, property titles, and the like) but as an effective instrument to relate the individual to the larger governance of state and nation. Even some local oligarchical character is preserved, though the oligarchy in modern times can be a city political machine or, in suburban America, an upper middle-class group of bankers, doctors, and lawyers.

Indeed, the details of politics should not obscure the most significant conclusion: the structure of provincial politics is that of a mature political system. By the 1760s the original colonies had been facing political problems for a century. The political experiences, the institutional structure of politics, and the appearance and confrontation of significant issues are indications that the colonies, at least politically, had become full-grown. This is why the leadership of the American Revolution seemed so much at home in the political arena. The Adamses of Massachusetts, the Clintons and Livingstons of New York, Jefferson in Virginia, and Pinckney in South Carolina had grown up in the mature political setting everywhere evident in provincial America. To them, the structure and exercise of political power and the experience of debating political issues were as familiar as life itself.

12

Contesting for a Continent

THE ONE POLITICAL POWER clearly recognized by the provincials and the British alike to be within the jurisdiction of the
mother country was diplomacy. There was never any question,
however, that the growing provincial self-interest, responding to
the evolution of indigenous economic, cultural, and political institutions, necessitated a deep involvement in the Atlantic community to achieve fulfillment. What happened in Europe, therefore, affected provincial America; what happened in America
profoundly influenced Europe.

This interrelationship was nowhere more apparent than in the
international competition for empire and power. The object of
eighteenth-century diplomacy was to maintain an equilibrium in
the balance of power, a balance which took into account not only
that force exerted in Europe by the major powers but also the
effective extension of this force in the American colonies. As the
eighteenth century advanced, the balance of power in Europe
became increasingly dependent upon the balance of power
achieved in America, the result in large measure of growing
colonial maturity, strength, and prosperity.

Diplomatic and military action was founded on the premise of
maintaining an equilibrium among the great powers. The almost
inexhaustible detail of diplomatic exchange does not conceal the
stark outline: from the late seventeenth century to the early

eighteenth century, the extension of French power in Europe and America was met by English-Spanish resistance in combination with allies from central Europe; by 1750 the growing power of Britain was resisted by an alliance of France and Spain. As a part of the Empire, the British colonies in North America were exposed to several diplomatic revolutions in the eighteenth century, which at times placed the provincial interest at cross-purposes with that of the mother country. Although the provinces continuously faced hostile French and Spanish colonial establishments on their borders, Britain considered these two nations at times as allies and at other times as enemies. The object of the provincials, in terms of diplomacy, remained relatively constant, but that of Britain, from the point of view of the colonies, vacillated.

The eighteenth-century wars in Europe were directly related to the so-called French-Indian Wars, sometimes described as the four intercolonial wars, in provincial America. Each conflict was a part of a world-wide struggle to conclude a stable balance of power. Although colonial empires in America constituted a significant element in this balance throughout the period, the decisive role of North America was not fully appreciated until the Great War for Empire, 1755-63.

What made the problem of maintaining international stability so difficult in the eighteenth century were the swift changes in Europe and in America which produced frequent imbalances. European nations expanded their trade at an uneven rate; colonies matured economically at a disproportionate pace; dynasties fell, creating instability and often the need for realignment. These and other developments required a constant revision of factors in order for eighteenth-century diplomatists to achieve their objective—maintaining an equilibrium. Diplomatic relationships were dynamic rather than static, fluid rather than fixed.

Commerce serves as an excellent example. The trade of each colonial empire in the New World became important not only in

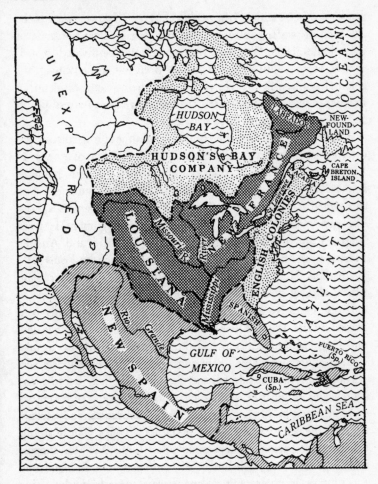

European Possessions in North America, 1750

relationship to the trade of its European parent, but also in relationship to the combined commerce of the European powers. Mercantilists had always held that trade resembled a pie, the size of the wedge obtained by a particular country determining its power. If a nation gained special commercial privileges, so the mercantilist concept continued, these were acquired at the expense of other nations. If a perfect balance of power were to be achieved in western Europe, including Britain, then the trade of the colonies in the Western Hemisphere must be divided in such a way as to confirm that balance. Securing an advantageous colonial position in the Western Hemisphere would result in an imbalance within Europe itself that would require redress, peacefully if possible but by force if necessary.

France first disturbed the equilibrium, although its thrust was directed principally toward extending its position of power in Europe rather than in America. During the forceful reign of Louis XIV (1643-1715), France expanded its boundaries and threatened to gain an unchallenged supremacy. France's aggressive policy seemed to call for a European alignment between England and the Hapsburg monarchies of Spain and Austria. Moreover, the hostile attitude and measures taken by Louis XIV against his Huguenot subjects suggested that England remain firmly aligned with the northern Protestant states of Europe to curb the excessive ambition of France, a policy supposedly confirmed by the Triple Alliance of 1668 between Holland, Sweden, and England for the defense of the Spanish Netherlands against French aggression. This likely alignment of forces was less successful than the outside prospects indicated, first, because the Dutch and English in the latter half of the seventeenth century were engaged in a fierce competition for commerce, and, second, because the later Stuarts were, in fact, Catholics. The Catholic Stuarts were personally dependent upon Louis XIV for support in the possible re-establishment of Catholicism in England and for support in their political maneuvers to restrain the rising power of Parliament, or, to restate the problem in slightly different form, to relax the restraint of Parliament upon the King.

Conditions changed when the Protestant, Dutch king, William III, and his wife, Mary, ascended the English throne after the Glorious Revolution (1688). Not only was the commercial rivalry between the Dutch and English subordinated— partly because the English had secured a much more favorable trading position by 1690 than they had enjoyed at mid-seventeenth century—but the issue of Protestantism found the two nations of a single mind. The English people were not especially anxious to expend money and lives in Europe for limited objectives, but the further extension of the French borders and the recognition of James II by Louis XIV as the legitimate English sovereign awakened latent English hostility. Two wars resulted, the first of which was concluded—perhaps "interrupted" would be a more appropriate term—by the Peace of Ryswick (1697) after nine years of fighting.

The anti-French campaign came to a climax, however, with the War of Spanish Succession (1701–14). The Hapsburgs of Austria and the Bourbons of France claimed succession to the Spanish throne. If either gained exclusive control of Spanish territory in Europe and the Spanish colonial possessions in the New World, the balance of power in Europe and America would be seriously imperiled. At first, attempts were made to "partition" Spanish power between the rival claimants, but when Charles II of Spain willed the Spanish dominions to Philip of Anjou, the grandson of Louis XIV, the alignment of France and Spain was sealed, and a counterforce coalition was formed.

The threat of Louis XIV that Philip might fall heir to the French as well as to the Spanish throne further alarmed the English, who quite correctly saw that equilibrium in Europe would be destroyed. A Grand Alliance, with the Hapsburgs of Austria and England at the core, joined by the Protestant countries of Europe, was formed. The war that followed was fought vigorously and tenaciously. Perhaps the most famous figure of this long struggle was the Duke of Marlborough, whose victory at Blenheim in 1704 was the greatest triumph of English arms from Agincourt to Waterloo.

The Peace of Utrecht (1713) concluding the major part of the struggle established the framework within which European diplomacy was to operate for almost four decades. First and foremost, the treaty specified that the Crowns of Spain and

France were to be separated. In Europe, England received Gibraltar, the gateway to the Mediterranean, and the island of Minorca. Britain also received unchallenged sovereignty over Hudson Bay, Newfoundland, and Acadia on the North American continent and St. Christopher in the West Indies. France and Britain agreed to guarantee the territorial *status quo* of the Spanish Empire, but Britain received from Spain the Asiento, or the right to supply slaves to the Spanish colonies for thirty years.

The terms of the treaty were designed to attain an equilibrium in three ways. First, a balance was achieved in Europe, especially by separating the thrones of France and Spain. Second, by adjusting the territorial dominions overseas, recognition was made that a balance of power could not be achieved in Europe without providing a balance in the New World. Third, a commercial balance was presumed to exist between the great powers of Europe; acknowledgment was made of this premise not only by the adjustments in colonial territory but by means of the Asiento.

The period from the Peace of Utrecht to the 1730s was one of transition. Presumably, a balance of power between the principal powers had been reached, and a Triple Alliance, including Britain, France, and Holland, was formed in 1717 to preserve this balance. In 1718 Austria joined the Alliance.

Underneath this seemingly stable structure, new developments took place which were to alter radically the alignment of the countries of western Europe. Britain became increasingly powerful; France became increasingly suspicious of British intentions. As early as 1716 a memorandum of the French Council of Regency envisioned Louisiana as "a sort of advance guard against the English colonies." Indeed, continued the memorandum, "it is not difficult to guess that their [the British] purpose is to drive us entirely out of the continent of North America." A move to curtail French power in America would admittedly have consequences for Europe, yet the natural tendency of the French to make common cause with Spain against Britain was delayed because Spain repeatedly acted against the French interest, especially by failing to provide a stable setting for French merchants in the Cadiz trade.

The founding of Georgia by Britain in 1733 revitalized a Spanish-French alignment. To the Spanish, Georgia represented a direct encroachment upon Spanish territory; to the French, the founding of Georgia substantiated their worst fears: that Britain planned to upset the European balance, not only by extending the colonial territory it held in the New World but by seizing, in time, the Spanish colonies.

The Family Pact of 1733 between France and Spain, in which the two nations agreed to a mutual guarantee of territory, affected the *rapprochement* of these great powers. Although the Pact had a strong continental emphasis, it clearly included an understanding with regard to the New World colonies. If Great Britain attacked Spain or the Spanish colonies, the French promised to support its ally. A second Family Pact (1743) included the provision that France would aid Spain in destroying Georgia and that France would support its ally in regaining any territory ceded to the British. As compensation, Spain agreed that it would not renew the Asiento with Great Britain.

By the 1750s colonial possessions in America—French, Spanish, and English—were becoming increasingly important in the diplomatic maneuverings of western Europe, and the New World colonies figured prominently in the minds of the European diplomatists as they attempted to maintain a balance of power, a diplomatic doctrine most clearly enunciated in the Treaty of Utrecht. Whereas in 1713 the doctrine was employed to curtail France, in the 1750s it was employed to counter Britain.* Writing in 1758, a French minister declared:

The King believes, Monsieur, that it is possessions in America that will in the future form the balance of power in Europe, and, that if the English invade that part of the world, as it appears they have

* A diplomatic revolution also took place in Europe at this time when previously implacable enemies, the Austrian Hapsburgs and French Bourbons, joined forces to oppose Britain and its ally, Prussia.

the intention of doing, it will result therefrom that England will usurp the commerce of the nations, and that she alone will remain rich in Europe.

Viewed within the larger frame of eighteenth-century diplomacy, the colonial wars of the late seventeenth and the first half of the eighteenth centuries gain special significance. In America, the first conflict, known as King William's War (1689–97), or the first of the French-Indian Wars, coincided with British efforts to curb the appetite of Louis XIV of France.

The major campaigns were waged in Europe; the campaigns in America, largely insignificant in European terms, were important only to the immediate participants. The American phase might well have taken place without the outbreak of war in Europe because the interests of France and England in America converged at numerous points: in the West Indies, where both held possessions; in the Hudson Bay area, where, in 1686, a French party captured three British outposts; in Newfoundland, where the two nations contested for fishing rights; and on the New York and New England frontiers, where the boundaries of the French and English claims had never been agreed upon. In the last area, the Indian relationships remained unsettled, from the powerful Iroquois in New York to the Abnaki Indians on the northern New England frontier.

Indeed, on the North American continent the contest at this early stage was concentrated in New England and New York; the rivalry between New France and New England was most acute because the buffer area was so narrow as to invite a major conflict. On the New York frontier, the Iroquois constituted a pre-eminent factor. At an early stage, the Iroquois had become skeptical of French intentions because of French commitments to tribes unfriendly to the Iroquois. The Iroquois, therefore, not the English, blocked French expansion into New York. The French tried to win the Iroquois by trade, by diplomacy, and by threats, but by the end of the seventeenth century the French effort had largely failed. In fact, because of the Iroquois, the French were forced to penetrate continental North America along a wide arc inland, through the Great Lakes and the Mississippi River basin.

The war in America was inconclusive. British fleets sent to the West Indies accomplished nothing of lasting importance, and the action on the North American continent was limited. The most significant effort, an expedition directed at Quebec, was undertaken exclusively by the English colonials, but its failure was the first of many unsuccessful attempts to capture that French citadel in subsequent decades.

The indecisive character of the American conflict was the result of a certain impotence on both sides. The English advantages of a larger colonial population and greater wealth were offset by their inability to marshal their forces. Political administration was in a turmoil, especially in New York with Leisler's Rebellion but also in Massachusetts where the new charter of 1691 was being tested. New France had more efficient leadership, especially in the person of Count Frontenac, a more effective centralized political administration, perhaps greater diplomatic capacity with the Indians, and perhaps better-trained soldiers, but it did not have the resources in North America to mount a sustained offensive.

Although the war in North America was inconclusive, it left a scar along the frontiers of New France on the one hand, and New York and New England on the other. A French war party led by Frontenac and consisting mainly of Indian allies, destroyed Schenectady, New York, in 1690. "The Cruelties committed at said Place," wrote a prominent Albany official, "no Penn can write nor Tongue expresse: the women bigg with Childe rip'd up and the Children alive throwne into the flames, and there heads dash'd in pieces against the Doors and windows." When New Englanders, led by Sir William Phips, left Boston in April, 1690, and captured Port Royal in Acadia, a base for French privateering operations, the stalwart Puritans damaged and sometimes destroyed unnecessarily the figures of faith in the Catholic chapel.

The second and more significant encounter between England and France, the War of the Spanish Succession, called Queen Anne's War in America (1702–13), marked a rather decisive turn in eighteenth-century international relationships. In America, England for the first time faced an alliance of its two great rival empires, those of France and Spain, each equipped with sufficient resources on the North American continent to harass the English settlements. South Carolina, with its limited white population, its extremely inadequate defenses, and its weak proprietary government, was particularly vulnerable, although the New York–New England frontier was seriously exposed. British naval superiority, a powerful factor in Europe, proved to be a frail support for the English colonials, who were frequently at the mercy of French privateers. It would not be too much to say that whatever success the English colonials experienced came about through their own effort.

From 1702 to 1709, the war in America took some strange but explicable turns. In New York the French had earlier made peace with the Iroquois, and they hesitated to alienate this powerful fighting force by attacking the English frontier in New York. New York was equally anxious to avoid provocative acts. It welcomed the income from the Indian trade, which a war would interrupt, as well as relief from war measures which would entail a high cost in money, matériel, and men. New York, therefore, became a neutral zone. Along the New England frontier, in contrast, the French instigated the Abnaki to attack, forcing the New Englanders to counterattack. This dark and bloody period is remembered for such incidents as the Deerfield Massacre (1704). South Carolina was twice besieged by assaults from Spanish Florida, supported by French and Indian allies, but with good luck and courage the Carolinians were able to defeat each attack; the colony sought reprisal against St. Augustine, but it was unable to win a decisive verdict.

From 1709 to 1713, Britain took a more active part in the war in America. Despite remarkable colonial co-operation and contributions, the results were disappointing because of inadequate British leadership and British mismanagement. The evidence on this point is so overwhelming that a single illustration will suffice. Samuel Vetch, a colorful and adventurous Scotsman who had resided briefly in New York and who had become a leading Boston merchant, proposed that a campaign, supported jointly by Britain and the colonies, be launched against New France, one attack to come by sea and pointed toward Quebec, and the second attack to be made overland to be directed toward Montreal. The plan drew enthusiastic support from New England; New York and New Jersey regarded the enterprise as a duty rather than as a crusade. In any event, the colonies made proper preparations, but the plans went awry when the contingent of regulars promised from Britain was dispatched to Portugal rather than to America. The colonies had lost time and money to no avail.

In the following year, 1710, colonial militia transported by British men-of-war captured Port Royal, and, as a result, Acadia became a British province, Nova Scotia. Francis Nicholson, the leader of this action, then sailed for England to obtain help for a second expedition to follow the grand scheme laid out earlier by Vetch, but despite unusual co-operation among the colonials and the British, the campaign failed when a navigational error piled a number of ships on the rocks along the northern shore of the St. Lawrence with serious losses. The British commanders, who were exceedingly inept, decided to abandon the enterprise before the expedition reached its military objective.

The next major French-Indian war began officially in the English colonies about 1744, the American phase of the War of the Austrian Succession in Europe. Some years previous to this date, a sharp and bitter conflict, the War of Jenkins' Ear, had broken out in 1739 between England and Spain, involving two significant colonial theatres, the West Indies and the territory in dispute between Georgia and Spanish Florida. An expedition in 1739 to the West Indies was manned in part by colonial volunteers under Governor Gooch of Virginia, but misjudgment on the part of the British fleet commander wasted lives and resources. Puerto Bello was captured, but loss by disease was heavy, and there was rank discrimination shown against American militiamen by British regulars. A series of highly disagreeable and disappointing campaigns marked the seesaw fate of the English and Spanish forces along the Georgia border. A campaign in 1740, with James Oglethorpe commanding British and colonial troops, failed to win the great prize, the capture of St. Augustine, but a Spanish counterblow, several years later, also failed. Nothing was changed by these expeditions, except to prove that the Georgia territory, contested by Spain, would remain a British possession.

The American phase of the War of the Austrian Succession particularly involved the New England colonials who took to the offensive in 1744. Assembled by Governor Shirley and commanded by William Pepperell, New England militiamen were dispatched to subdue the powerful French fortress of Louisbourg on the island of Cape Breton, guarding the entrance to the Gulf of St. Lawrence. Louisbourg had been abuilding since the Treaty of Utrecht of 1713 when the French lost Port Royal and Acadia to the English. To believe that an army of untrained colonials would be able to conquer the great fortress seemed sheer madness, but through good fortune and good judgment, the impossible became the fact. Peter Warren, the English fleet commander, and Pepperell, commanding the land forces, were well matched in temperament, and the citizen soldiers showed surprising skill in exploiting French ineptness. Capturing the largest French batteries, and bringing along shot to fit these guns, proved the energy and imagination of the militiamen and the astonishing foresight of the planners. Louisbourg was a great victory for the colonials, but in the Treaty of Aix-la-Chapelle (1748) that concluded the struggle, this strategic bastion was returned to France, to the great disappointment of the colonials.

The contest for global supremacy between France and England reached its peak shortly after mid-century with the Great War for Empire (1755–63), known in each section of the world by a different name. To understand the full significance of this mighty conflict, a comparison must be made between it and the earlier wars, emphasizing particularly the decided alteration in the British position toward the respective theatres of war.

In the early wars, the great British victories had occurred in Europe, notably the Battle of Blenheim in 1704 and the capture of Gibraltar the same year. In the Great War for Empire, the crucial victories were gained outside of Europe, notably on the North American continent and in India. In part, this can be explained on the basis of the growing British naval strength, which was, in proportion to the other great Western countries, much more powerful in 1750 than it had been in 1690. In part, the explanation lies in the recognition by Britain and France that the economic stake in outlying possessions was rising, in the North American continent because of the obvious provincial maturity and in India because possessing rather than sharing trading centers could alone serve as the basis for continued commercial expansion. Before the 1750s, for example, neither Britain nor any other European power had had sufficient resources to control the rich trade from India by capturing the key territories.

In the early colonial wars of the eighteenth century, the American provincials fought with a minimum of aid from Britain. Co-operation, at least on the part of those colonies in proximity to the immediate danger, was adequate and at times remarkable. Moreover, the provincials captured Port Royal and much later Louisbourg, both noteworthy achievements. In the Great War for Empire, in contrast, the British furnished regulars even in the initial stages. In the climactic battle before Quebec on the Plains of Abraham, British regulars, not citizen soldiers, faced the French. Moreover, Britain furnished supplies and transportation, and reimbursed the colonies for the expense incurred during the struggle. Obviously, Britain recognized that the stakes on the North American continent were much higher in the Great War for Empire than in any previous contest, that global supremacy depended upon supremacy not only in Europe but in the non-European territories, and that the balance of power in Europe would be determined principally by what happened outside Europe.

For this reason, therefore, the notion that the American provincials should have been "grateful" for the British expenditure of men and money is, at best, misleading and, at worst, nonsense. Britain, by concentrating a major share of its effort in the contest for the North American continent, was merely serving its own best interest. It was a decision based upon unalterable facts and circumstances, not upon parental affection or emotionalism. If the stakes had been higher in some other theatre of operations, priority of men and materials, quite properly, would have been assigned accordingly.

On the continent of North America, the relative positions of the great powers by the 1750s were clearly defined. France since 1660 had taken steps to strengthen its colonies on the North American continent. Using Louisbourg and Quebec as northern anchors, one giant arm of French expansion reached southwest along the St. Lawrence River to the Great Lakes and behind the Appalachian Mountains toward the sources of the Ohio River. A second arm, anchored at the mouth of the Mississippi River, reached north to converge with the expansion from France's northern outposts. Thus, French expansion tended to envelop the British colonies, colonies which were no longer minor appendages of the mother country but strong, mature provinces backed by British power.

The strategic importance of the North American continent

is heightened by a comparison of the military roles of France and England. France, whose great armies reflected its position as a continental power, and England, whose great naval strength reflected its position as an island power, could not easily come to grips in Europe except by fighting on the soil of their respective European allies. In America, and to a more limited extent in India, British and French territory was contiguous, enabling these two great powers to confront each other directly. In order to score a decisive victory, one of these powers must seriously impair if not destroy the colonial power of the other.

On the surface the English appeared to possess superior strength. The English colonial population greatly outnumbered the French colonials, perhaps as much as 15 to 1. The rate of immigration, together with normal fertility, might alone overwhelm the French. Nevertheless, France had a larger military establishment in America, and the nucleus of its soldiery was more carefully trained. The French enjoyed a general unity of command and political direction, although it should be added that quarrels arose between political and military leaders. The French had also developed more reliable Indian allies. In short, the French in America were better prepared for war.

The best prospect for a British and British-colonial victory lay in a war of attrition. The British fleet could seriously hamper, if not sever, the flow of supplies which nourished French strength. Combined with a build-up of the latent resources of the colonies and the mother country, this strategy promised success. Strangely enough, no British or colonial leader comprehended these essentials at the beginning of the war. There was instead an instinctive response to break out of the French encirclement—witness the Braddock expedition to Fort Duquesne, where the French expansion from Canada and Louisiana converged. The strategic importance of the navy and the build-up of the military potential were initially given inadequate attention. That the struggle opened in the middle colonies rather than along the New York or New England frontier reveals in itself the high stakes: control of the continent and dominance of the Mississippi River basin.

The first years of the war went badly for the British and the American provincials. The capitulation of George Washington at Fort Necessity before the main conflict got under way and the much-remembered defeat of Braddock marked the beginning of tragic years. Bungling, apathy, and defeatism sat in the saddle as the English forces fell back along the entire perimeter. With victories at Oswego and at Fort William Henry, French prestige and power gradually swelled until it seemed as if France would surely triumph. Its brilliant commander in New France, the Marquis de Montcalm, was toasted wherever Frenchmen gathered, and his name was on everyone's lips at the court of Louis XV.

To most Frenchmen and to many Englishmen, the verdict of those early years needed only to be confirmed by a treaty favorable to the French, but such a judgment was premature. The most important fact about the development of the war was largely overlooked. The French in America had rolled back the English perimeter, but they had not pierced the English defenses; therefore, the English build-up of resources in men, food, or munitions could and did take place. One man, William Pitt, grasped this important fact with clarity. Egocentric, pompous, but incorruptible in an age when it was the fashion to be otherwise, William Pitt formed a government which drove Britain to heights of success, and many would say greatness, unparalleled in its history.

Pitt realized that the battle for empire was being fought on the North American continent rather than in Europe, but he also recognized that although an empire could not be gained by the fighting in Europe, it could be lost there if the French failed to be contained. Consequently, Pitt urged additional support for Prussia because the activities of Frederick the Great diverted the power of France. British power, however, was principally directed toward defeating the French in America. Pitt molded the colonial governments, whose lack of enthusiasm had been a persistent burden, into important agencies for supporting the war.

He reconciled many of the differences between the colonies and the British forces in America, another factor which previously had hampered the war effort. He strengthened the fleet; he sent over additional trained British regulars; he also increased the supply of arms. He uncovered superior military leadership by reaching down within the officer ranks, a somewhat unusual action for the eighteenth century, when it was the custom to purchase a commission and to reach high rank either by buying it or by political influence. Finally, and perhaps most important of all, Pitt brought all these efforts to an effective unity by formulating an over-all strategic plan, one which perceived the essentials within the complexities of the world-wide conflict.

Pitt's war plans were not unlike those advanced as early as 1690 and reconfirmed by Vetch in 1709: a sea and land force was to approach the St. Lawrence, in this case, first by capturing Louisbourg, which protected the vital northern arm of the French envelopment; a large land force was to storm the French defenses along Lake Champlain, the most prominent of which was Ticonderoga. General James Abercromby, in command of over fifteen thousand British and colonial troops, led a frenzied attack on that stronghold before he had made adequate preparations. He failed to bring up his artillery, and he neglected to use effectively his decided superiority of troops. A much smaller but staunch French foe under the superb leadership of Montcalm beat off the attack, and Abercromby was forced to retire to the southern tip of Lake George.

In contrast, the Louisbourg expedition, under the immediate command of Lord Jeffrey Amherst succeeded. Over 150 vessels assembled at the English base at Halifax for the campaign. In a fashion strikingly similar to modern invasion techniques, the assault troops stormed ashore from small boats and established a beachhead. They soon gained the high ground and after a siege captured the fort. The St. Lawrence was exposed to the English navy; the entire French defense line in America was in jeopardy.

Pitt's military plan for the following year, 1759, took advantage

U

of the new British position. It called for a large land and sea force to strike at the heart of New France—Quebec. Details were soon worked out to implement the plan. Additional British regulars were dispatched to America, and the naval force was augmented. Pitt offered the command to young James Wolfe, a splendid professional soldier and a person of learning and intelligence. Although only thirty-two, Wolfe enjoyed a distinguished reputation because of his combat and command experience. His most recent action had been at Louisbourg as a brigadier under General Amherst.

The size of the expedition was impressive. Some 250 ships (about one-fifth warships and the remainder transport and supply ships), carrying about 8,500 regulars and twice as many sailors and marines, sailed cautiously up the St. Lawrence. Spread out for an expanse of fifty miles, this battle force displayed the most imposing show of strength the North American continent had ever witnessed. A series of fire signals along the shore—prearranged by the French—warned Montcalm of the approach of Wolfe. By June 25, 1759, most of the fleet had anchored below Quebec, and the contest for the continent was reaching its climax.

Quebec wore an air of defiance. Nature had endowed it with an almost insurmountable protective cover. The broad, swift-flowing St. Lawrence with its treacherous current formed a natural moat, while the steep, jagged cliffs which formed its northern shore provided a formidable natural wall. In some respects, Quebec resembled an island fortress with no beaches.

Outside Quebec, the French defenses extended along the Beaufort shore, that is the northern shore of the St. Lawrence River, stretching out some five or six miles to the Montmorency River, which flowed into the St. Lawrence. All along this line, slick tidal flats, which were covered with water at high tide, met steep, rugged cliffs; together they served as an almost impassable barrier. The Falls of Montmorency provided a superb anchor to this defense line. The defenses inside and outside Quebec were manned by the best units within the French command, supported by local militia from the surrounding area.

Wolfe landed a segment of his force on the southern shore of the St. Lawrence, another part on the Island of Orleans, and the remainder on the east bank of the Montmorency River, opposite Montcalm's defense units at that point. Wolfe followed a scorched earth policy by burning French crops and supplies in the area surrounding Quebec, but this action did not strike at the vitals of the Quebec defenses. When Wolfe attempted to penetrate the French defense line along the Montmorency River, he failed miserably.

By September—over two months after the British forces had arrived—the military situation had reached something of an impasse. Wolfe himself became ill and despondent. It looked as if the campaign would prove abortive and its prime object, the capture of Quebec, would not be accomplished.

As Wolfe sailed for days slowly up and down the St. Lawrence, looking for some hint of weakness, he noticed some women on the northern shore washing clothes in the river. Later, he saw these identical clothes hanging up to dry at the rim of the cliff. After further investigation, Wolfe detected a small pathway, strewn with obstacles to impede an ascent, winding its way upward to the heights from a small bay known as The Foulon.

In this small bay Wolfe planned the most dramatic and significant action of the war. Acting secretly—he did not even inform his brigadiers—Wolfe ordered the fleet to bombard the Beaufort shore, and just before sunset, men were lowered into small boats as if a landing were to be attempted at that point. Another squadron of the fleet, together with shore batteries on Point Levy, were ordered to confront Quebec itself. A third feint consisting of small vessels sent upriver encouraged the French to think that Montreal might be attacked. These actions served their purpose by diverting attention from The Foulon where the real assault was planned.

At the stroke of 2 A.M., assault craft, with Wolfe at the head, floated quietly down the St. Lawrence, approaching the northern shore. Changing tides and the indispensable element of surprise dictated the hour. Under the cover of darkness, troops stationed at Point Levy on the south bank of the St. Lawrence were marched to an area opposite the bay, and the ships standing off the tidal flats, plus all the ships and men participating in the feinting maneuvers, were eventually directed to the main point of attack.

Wolfe and his men, after successfully deceiving a French guard who challenged them as they silently floated downriver, reached the historic bay at 4 A.M. The cliffs, which abruptly towered some 180 feet overhead, dwarfed the landing party. Wolfe whispered last-minute instructions and encouragement to a picked group of volunteers who were assigned the task of scaling the cliffs to surprise and overpower the lax French guard. They were successful, and the whole operation was carried off with remarkable precision. By eight o'clock the following morning some four thousand British regulars (the estimates vary) with a sprinkling of colonials had taken up a position on the heights above Quebec— on the Plains of Abraham. In modern warfare such an operation would be heralded as a splendid achievement; in the eighteenth century the precision was phenomenal.

On the Plains of Abraham, the contest which had been shaping up for over a century on the North American continent suddenly reached its culmination. Within a few hours, the outcome was evident. Wolfe's regulars waited tensely while the French pressed the attack. At the right moment, when the flower of the French troops had advanced within easy musket range, the British troops poured forth a fire of hell. Some of the French troops later remarked that it sounded as if cannon were being discharged. Montcalm's men faltered; then the ranks broke. Finally, the French troops fled in full retreat. Quebec was soon captured and with it the main forces of Montcalm; the two superb soldiers, Wolfe and Montcalm, received fatal wounds. This momentous battle determined the fate of the war, and the following autumn (1760) Montreal fell. Great Britain now dominated the North American continent, reducing the French holdings to the little islands of St. Pierre and Miquelon. With its victories in North America and India, Britain became the leading colonial and maritime power of the world. Britain had won the contest for global supremacy.

For the provincial Americans, the results of the war were far-reaching. The English colonials had been hemmed in along the Atlantic seaboard largely because of the French menace. Now the colonials could freely exploit the regions beyond the Appalachian mountain range—that is, if the mother country did not prevent them. No substantial checks remained on the advancing provincial society except for the natural barriers of mountain, stream, and forest. And by losing their strategic advantage of playing off the English against the French, the Indians were destined to be swept aside by the growing English-American settlement. Therefore, British political and cultural institutions were fated to be implanted upon the region west of the Appalachian Mountains.

A second consequence deserves equal if not greater stress. The Great War for Empire was of paramount importance as an indispensable preliminary to the American Revolution. Without it, the Revolution simply could not have taken place. The elimination of the French menace freed the American provincials from the need for excessive protection from the mother country. They were less dependent. In any dispute within the Empire, they would be more disposed to battle for their interests and their rights, as they conceived them. For the British, winning the contest for a continent resulted eventually in the loss of an Empire.

Third, many of the disputes within the Empire which arose between 1763 and 1776 sprang out of the problems created by the victory—the problem of the West, the administration of the expanded Empire, the burden of war debts. Moreover, the Great War for Empire, in contradiction to what many historians suggest, acted as a unifying force for the American colonies. It is interesting to note that in 1754—before the Great War for Empire —a conference was held in Albany at which Franklin presented his Plan of Union, but the response in the colonial legislatures was, at best, indifferent, and, at worst, hostile. In contrast, when the Stamp Tax was imposed on the American colonies in 1765— after the Great War for Empire—the response was direct, passionate—and united. Provincial experience in this instance, as in so many others, had been elevated to the status of principle.

13

Epilogue: Experience
Elevated to Principle

THE FORMATIVE YEARS concluded a cycle. The synthesis
of Western civilization, channeled through Elizabethan England,
had been fragmented in the American wilderness where, in the
course of a century and a half, the parts re-formed to produce a
new provincial American synthesis, distinctive in institutions, in
social and economic patterns, and in its intellectual attitudes. In
the process, a group of colonies, isolated, dependent, and frail, approached the threshold of nationhood. A few Englishmen, barely
able to survive in the 1620s, had grown into a vigorous energetic
American society of almost two million, nearly one half the population of the mother country. A primitive economic life had been
replaced by a mature commercial capitalism; colonial dependency
had given way to a mature provincial society.

These changes clearly marked the pathway, but it was the
American Revolution which enabled this experience and these
practices to be elevated into principles and precepts. The setting
for the elevation of experience to principle on a grand scale lay in
the three silent but sweeping revolutions of the eighteenth century: (1) the political and economic transition within Britain,
which placed Parliament in a position of ascendancy in its relationship to the executive authority, and which witnessed the

consummation of the spirit of commercial capitalism and the emergence of industrialism; (2) the diplomatic revolution in Europe, which not only caused the polarity of Britain and France as the chief antagonists for world dominion, but which required France, after the British gained supremacy in 1763, to take the unprecedented step of cultivating a friendship with the English colonies in America, their bitter rival for two centuries; and (3) the maturation—politically, economically, and culturally—of the English colonies in America.

These three major revolutions were destined to bring friction and to demand a drastic adjustment of theory and practice in the relationship between the American provinces and Great Britain, regardless of whether or not a War for Independence ever took place. The rising importance of the provinces as an English market and the evolution of an indigenous provincial economy required a thorough revision of imperial policy and attitudes, especially in relation to finance and trade. The supremacy of Parliament necessitated a redefinition of the constitutional ties between the mother country and the colonies. The realignment of great powers in the Atlantic community and the increasing part played by the New World in the balance of power required a re-examination of the diplomatic role of the American provinces.

Even the British recognized that a new day had dawned by 1763, but they failed to realize that this unusual opportunity required experimentation, a fresh approach, rather than the vigorous application of theories which the American experience had already proved to be outmoded. Criticizing the British for their lack of foresight can be quite meaningless, for they employed the best contemporary theory in administering the provinces. In their colonial establishment, the British granted more privileges in self-government and exercised a greater indulgence toward personal provincial enterprise than did any other country, a liberality unparalleled elsewhere in the world. However, the situation confronting the British was so new and different that past experience in managing colonial possessions obscured rather than lighted the way toward the future. A new vision based on a realistic appraisal of the contemporary situation was imperative.

By looking back rather than ahead, the British triggered a response in the American provinces that has yet to run its course. Within a decade and a half, the provincial experience of a common structure of politics, a common language, intercolonial communication, intercolonial political experience, intercolonial religious organization, and intercolonial intellectual and social ties was translated into American nationhood, elevating these diverse currents into the principle of national sovereignty for which many men in the civil war of the nineteenth century made the ultimate sacrifice.

When nationhood became a reality, political patterns that had been practiced for a century were institutionalized. When an American intellectual life matured, an attitude of mind was revealed that was clearly foreshadowed by the intellectual developments of the provincial eighteenth century. When Americans began to reflect upon their social patterns, they discovered that most of the indigenous characteristics had been set by the conclusion of the formative years. When men spoke of the workings of American economy, either to praise it or to condemn it, they were merely expressing in words what had been practiced in the colonial and provincial period for a hundred years.

Almost every aspect of life in the formative years underscores the truth of this generalization. Direct representative government, the distribution of power between the respective levels of government, the significant role of local government, and the evolution of a political structure that was eventually to be institutionalized as a federal system of government are all legacies of the formative years. The diversity of religions, implanted at the outset, and the subsequent history of faiths in colonial-provincial America made toleration, and eventually freedom of religion, a necessity—practice, to be sure, elevated to principle by its codification in constitutional documents—without the diminution of religion, as de Tocqueville and others recognized, as a pre-eminent theme in American life.

The premises upon which the American economic system were based had been precisely formulated by the end of the provincial period: a money economy, vigorous individual enterprise coupled with a close relationship between the government and the economy especially in the more advanced and sophisticated sectors of the economy. The concept of property, too, was defined by practice. Land was generally obtained in fee simple with no reservations made by the Crown or other governing authority to retain mineral rights or resources, mainly because of the scarcity of precious metals in the early settlements. The result was to continue in law and in practice the doctrine that a man not only owned the land but the mineral rights under the land. This interpretation of land ownership was to be important for the future when later discoveries of gold, silver, iron, oil, and other subterranean treasures, which under a different regime would have become a source of income for the government, were in the United States included among the property rights of the individual. The freedom of enterprise encouraged in the formative years unleashed at one and the same time a tradition of creative action and a tradition of exploitation that consistently raised contradictory problems, as might be expected in such a peculiar blend of opportunity and opportunism.

The adjectives used by historians to describe Americans of the nineteenth and early twentieth centuries—optimistic, self-confident, buoyant, pragmatic—are the same as those applied to provincial Americans and, before them, to the sixteenth- and early seventeenth-century English yeomen. These adjectives reflected the immense success of the English colonies; they were not the product of a preconceived philosophy. The ideas of progress and perfectibility in American thought did not arise out of the Enlightenment, rather the Enlightenment supplied words and concepts for expressing an attitude of mind to which Americans had, in fact, subscribed for several centuries. A clergyman and his parish might hold the doctrinal position that humanity was forever condemned and doomed to inconsequence, but their daily lives revealed a commitment to the idea of progress and betterment that belied their expressed views.

The provincial American recognized his relationship to the Atlantic community; nonetheless, he viewed his colony as his country, his home, his native land. He had developed his own leadership, so he was free from a dependence upon the leadership supplied by Britain. The provincial American, like his nineteenth- and twentieth-century successor, was accustomed to rapid and dramatic changes. The events of his lifetime made him temperamentally suited to change, for each man witnessed remarkable transformations, whether it be John Alden of Plymouth, a settler born in England who lived to see a flourishing New England society, or George Washington, a provincial originally devoted to Britain who eventually presided over a new nation.

Because of this ready adaptation to change, to unfamiliar modes, the strain of pragmatism in provincial life was deep-seated. As the Puritans bear witness, pragmatism did not mean that ideas failed to take root or that ideas failed to influence the life of a community. But, generally, provincial Americans were attracted only to those ideas that seemed useful to them, the same attitude that was to govern their nineteenth- and twentieth-century descendants.

Ideas and precepts espoused in early seventeenth-century England were the basis for many of the early colonial practices. The realities of colonial and provincial America modified these practices, and, as a consequence, the premises on which they were based. New practices became the foundation for the creation of new principles, a re-structured set of ideas. The new principles were seldom enunciated clearly and vigorously until the crisis of the Revolution forced men to define their views and attitudes and to institutionalize their practices, but in this manner experience was elevated to principle. The formative years represent the first period in American history in which this process—principles to practice to new principles—comes full turn, and this period is, therefore, a model for a synthesis of ideas and practice which has an application for the whole of American history.

During the American Revolution, practice was elevated to principle when embodied in an official written consensus. Such a statement of principles—the Declaration of Independence, the state and national constitutions, and the Bill of Rights are the most obvious examples—became in turn the touchstone from which new practices were derived. Once adopted, these formulations assumed a life of their own, becoming, in many cases, the fountainhead for an American democratic ideology which has had world-wide repercussions.

The formative years, then, concluded a giant cycle in which ideas and practices transplanted from the Old World to the New were modified by experience to emerge as American principles, redefined particularly in the crisis of Revolution, but predictable within the framework of provincial society.

Bibliographical Essay

I. General

No synthesis as sweeping as *The Formative Years* could be written without the unceasing stream of historical studies, monographs, and articles produced over the past century by industrious, imaginative co-workers. However, a synthesis can still reveal the author's point of view by his selection of mainstreams, his approach to issues, his interpretation of events, and finally by the distinctive historical structure in which he discusses this continuum of events. In these respects, this synthesis reflects the researches of the author, frequently unpublished, and the consistent honing process that takes place in the classroom where alert students demand more persuasive explanations and analyses than the traditional historian has provided.

Because of space limitations and the extent of the period, the bibliography that follows must be selective. Articles in journals will rarely be cited, although the quality of such articles in the past two decades has consistently improved and the impact of such findings is reflected in this book. Unpublished dissertations read by the author do not receive the attention they deserve because the reader who consults this selected bibliography generally will not have access to this material. Those manuscript materials that have frequently influenced my assessment of an historical development are not cited because, once again, they are not readily available. The materials cited are those reasonably available to interested readers and are considered desirable first reading for students who wish to pursue a particular line of inquiry.

The standard multivolume works, so often cited but so seldom consulted, much less read in full, help to bring a measure of order out of a mass of material. Charles M. Andrews' *The Colonial Period of American History* (4 vols., 1934–40) is the product of a lifetime of work. Except for the fourth volume, which is devoted to England's commercial and colonial policy, Andrews' work is a history of the seventeenth-century settlements. The first two volumes are especially incisive; Andrews' judgments stand up well, even though the more recent emphasis is upon intellectual and social history rather than the political-institutional structure that gives form to his work. The statement is commonly and erroneously made that Andrews' multi-volume work replaced Herbert Levi Osgood's *The American Colonies in the Seventeenth Century* (3 vols., 1904–07). Osgood is the unread historian of early America; it does not require an extensive investigation to discover that his point of view and his discussion of internal colonial political and economic development supplements rather than supplants Andrews'. Osgood's *The American Colonies in the Eighteenth Century* (4 vols., 1924–25) stands as a work apart, not because of its narrative or analytical or organizational force, but because no other historian has written about the colonial eighteenth century on such a massive scale. Internally, these volumes vary greatly in quality. His chapters on New York, for example, provide more revealing insight than his chapters on the southern colonies. His organization, which is principally based upon the consecutive intercolonial wars, gives chronological form to the narrative, but the most significant themes of the period fail to emerge within such an unimaginative regimen. It should be added, however, that no period in American history is more difficult to organize coherently because historical issues have seldom been meaningfully articulated. Edward Channing's *History of The United States* (6 vols., 1905–25), the first two volumes cover the period up to 1760, is good on those topics that he has chosen to discuss; but his selection of topics is sometimes so arbitrary that he creates a serious problem of imbalance. Lawrence H. Gipson's *Southern Plantations*, Vol. II, and *Northern Plantations*, Vol. III, in *The British Empire Before the American Revolution* (10 vols., 1936–62), a project not yet completed, provides one of the best scholarly résumés of the colonies and their relationship to Britain at about 1750. *British Isles and the American Colonies*, Vol. I, provides an instructive summary of the eighteenth-century British background.

For the general English background, G. N. Clark, ed., *Oxford History of England* offers a useful point of departure. The appropriate volumes are: J. D. Mackie, *The Earlier Tudors, 1485–1558* (1952); J. B. Black, *The Reign of Queen Elizabeth, 1558–1603* (1936, rev. 1959); Godfrey Davies, *The Early Stuarts, 1603–1660* (1937, rev. 1959); G. N. Clark, *The Later Stuarts, 1660–1714* (1934, rev. 1955); Basil Williams, *The Whig Supremacy, 1714–1760* (1939, rev. 1962); and J. Steven Watson, *The Reign of George III, 1760–1815* (1960).

The books on Tudor, Stuart, and Hanoverian England, without

which any student of early American history loses perspective, are almost without number; but the shortcut is to select the books found in the celebrated bibliographies provided in Conyers Read, *Bibliography of British History: Tudor Period* (1933, rev. 1950); Godfrey Davies, *Bibliography of British History: Stuart Period* (1928); and Stanley Pargellis and D. J. Medley, *Bibliography of British History: Eighteenth Century* (1951).

More than fifty book-length studies on British history, published in the last decade, have a bearing upon an understanding of *The Formative Years*. The following are a selected sample of these books: J. O. Lindsay, ed., *The Old Regime, 1713–63* (1957); Dorothy Marshall, *English People in the Eighteenth Century* (1956); J. H. Plumb, *The First Four Georges* (1957); D. Harris Willson, *King James VI and I* (1956); J. H. Plumb, *Sir Robert Walpole: The King's Minister* (1961); Charles H. George and Katherine George, *The Protestant Mind of the English Reformation* (1961); William Charles Braithwaite, *The Beginnings of Quakerism* (1955); Stephen B. Baxter, *The Development of the Treasury, 1660–1702* (1957); W. E. Minchinton, ed., *The Trade of Bristol in the Eighteenth Century* (1957); Kenneth Ellis, *The Post Office in the Eighteenth Century: A Study in Administrative History* (1958); O. A. Sherrard, *Lord Chatham and America* (1958); T. S. Ashton, *An Economic History of England: The 18th Century* (1955); G. D. Ramsey, *English Overseas Trade during the Centuries of Emergence: Studies in Some Modern Origins of the English-Speaking World* (1957); Norman Sykes, *William Wake: Archbishop of Canterbury, 1657–1737* (2 vols., 1957); William Haller, *The Rise of Puritanism* (1957); Dora Mae Clark, *The Rise of the British Treasury: Colonial Administration in the Eighteenth Century* (1960); and A. P. Thornton, *West-Indian Policy under the Restoration* (1956).

For a general American background, the bibliographical tool to explore first is, of course, Oscar Handlin, and others, eds., *Harvard Guide to American History* (1954). The annual publication *Writings on American History* (1906–40), edited by Grace G. Griffin, and others, is unsurpassed; but its progress has not kept pace with the scholarship of the past few decades. For secondary works printed before 1900, a student should not overlook Justin Winsor's *Narrative and Critical History of the United States* (8 vols., 1884–89), an outstanding work for its time and too often disregarded. In the American Historical Association's *Guide to Historical Literature* (1961), edited by George Howe, and others, the sections on "British and Dutch America" and the "United States of America" constitute a useful point of departure. The bibliographies provided in H. I. Priestley's *The Coming of the White Man, 1492–1848* (1929), Thomas J. Wertenbaker's *The First Americans* (1927), and J. T. Adams' *Provincial Society* (1928) in the *American Life Series,* edited by Arthur M. Schlesinger, Sr. and Dixon Ryan Fox, are valuable as of the date of publication. For its subject matter, Louis B. Wright's *Cultural Life of the American Colonies: 1607–1763* (1957) in *New American Nation Series,* edited by Henry Steele Commager and Richard B. Morris, has a remarkably complete bibliography. Wallace Notestein's *The English People on the Eve of Colonization* (1954) has a useful one.

Individual states have compiled their own bibliographies. Among the most useful are the following: J. H. Easterby, comp., *Guide to the Study and Reading of South Carolina History* (1950); Norman B. Wilkinson and others, comps., *Bibliography of Pennsylvania History* (2nd ed., 1957); and Mary Thornton, *A Bibliography of North Carolina* (1958). The best single volume of documents is Merrill Jensen, ed., *American Colonial Documents to 1776* (1955), Vol. IX, in *English Historical Documents.* For the most ardent students, there are Philip Hamer, ed., *A Guide to Archives and Manuscripts in the United States* (1961) and Richard Hale, ed., *Guide to Photocopied Historical Materials in the United States and Canada* (1961).

The bibliography on explorations is extensive. A good point of departure is John B. Brebner's *The Explorers of North America, 1492–1806* (1933). See also George B. Parks, *Richard Hakluyt and the English Voyages* (1928); C. R. Boxer, *Four Centuries of Portuguese Expansion, 1415–1825* (1961); A. L. Rowse, *The Elizabethans and America* (1959) and *Sir Walter Raleigh* (1962); Willard Wallace, *Sir Walter Raleigh* (1959); Hjalmar R. Holland, *Explorations in America Before Columbus* (1956); Samuel E. Morison's magnificent *Admiral of the Ocean Sea* (2 vols., 1942); David B. Quinn, *The Roanoke Voyages, 1584–90* (2 vols., 1955); Charles G. Nowell, ed., *Magellan's Voyages Around the World: Three Contemporary Accounts* (1962); and J. A. Williamson, *The Age of Drake* (1938).

Significant as background are the following books: A. P. Newton, *The Colonizing Activities of the English Puritans* (1914); Louis B. Wright, *Religion and the Empire: The Alliance Between Piety and Commerce in English Expansion, 1558–1625* (1943); Allen French, *Charles I and the Puritan Upheaval* (1955); and Mildred Campbell's splendid *The English Yeoman under Elizabeth and the Early Stuarts* (1942).

II. The Seventeenth-Century Colonies

New England. The Puritan settlement has received the most attention of the seventeenth-century settlements. J. T. Adams' *The Founding of New England* (1921) received ecstatic reviews upon its appearance in the 1920's because of its literary style and of its jaundiced view of the Puritan Fathers. It is the first volume of a trilogy; the other two volumes are *Revolutionary New England, 1691–1776* (1923) and *New England in the Republic, 1776–1850* (1926). Earlier studies had foreshadowed Adams' point of view; not the least significant was C. F. Adams' *Three Episodes of Massachusetts History* (2 vols., 1892). Since J. T. Adams' day, the Puritans and the Puritan community have been under constant scholarly reconsideration, in which conflicting points of view, and in which "revisionists" are revised, become commonplace. Whether or not the Puritans have been "restored" is not the critical issue; the critical issue is whether they have been reviewed with a greater understanding of their contemporary intellectual, social, and political environment. A great number of distinguished historians have contributed to the reappraisal. Among the most prominent is Samuel Eliot Morison; and his works are *Builders of Bay Colony* (1930), *Puritan Pronaos* (1936), *The Founding of Harvard College* (1935), *Harvard College in the Seventeenth Century* (2 vols., 1936). Works of penetration and brilliance, influencing a generation of scholars, have come from one of the nation's most eminent intellectual historians, Perry Miller; a few of these are *Orthodoxy in Massachusetts* (1933), *The New England Mind* (1939), and *New England Mind: From Colony to Province* (1953). Thomas J. Wertenbaker's *The Puritan Oligarchy* (1947) takes a cultural approach to the Puritans; and Alan Simpson's *Puritanism in Old and New England* (1955) compares the development of the Age of Faith in the New England colonies and in the mother country.

A few of the principal figures in the development of Puritanism in America have attracted biographers; but compared with other periods of history, the number of biographies is small and the quality is poor because of a scarcity of material. The biographies of Roger Williams are based on similar sources with somewhat different results depending upon current historical thought prevailing at the time of writing. J. E. Ernst's *The Political Thought of Roger Williams* (1929) and Samuel H. Brockunier's *The Irrepressible Democrat: Roger Williams* (1940) are good illustrations. Two contributions which should not be

x

neglected are Perry Miller's *Roger Williams and His Contribution to American Tradition* (1953), a source book of Williams' key writings, with introductions by Perry Miller which make clear for the first time the devious route by which Williams entered into the "principle" of religious liberty; and Ola Winslow's *Master Roger Williams, A Biography* (1957), the best general biography currently available. John Winthrop, perhaps the outstanding Puritan leader, has attracted only two noted biographers: Robert C. Winthrop, *Life and Letters of John Winthrop* (2 vols., 1869), and Edmund S. Morgan, *The Puritan Dilemma: The Story of John Winthrop* (1958). Clifford K. Shipton's *Roger Conant* (1944) is a study of great merit; and a recent work on Anne Hutchinson and the Antinomian Controversy, Emery Battis' *Saints and Sectaries* (1962), provides an unusual insight into Puritanism through an examination of that controversial Puritan figure. Of special merit are these biographies: Raymond P. Stearns, *The Strenuous Puritan: Hugh Peter, 1598–1660* (1954); Lawrence Mayo, *John Endicott* (1939); C. W. Tuttle, *Captain John Mason, Founder of New Hampshire* (1887); and G. P. Insh, *Gorges and the Grant of the Province of Maine* (1923). Writings autobiographical in nature are included in J. F. Jameson, ed., *Original Narratives of Early American History* (19 vols., 1906–17), the full set serving as a useful introduction into the character of many contemporary general source materials.

A secondary work, of a somewhat different caste, Ola Winslow's *Meetinghouse Hill* (1954), describes the establishment of a church congregation and then proceeds to narrate the history of the churches of colonial New England. The best insight into the Plymouth Colony is still William Bradford's enduring *Of Plymouth Plantation, 1620–1647;* the most readable edition is that compiled by Samuel E. Morison (1952). George Willison's *Saints and Strangers* (1945) is an excellent authoritative, modern account of the history of Plymouth; and Bradford Smith's *Bradford of Plymouth* (1951) is an unpretentious biography of that imperishable figure.

A number of significant monographic studies have greatly extended the range of understanding of seventeenth-century New England. Among the most important are the following: Edmund S. Morgan, *The Puritan Family* (1944); Bernard Bailyn, *The New England Merchants in the Seventeenth Century* (1955); Harry M. Ward, *The United Colonies of New England, 1643–1690* (1961); Babette Levy, *Preaching in the First Half Century of New England History* (1945); E. N. Hartley, *Ironworks on the Saugus: The Lynn and Braintree*

Ventures of the Company of Undertakers of the Ironworks in New England (1957); Emil Oberholzer, Jr., *Delinquent Saints: Disciplinary Action in the Early Congregational Churches of Massachusetts* (1956); Kenneth B. Murdock, *Literature and Theology in Colonial New England* (1949); Isabel M. Calder, *The New Haven Colony* (1937); Richard S. Dunn, *Puritans and Yankees: The Winthrop Dynasty of New England, 1630–1717* (1962); William Haller, Jr., *The Puritan Frontier, Town Planting in New England Colonial Development, 1630–1660* (1951); James Duncan Phillips, *Salem in the Seventeenth Century* (1933); Larzer Ziff, *The Career of John Cotton: Puritanism and the American Experience* (1962); and Norman S. Grabo, *Edward Taylor* (1961). In a slightly different category are William A. Baker's *Colonial Vessels: Some Seventeenth Century Sailing Craft* (1962), Zoltan Haraszti's *The Bay Psalm Book* (1956), and Charles Andrews' *The River Towns of Connecticut* (1889).

Some older studies of seventeenth-century social life continue to be consulted. In some instances, as their titles indicate, these studies include the provincial period. They are the following: G. P. Dow, *Domestic Life in New England in the Seventeenth Century* (1925); Alice Morse Earle, *Home Life in Colonial Days* (1898) and *Child Life in Colonial Days* (1899); W. B. Weeden, *Economic and Social History of New England, 1620–1784* (2 vols., 1890); Elizabeth Dexter, *Colonial Women of Affairs* (1931); and A. W. Calhoun, *A Social History of the American Family* (3 vols., 1917–19).

A book with essays by authorities in a number of important subjects, not confined to New England, is James M. Smith, ed., *Seventeenth Century America: Essays in Colonial History* (1959). The classic monograph of Curtis Nettels, *The Money Supply of American Colonies Before 1720* (1934), must be mentioned.

CHESAPEAKE COLONIES. An analysis of the Chesapeake society continues to be based, with significant revision of course, upon the framework laid out by Philip A. Bruce's *Economic History of Virginia in the Seventeenth Century* (2 vols., 1907), *Institutional History of Virginia in the Seventeenth Century* (2 vols., 1910), and the least persuasive volume, *Social Life of Virginia in the Seventeenth Century* (1927). Although many books have modified Bruce's contribution, not one has entirely dislodged him because of his invaluable work in the local records.

Among the historical studies that have since amplified or altered Bruce's investigations is Thomas J. Wertenbaker's *The Planters of*

Colonial Virginia (1922), which rightly emphasized in contrast to Bruce that in the seventeenth century the characteristic plantation was small and that the evolving social structure, especially the rising gentry, was the outgrowth of conditions native to the region, and not a direct transplant from England. *The Planters* was an outgrowth of a previous study by Wertenbaker entitled *Patrician and Plebian* (1910). These volumes and his *Virginia under the Stuarts* have been published under a single title *The Shaping of Colonial Virginia* (1958). Wertenbaker has also written *The Old South; The Founding of American Civilization* (1942), which reviews certain cultural aspects of the Chesapeake colonies.

The first volume of C. M. Andrews' *Colonial Period of American History*, cited earlier, makes a significant contribution to an understanding of the Chesapeake society. There is also Wesley Frank Craven's *The Southern Colonies in the Seventeenth Century* (1949), in *History of the South Series*, edited by Wendell H. Stephenson and E. Merton Coulter. Wesley Frank Craven's *Dissolution of the Virginia Company* is an important monograph on the later years of the Virginia Company. Louis B. Wright's *The First Gentlemen of Virginia* (1940) contributes to an understanding of that colony's gentry class in the late seventeenth and early eighteenth centuries, especially its social and cultural aspirations. The best single work at the level of local history is Susie Ames' *Studies of the Virginia Eastern Shore in the Seventeenth Century* (1940).

Aside from Craven's *The Southern Colonies in the Seventeenth Century*, Maryland's early history has been slighted despite the relative abundance of source material. A dated, but useful, work is John T. Scharf's *History of Maryland, from the Earliest Period to the Present Day* (3 vols., 1879). A number of older books by Bernard Steiner, *Beginnings of Maryland 1631–39* (1903), *Maryland During the English Civil Wars* (2 vols., 1906–07), and *Maryland under the Commonwealth: A Chronicle of the Years 1649–58* (1911), continue to be consulted, together with Clayton C. Hall's *The Lords Baltimore and the Maryland Proprietors* (1902). Newton D. Mereness' *Maryland as a Proprietary Province* (1901) is another of the standard monographs, written a half-century ago. A volume intended for a popular audience, Matthew Page Andrews' *The Founding of Maryland* (1933), is serviceable, and so is Elizabeth Baer's *Seventeenth Century Maryland* (1949); but modern scholars, equipped with the new tools and approaches, have been unduly hesitant in re-examining the period.

Because of the agrarian economy of the seventeenth-century settlements, agricultural histories are valuable. Lewis C. Gray's *History of Agriculture in the Southern United States to 1860* (2 vols., 1933) is a remarkable reference to consult constantly. Percy W. Bidwell and J. I. Falconer's *History of Agriculture in the Northern United States, 1620–1860* (1925) is less penetrating and less thorough, but it is an important reference. Land policy is, of course, fundamental to settlement; but penetrating monographic studies are almost unknown. Beverley W. Bond's *The Quit Rent System* (1919) and Roy Akagi's *Town Proprietors of New England* (1924) were pioneer works of their time. Not to be neglected is the significant work of Avery Craven, *Soil Exhaustion as a Factor in Virginia, 1607–1860* (1925). The pioneer study of R. B. Morris, *Studies in the History of American Law* (1930), has implications that touch upon property and the like. For general economic thought, E. A. J. Johnson's *American Economic Thought in the Seventeenth Century* (1932) must be consulted; but it should be supplemented by general studies of mercantilist thought in western Europe and by the first volume of Joseph Dorfman's *History of American Economic Thought* (5 vols., 1946—).

Marcus Jernegan's *Laboring and Dependent Classes in Colonial America 1607–1783* (1931) is a rather standard treatise on that subject, which can be supplemented by numerous monographs on servitude in individual colonies, such as James Ballagh's *White Servitude in Virginia* (1895) and E. I. McCormac's *White Servitude in Maryland* (1904). Most of these monographs require extensive revision. More recently, Abbot E. Smith's *Colonists in Bondage: White Servitude and Convict Labor in America 1607–1776* (1947) emphasizes the English and European background to working groups. Richard B. Morris' *Government and Labor in Early America* (1946) is an exceedingly thorough and substantial contribution to the subject.

The investigations of slavery in colonial as well as provincial America have been much too restrictive. James Ballagh for Virginia (1902), Jeffrey Brackett for Maryland (1889), and John Russell for the free Negro in Virginia (1913) are frequently cited; but they are disappointing. The sweeping work of Elizabeth Donnan, ed., *Documents Illustrative of the History of the Slave Trade to America* (4 vols., 1930–35), stands in magnificent contrast to the limitations of the monographic studies. A more general study is John Hope Franklin's *From Slavery to Freedom: A History of American Negroes* (1947). Older works, such as U. B. Phillips' *American Negro Slavery* (1929), are not too valuable for the colonial-provincial period. Oscar and Mary Handlin's "Origins of the Southern Labor System," *William and*

Mary Quarterly, 3rd Ser., Vol. VII (1950) challenges the accepted version of the early rise of slavery as a legal institution. K. G. Davies' *The Royal African Company* (1957) is not particularly illuminating from the point of view of the growth of slavery in the American colonies. Lack of adequate studies of the evolution of slavery in the seventeenth and eighteenth centuries is a serious shortcoming of American scholarship.

There are a number of separate studies on Virginia and Maryland that illuminate various aspects of society. They are as follows: Cyrus H. Karraker, *The Seventeenth Century Sheriff in England and the Chesapeake Colonies, 1607–1689* (1930); O. P. Chitwood, *Justice in Colonial Virginia* (1905); A. P. Scott, *Criminal Law in Colonial Virginia* (1930); P. S. Flippin, *Royal Government in Virginia* (1919); and Annie L. Sioussat, *Old Manors in the Colony of Maryland* (2 vols., 1911–13). Other miscellaneous works should be mentioned as follows: Howard M. Jones, *The Literature of Virginia in the Seventeenth Century* (1946); Thomas E. Drake, *Quakers and Slavery in America* (1950); and Edwin W. Beitzell, *The Jesuit Missions of St. Mary's County Maryland* (1960).

GENERAL ENGLISH COLONIAL POLICY. For the seventeenth-century English colonial system, the important studies are Lawrence Harper's *The English Navigation Laws* (1939), which focuses upon English policy-making, and George Louis Beer's *The Origins of the British Colonial System 1578–1660* (1908) and *The Old Colonial System 1660–1688* (2 vols., 1912). Viola Barnes' *The Dominion of New England* (1923) is a good book. Still a useful book is C. M. Andrews' *British Committees of Trade, 1622–75* (1908). Some books on the West Indian colonies offer important background. They are Wesley F. Craven's *An Introduction to the History of Bermuda* (1938), Vincent T. Harlow's *A History of Barbados 1625–85* (1926), and Charles S. Higham's *The Development of the Leeward Islands Under the Restoration 1660–1688* (1921). Mention should also be made of James E. Gillespie's *The Influence of Overseas Expansion on England to 1700* (1920).

III. THE EIGHTEENTH CENTURY

THE TRANSITION FROM COLONIES TO PROVINCES. Many of the works previously cited for the seventeenth-century colonies span the period of the early eighteenth century, but no specific bibliography exists that quite parallels the principal theme of transition from seventeenth-century settlements to eighteenth-century provinces. A few books in particular suggest the possibilities of this theme without fully recognizing it. They are Perry Miller's *The New England Mind: From Colony to Province* (1953); Charles M. Andrews, ed., *Narratives of the Insurrections* (1915) in the series *Original Narratives of Early American History*, edited by J. F. Jameson; and Louis B. Wright's *The First Gentlemen of Virginia* (1940).

A number of studies, though not written for this purpose, contribute to the theme of transition. They are as follows: Marion Starkey, *The Devil in Massachusetts* (1949), an account of the witch trials in Massachusetts; Jerome R. Reich, *Leisler's Rebellion; A Story of Democracy in New York, 1664–1720* (1953), a useful rather than a finished work; Lawrence Leder, *Robert Livingston, 1654–1728 and the Politics of Colonial New York* (1961); Dixon Ryan Fox, *Caleb Heathcote, Gentleman Colonist: The Story of a Career in the Province of New York, 1692–1721* (1926); Lilian T. Mowrer, *The Indomitable John Scott: Citizen of Rhode Island, 1632–1704* (1960); B. C. Steiner, *The Protestant Revolution in Maryland* in the American Historical Association, *Annual Report* (1898); and F. E. Sparks, *Causes of the Revolution of 1689 in Maryland* (1896). William R. Shepard's *History of the Proprietary Government in Pennsylvania, 1696–1765* (1896), Frederick Tolles' *James Logan and the Cultures of Provincial America* (1957), and Edwin P. Bronner's *William Penn's "Holy Experiment"; The Founding of Pennsylvania 1681–1701* (1962) are more appropriate for the study of provincial America, but they are also useful for this early stage. Two rather recent books which have an external rather than internal impact are Vincent Buranelli's *The King & the Quaker: A Study of William Penn and James II* (1962) and Catherine Owens Peare's *William Penn, A Biography* (1957). E. P. Tanner's *The Province of New Jersey, 1664–1738* (1903) is a standard work, but it must be supplemented by John Pomfret's *The Province of West New Jersey, 1609–1702* (1956) and *The Province of East New Jersey, 1609–1702* (1962), the first of which is important for the background of Pennsylvania as well.

For South Carolina in the period of transition as well as all phases of South Carolina history, consult J. H. Easterby's *Guide to the Study of South Carolina History* (1950). For the earlier stages of South Carolina history, it is difficult to find anything better than the old volume of William J. Rivers, *A Sketch of the History of South Caro-*

lina to the Close of Proprietary Government by the Revolution of 1719 (1856), although these years are a part of more recent general accounts, to be cited subsequently. Edward McCrady's ill organized *History of South Carolina as a Proprietary Province* (1897) and Louise F. Brown's *The First Earl of Shaftesbury* (1933) are useful. Verner Crane's *The Southern Frontier, 1670–1732* (1928) is a classic monograph, partly involved in the transition, but its principal contribution lies elsewhere.

An interesting historical discussion has been carried on with regard to key events in the history of Virginia in the late seventeenth century, but the focus has usually been confined to internal developments in the colony rather than in relation to their affinity with similar instability in other colonies. Thomas J. Wertenbaker's biography of Nathaniel Bacon, *Torchbearer of the Revolution* (1940), has its counterweight in Wilcomb Washburn's *The Governor and the Rebel* (1957). Wesley F. Craven's *Southern Colonies in the Seventeenth Century,* previously cited, discusses some of the issues involved, as does contemporary historian Robert Beverley's *The History and Present State of Virginia* (1705), the best modern edition of which was made available by Louis B. Wright (1947).

In the period of transition, events in England became exceedingly important. A work of lasting quality is Viola Barnes' *The Dominion of New England,* previously cited, with its full bibliography as of the time of publication. Michael G. Hall's *Edward Randolph and the American Colonies, 1676–1703* (1960) supplements the story of the colonial-mother country relationship, and his bibliography supplements Viola Barnes' bibliography. But the full extent of the colonial-mother country relationship from the 1670's to the 1720's requires further exploration on a more imaginative scale than trade relationships. The following selected studies do not exhaust the list: Everett Kimball, *The Public Life of Joseph Dudley* (1911); Gertrude Jacobsen, *William Blathwayt: A Late Seventeenth Century Administrator* (1932); Margaret S. Morriss, *The Colonial Trade of Maryland 1688–1715* (1914); George H. Guttridge, *The Colonial Policy of William III* (1922); Maurice Cranston, *John Locke* (1957); Lawrence Harper, *The English Navigation Laws,* previously cited; and Ralph P. Bicker, *The Lords of Trade and Plantations, 1675–96* (1919).

The whole issue of privateers, not discussed at any length in *The Formative Years,* is another symptom of the social instability at the end of the seventeenth century. See J. F. Jameson, ed., *Privateering and Piracy in the Colonial Period* (1923).

COLONY-STATE HISTORIES. Most of the Atlantic coast states have multivolume state histories that usually devote a volume to the colonial period. These state histories are seldom if ever interpretative in nature, and they usually fail to relate the developments within their particular colony to the larger framework of colonial and provincial society. However, these multivolume histories sometimes provide a summary of the monographic studies available at the time of publication. The following are most useful for the colonial and provincial periods of the state histories: A. B. Hart, ed., *Commonwealth History of Massachusetts* (5 vols., 1927-30); A. C. Flick, ed., *History of the State of New York* (10 vols., 1933-37), the first two volumes of which are appropriate to this study; J. T. Scharf, *History of Maryland from the Earliest Period to the Present Day,* previously cited, a somewhat jumbled but helpful work; R. D. W. Connor, and others, *History of North Carolina* (6 vols., 1919); and David D. Wallace, *History of South Carolina* (4 vols., 1920). A work of unusual merit that must be classified somewhat differently is Richard L. Morton's *Colonial Virginia* (2 vols., 1960). Oscar Handlin, and others, *Harvard Guide to American History,* previously cited, includes a bibliographical section on the state histories.

BRITISH-COLONIAL EIGHTEENTH CENTURY RELATIONSHIPS. In discussing British-colonial ties, the point of departure must be two multivolume series: Herbert L. Osgood, *The American Colonies in the Eighteenth Century* (4 vols., 1924-25) and Lawrence Gipson, *The British Empire Before the American Revolution* (10 vols., 1936—) to be completed in eleven volumes. Osgood and Gipson also provide enlightening material on internal colonial development. Additional studies are needed to explore more fully the relationship between individual colonies and the mother country, after the fashion of W. T. Root's standard monograph, *Relations of Pennsylvania with British Government 1696-1765* (1923). There are also George Louis Beer's *British Colonial Policy 1754-65* (1907); Oliver P. Dickerson's *The Navigation Acts and the American Revolution* (1951), which extends beyond the provincial period; and Leonard Labaree's *Royal Government in America* (1930), an indispensable, classic study. The early sections of Jack M. Sosin's *Whitehall and the Wilderness: The Middle West in British Colonial Policy, 1760-75* (1961) are provocative, for he challenges previous writers on this subject.

A number of supplementary works still guide the modern student. For colonial agents representing assembly interests, see Ella Lonn,

The Colonial Agents of the Southern Colonies (1945); J. J. Burns, *Colonial Agents of New England* (1935); M. P. Wolff, *Colonial Agency of Pennsylvania* (1933); and Edward P. Lilly, *The Colonial Agents of New York and New Jersey* (1936). For administrative structure, see A. H. Basye, *Lord Commissioners of Trade and Plantations, 1748–1782* (1925); J. D. Doty, *British Admiralty Board in Colonial Administration, 1689–1763* (1932); M. A. Thomson, *Secretaries of State, 1681–1782* (1932); Margaret M. Spector, *The American Department of the British Government* (1940); and D. B. Horn, *The British Diplomatic Service, 1689–1789* (1961). For a review of colonial legislation, see E. B. Russell, *Review of American Colonial Legislation by King in Council* (1915), a somewhat outdated study; G. A. Washburn, *Imperial Control of Administration of Justice, 1684–1776* (1923); Joseph Smith, *Appeals to the Privy Council From the American Plantations* (1950); and the initial sections of Carl Ubbelhode, *The Vice-Admiralty Courts and the American Revolution* (1960). For the evolution of the West Indian colonies, see the somewhat outdated book of F. W. Pitman, *The Development of the British West Indies, 1700–1763* (1917).

Again the significant general works referred to early in the bibliographical essay must be consulted, because the tremendous change taking place in eighteenth-century England must be understood if the mother country-colonial relationship is to be analyzed.

PROVINCIAL EXPANSION. Every scholar begins with the standard works, such as Frederick J. Turner's "The Old West," first printed in the *Proceedings* of State Historical Society of Wisconsin in 1908 and then reprinted in *The Frontier in American History* (1920). The general themes are supported by the following books: Louis Koontz, *Robert Dinwiddie* (1940); the classic monograph of Verner Crane, *The Southern Frontier,* cited previously; and the fascinating travel account of Charles Woodmason, *The Carolina Backcountry* (1953), edited with an illuminating introduction by Richard Hooker, to be supplemented and corrected in part by Robert M. Brown, *The South Carolina Regulators* (1963). No systematic synthesis has yet been written of eighteenth-century provincial expansion, although several are underway. The best general work on the entire frontier is Ray A. Billington's *Westward Expansion* (1949).

Two books supply significant modern bibliographies. They are R. W. G. Vail's *The Voice of the Old Frontier* (1949) and William N.

Fenton, and others, *American Indian and White Relations to 1830: Needs and Opportunities for Study* (1957).

A number of biographies of principal figures who frequently spent their lives and certainly made their fame on the frontier are helpful. They are as follows: James T. Flexner, *Mohawk Baronet: Sir William Johnson of New York* (1959); Nicholas Wainwright, *George Croghan: Wilderness Diplomat* (1959); Paul A. W. Wallace, *Conrad Weiser, 1696–1760: Friend of Colonist and Mohawk* (1945); and John Alden, *John Stuart and the Southern Frontier* (1944).

The quality of the monographs vary, and additional research is badly needed. An invaluable work such as Robert L. Meriwether's *The Expansion of South Carolina, 1729–65* (1941) could profitably be imitated by like studies in every colony. There are other important monographs: Nathaniel C. Hale, *Pelts and Palisades: The Story of Fur and the Rivalry for Pelts in Early America* (1959); William A. Hunter, *Forts on the Pennsylvania Frontier, 1753–1758* (1960); Hugh Cleland, *George Washington in the Ohio Valley* (1955); Robert L. D. Davidson, *War Comes to Quaker Pennsylvania, 1682–1756* (1957); David H. Corkran, *The Cherokee Frontier: Conflict and Survival, 1740–1762* (1962); Louis K. Koontz, *The Virginia Frontier, 1754–63* (1925); Murray G. Lawson, *Fur: A Study in English Mercantalism* (1943); and Ruth Higgins, *Expansion in New York with Especial Reference to the Eighteenth Century* (1931). A special work is Lloyd A. Brown's *Early Maps of the Ohio Valley: A Selection of Maps, Plans, and Views Made by Indians and Colonials from 1673 to 1783* (1959). A more general, popular, and dependable work is Dale Van Every's *Forth to the Wilderness: The First American Frontier, 1754–1774* (1961).

A rather large number of records emphasizing particularly the Indian relations has recently appeared: Wilbur R. Jacobs, ed., *Indians of the Southern Colonial Frontier: The Edmond Atkin Report and Plan of 1755* (1954); Lawrence H. Leder, ed., *Pennsylvania History: The Livingston Indian Records, 1666–1723* (1956); W. L. McDowell, ed., *The Colonial Records of South Carolina: Journals of the Commissioners of the Indian Trade, September 20, 1710–August 29, 1718* (1955) and *The Colonial Records of South Carolina: Documents Relating to Indian Affairs, May 21, 1750–August 7, 1754* (1958); and Milton W. Hamilton, ed., *The Papers of Sir William Johnson*, Vol. XII (1957). Older works include Cadwallader Colden's contemporary *History of the Five Indian Nations. . . .* (London, 1747), Peter Wraxall's *An Abridgement of Indian Affairs . . . 1678–1751* (1915), and Lily Lee Nixon's *James Burd, Frontier Defender 1726–93* (1941).

Specific books on the Indians are as follows: Roy H. Pearce, *The Savages of America: A Study of the Indian and the Idea of Civilization* (1953); Allen W. Trelease, *Indian Affairs in Colonial New York: The Seventeenth Century* (1960); Harold E. Driver, *Indians of North America* (1961); Paul A. W. Wallace, *Indians in Pennsylvania* (1961); Howard A. Peckham, ed., *Captured by Indians: True Tales of Pioneer Survivors* (1954); and Anthony F. C. Wallace, *King of the Delawares: Teedyuscung* (1949).

A more general work is Ruth M. Underhill's *Red Man's America: A History of the Indians in the United States* (1953). Except for the work of scholars, such as William Fenton and Paul Wallace, not enough work is being done by historians on Indians in early America from an anthropological point of view. The Indians are usually seen through the eyes of the white settler; therefore, the point of view is frequently either one of shock and abhorrence of Indian cruelty or imprecise sentimentality about the ill-treatment of the Indians by whites without trying to understand the Indian culture on its own terms.

Intimately related to expansion and to social history and change is the migration of peoples. Inquiry into this subject has, at certain periods in America's subsequent history, been intense. As pride in forebearers who migrated diminished and as pride in being "an American" increased, the nature of the historical inquiry and thus the character of historical studies changed. Among the older works, important reference books are the following: Albert B. Faust, *The German Element in the United States* (2 vols., 1927); Frank R. Diffenderffer, *German Immigration into Pennsylvania through the Port of Philadelphia* (1900); Levi Oscar Kuhns, *The German and Swiss Settlements of Colonial Pennsylvania* (1914); Adelaide L. Fries, *The Moravians in Georgia, 1735–1740* (1905); Wayland F. Dunaway, *The Scotch-Irish in America* (1915); Henry J. Ford, *The Scotch-Irish in America* (1915); Charles A. Hanna, *The Scotch-Irish or The Scot in North Britain, North Ireland, and North America* (2 vols., 1902); Charles W. Baird, *History of the Huguenot Emigration to America* (1885); and C. H. Browning, *The Welsh Settlement of Pennsylvania* (1912).

Somewhat more recent studies include: Arthur H. Hirsch, *The Huguenots of Colonial South Carolina* (1928); W. A. Knittle, *Early Eighteenth Century Palatine Emigration* (1936); Dieter Cunz, *The*

Maryland Germans: A History (1948); Paul A. Wallace, *The Muhlenbergs of Pennsylvania* (1950); Ian C. C. Graham, *Colonists from Scotland: Emigration to North America, 1707–1783* (1956); Duane Meyer, *The Highland Scots of North Carolina, 1732–1776* (1961); Warren C. Scoville, *The Persecution of Huguenots and French Economic Development, 1680–1720* (1960); Jacob R. Marcus, *Early American Jewry: The Jews of New York, New England, and Canada, 1649–1794* (1951) and *Early American Jewry: The Jews of Pennsylvania and the South, 1655–1790* (1953); Hymah B. Grinstein, *The Rise of the Jewish Community of New York, 1654–1860* (1945); and Edwin Wolf, II, and Maxwell Whiteman, *The History of the Jews of Philadelphia from Colonial Times to the Age of Jackson* (1957).

Many of the more recent works include an important and necessary emphasis on the European background. English migration tends to be neglected in specific studies, so it is well to mention Mildred Campbell's important article "English Migration on the Eve of the American Revolution," *The American Historical Review,* Vol. LXI (1955).

It is proper to repeat that the forced Negro migration should be considered within the larger context of immigration, and the works cited for the seventeenth century are appropriate here. Moreover, the lack of reliable and thorough studies of the Negro migration is distressing to the historical scholar. See, however, Frank J. Klingberg, *The Negro in Colonial South Carolina* (1941).

Of course, labor supply is closely related to migration. Many of the studies cited for the seventeenth century carry through the provisional period. The following studies are representative: Richard B. Morris, *Government and Labor in Early America* (1946); Abbot E. Smith, *Colonists in Bondage: White Servitude and Convict Labor in America, 1607–1776* (1947); Marcus W. Jernegan, *Laboring and Dependent Classes in Colonial America, 1607–1783* (1931); A. Cheesman Herrick, *White Servitude in Pennsylvania* (1926); Carl Bridenbaugh, *The Colonial Craftsman* (1950); Warren B. Smith, *White Servitude in Colonial South Carolina* (1961); Ulrich B. Phillips, *Life and Labor in the Old South* (1929); J. Harry Bennett, Jr., *Bondsmen and Bishops: Slavery and Apprenticeship on the Codrington Plantation of Barbados, 1710–1838* (1958), which provides an insight into an English possession outside continental North America; Lawrence C. Wroth, *Abel Buell of Connecticut: Silversmith, Type Founder & Engraver* (1958); and Penrose R. Hoopes, *Shop Records of Daniel Burnap, Clockmaker* (1958).

PROVINCIAL ECONOMIC STRUCTURE. The economic structure of provincial America must be pieced together from a great variety of sources. The agricultural histories of Lewis Gray and Percy Bidwell, cited for the seventeenth century, and the older general works, such as William B. Weeden's *Economic and Social History of New England,* cited previously, provide background. More significant are the investigations in recent decades into the activity of merchants. James B. Hedges's *The Browns of Providence Plantations: Colonial Years* (1952) is a model volume of its kind. This should be broadened by a number of pertinent studies: James D. Phillips, *The Life and Times of Richard Derby, Merchant of Salem, 1712–1783* (1929); W. T. Baxter, *The House of Hancock: Business in Boston, 1724–1755* (1945); Glenn Weaver, *Jonathan Trumball: Connecticut's Merchant Magistrate (1710–1785)* (1956); Byron Fairchild, *Messers. William Pepperell: Merchants at Piscataqua* (1954); Philip L. White, *The Beekmans of New York in Politics and Commerce, 1647–1877* (1956), perhaps more important as a study of social rather than economic history; and, in the same category, Frederick B. Tolles, *Meeting House and Counting House: The Quaker Merchants of Colonial Philadelphia, 1682–1763* (1948); and finally, a statistical analysis by Bernard and Lotte Bailyn, *Massachusetts Shipping 1697–1714: A Statistical Study* (1959).

Early chapters of studies that are principally focused on the revolutionary generation of merchants provide helpful suggestions for the provincial period. These include the following: Virginia D. Harrington, *The New York Merchant on the Eve of the Revolution* (1935); Mary A. Hanna, *Trade of the Delaware District before the Revolution* (1917); Benjamin W. Labaree, *Patriots and Partisans: The Merchants of Newburyport, 1764–1815* (1962); Margaret E. Martin, *Merchants and Trade of the Connecticut River Valley, 1750–1820* (1938–39); and Mack Thompson, *Moses Brown, Reluctant Reformer* (1962).

In those parts of the American provinces where the structure of the economy was not built upon an indigenous group of merchants, other approaches are necessary. See Arthur P. Middleton, *Tobacco Coast: A Maritime History of Chesapeake Bay in the Colonial Era* (1953); Jacob Price, "The Rise of Glasgow in the Chesapeake Tobacco Trade, 1707–1775," *The William and Mary Quarterly,* 3rd Ser., Vol. XI, (1954); and Jacob Price, *The Tobacco Adventure to Russia: Enterprise, Politics, and Diplomacy in the Quest for a Northern Market for English Colonial Tobacco, 1676–1722* (1962).

The British background is also significant because of the close interrelationship between the markets of England and America. The following are helpful for some external studies: Richard Pares, *Merchants and Planters* (1960), *Yankees and Creoles: The Trade Between North America and the West Indies Before the American Revolution* (1956), and an earlier work, *War and Trade in the West Indies, 1739–63* (1936); T. S. Ashton, *Economic Fluctuations in England, 1700–1800* (1959); and K. G. Davies, *The Royal African Company,* cited previously.

A number of books treat special aspects of economic life. Representative monographs include the following: A. C. Bining, *Iron Manufacturing in the Eighteenth Century* (1938) and *British Regulation of the Colonial Iron Industry* (1933); Vertrees J. Syckoff, *Tobacco Regulation in Colonial Maryland* (1936); Margaret S. Morriss, *Colonial Trade of Maryland, 1689–1715,* cited earlier; M. A. Hanna, *Trade of the Delaware District Before the Revolution* (1917); K. L. Behrens, *Paper Money in Maryland 1727–89* (1923); C. P. Gould, *The Land System in Maryland 1720–65* (1913) and *Money and Transportation in Maryland* (1915). Finally, there is the remarkable study of Anne Bezanson, and others, *Prices in Colonial Pennsylvania* (1935).

Careful economic studies are still required—and in depth. Currently, conclusions must be drawn from sampling the printed sources and from an impressionistic analysis of sources.

SOCIAL AND INTELLECTUAL LIFE. If a man is a doer, read his biography; if a man is a thinker, read what he has written. This simple and useful dictum cannot be applied in the eighteenth century because these men, more often than not, were doers *and* thinkers. This duality is inadvertently reflected in the types of historical studies that characterized the intellectual life of provincial America. Few studies represent a true history of ideas in the manner of Perry Miller's brilliant works on Puritanism; instead, most studies are a blend, sometimes a peculiar blend, of intellectual and social history. Even the social histories of the provincial period do not represent a pure strain; that is, directed toward questions normally regarded as proper subjects for inquiry: the structure of society; the mobility between class groupings; the nature, role, and significance of family groups; and the like; instead, the social histories become generalized social-cultural studies. The reason for this blurring of lines is often the inadequacy of the source, but frequently historians have neglected to focus their investigations, relying instead on a general nonpolitical category. As a result, the answers currently available to historians as to the specific character of provincial society lack precision.

Among the outstanding general works covering the social-intellectual-cultural life of provincial America are the following: Max Savelle, *Seeds of Liberty* (1948), in which each chapter is devoted to an aspect of provincial thought; Clinton Rossiter, *Seedtime of the Republic* (1953), which encompasses a general background of ideas centered upon political thought; Daniel Boorstin, *The Americans: Their Colonial Experience* (1958), which deflates the importance of ideas in early America and contributes a fresh point of view toward standard subjects, such as the evolution of American laws, education, and science. Boorstin's book also includes a thorough and valuable bibliography. Carl Bridenbaugh's *Cities in the Wilderness, 1625–1742* (1938, reissued in 1955) and *Cities in Revolt: Urban Life in America, 1743–1776* (1955) are pioneer studies, so thorough and informative that they must be consulted constantly. James T. Adams' *Provincial Society* (1927) is a synthesis that continues to be valuable, and Louis B. Wright's *The Cultural Life of the American Colonies, 1607–1763* (1957) is an up-to-date survey on a variety of subjects, such as communication, education, and religion. Wright's book also includes a first-rate bibliography broken down into subject areas. Michael Kraus' *The Atlantic Civilization: Eighteenth-Century Origins* (1949) underscores the intellectual and cultural interrelationship between the colonies and England. Moses Coit Tyler's *A History of American Literature During the Colonial Period, 1607–1765* (2 vols., 1878), since reissued, is a literate, readable work that summarizes and, to a limited extent, evaluates the writing in early America. Vernon Louis Parrington's *The Colonial Mind* (Vol. I) in *Main Currents in American Thought* (3 vols., 1927–30), is a controversial and important book that takes strong positions on contributors to early American thought. Edward Eggleston's *The Transit of Civilization* (1900), though concentrating on seventeenth-century America, is a pioneer work which has influenced scholars of provincial culture.

Thomas J. Wertenbaker's *The Old South: The Founding of American Civilization* (1949) and *The Founding of American Civilization: The Middle Colonies* (1949) are generalized accounts of the evolving American culture. Other regional, or local studies, include Frederick P. Bowes' *The Culture of Early Charleston* (1942) and Carl Bridenbaugh's *Myths and Realities: Societies of the Colonial South* (1952). In this category, see also Carl and Jessica Bridenbaugh's *Rebels and Gentlemen: Philadelphia in the Age of Franklin* (1942) and Frederick

Tolles' perceptive study, *Meeting House and Counting House: The Quaker Merchants of Colonial Philadelphia, 1682–1763,* previously cited. Tolles' *James Logan,* previously cited, also is useful. Tolles has contributed a more general work, *Quakers and the Atlantic Culture* (1960), and so has Howard M. Jones, *America and French Culture* (1927).

The outpouring of books on early American cultural life is truly phenomenal, as if somehow American scholars are trying to prove the richness and variety of their cultural origins. Another possible explanation of this abundance is the reawakening of interest in the indigenous character of Americans. When did the provincials become Americans? The indigenous character of Americans could be demonstrated in terms of economic or political institutions as easily as in terms of culture and intellect, but somehow this approach has not held the same attraction for scholars. For my personal views on this matter, see my bibliographic essay, "The North American Colonies in the Eighteenth Century, 1688–1763," in the *Thirty-First Yearbook, National Council for Social Studies* (1961).

Obviously, the abundance of special studies prevents completeness in citation. The following books, therefore, represent a useful sampling. For education, see Bernard Bailyn's *Education in the Forming of American Society: Needs and Opportunities for Study* (1960), which also contains the most valuable and complete modern bibliography on this subject. For painting, see James T. Flexner's *American Painting: First Flowers of Our Wilderness* (1947), supplemented by special studies, such as Henry W. Foote's *John Smibert* (1950); Margaret S. Middleton's *Jeremiah Theus, Colonial Artist of Charles Town* (1953); George Evans' *Benjamin West and the Taste of His Times* (1959); and general works, such as Oliver W. Larkin's *Art and Life in America* (1949); and such important tools as *The New York Historical Society's Dictionary of Artists in America, 1564–1860* (1957).

A general book is not so readily available for architecture. Two books of note are Anthony N. B. Garvan's *Architecture and Town Planning in Colonial Connecticut* (1951) and Carl Bridenbaugh's *Peter Harrison: First American Architect* (1949). Thomas T. Waterman's *The Dwellings of Colonial America* (1950) and Marcus Whiffen's *The Eighteenth Century Houses of Williamsburg* (1960) are useful introductions. Older treatments, such as Fiske Kimball's *Domestic Architecture of the American Colonies and the Early Republic* (1927) and Talbot F. Hamlin's *The American Spirit in Architecture* (1926), are still worth consulting. John Gloag's *Georgian Grace: A Social*

Y

History of Design from 1660–1830 (1956) and Rosamund R. Beirne and John H. Scarff's *William Brickland, 1734–1774: Architect of Virginia and Maryland* (1958) can be consulted. Almost every region and many colonial cities have had their share of devotees who have produced books of somewhat uneven quality on the architecture of early America. Most of these works are uncritical in either an historical or an aesthetic sense.

On printed matter—books, newspapers, pamphlets, and the like—for the provincial period, the number of studies available is large, and their quality is generally high. The first chapters of Robert E. Spiller, ed., *Literary History of the United States* (3 vols., 1948) should be consulted, and all the outstanding general works mentioned earlier in this section of the bibliographical essay. A number of special studies of excellent quality should be mentioned. Lawrence Wroth's *An American Bookshelf, 1955* (1934) and *Colonial Printer* (1938) are discriminating pieces of work, and so is Clarence Brigham's *Journals and Journeymen, A Contribution to the History of Early American Newspapers* (1950). Brigham is also the compiler of the invaluable *History and Bibliography of American Newspapers, 1690–1820* (2 vols., 1947). A general work, such as Sidney Kobre's *The Development of the Colonial Newspaper* (1944), is helpful and special studies, such as Anna J. De Armond's *Andrew Bradford, Colonial Journalist* (1949), are of value. No one can neglect Benjamin Franklin, either his papers (5 vols., 1959–63), edited by Leonard Labaree and Whitfield Bell, or his biography, written by Carl Van Doren (1938). There also is the ingenious bit of historical detective work reflected in Verner Crane's *Franklin's Letters to the Press* (1950). Henning Cohen's *The South Carolina Gazette, 1732–1775* (1953) is a quick way to get the flavor of a colonial newspaper.

The evolution of the public library in the provincial period as compared with the exclusive private library in the seventeenth century makes C. Seymour Thompson's *Evolution of the American Public Library, 1653–1876* (1952) a useful book to consult. In this regard, the work of Thomas Bray is important, which makes H. P. Thompson's *Thomas Bray* (London, 1954) a book to examine; a number of articles on Bray were also published by Samuel C. McCulloch. A book to consult is Donald H. Mugridge and Blanche P. McCrum, comps., *A Guide to the Study of the United States of America; Representative Books Reflecting the Development of American Life and Thought* (1960).

The development of science was, of course, a part of eighteenth-century intellectual life. Each of the general books cited earlier in this section takes a measure of this subject and many include ample bibliographies. For special studies, see the following books: Brooke Hindle, *The Pursuit of Science in Revolutionary America, 1735–1789* (1956); Dirk J. Struik, *Yankee Science in the Making* (1948); John B. Blake, *Public Health in the Town of Boston, 1630–1822* (1959); Richard H. Shryock, *Medicine and Society in America, 1660–1860* (1960); I. Bernard Cohen, *Some Early Tools of American Science* (1950); John Duffy, *Epidemics in Colonial America* (1953); and Harry Woolf, *The Transit of Venus: A Study of Eighteenth-Century Science* (1959).

Certain scientific figures in addition should be mentioned. They are covered in the following books: Otho T. Beall, Jr. and Richard H. Shryock, *Cotton Mather: First Significant Figure in American Medicine* (1954); Helen Gere Cruickshank, ed., *John and William Bartram's America* (1957); George F. Frick and Raymond P. Stearns, *Mark Catesby: The Colonial Audubon* (1961); and Edward Ford, *David Rittenhouse, Astronomer-Patriot, 1732–1796* (1946).

The constant impact of English thought and social life on the colonies can be seen in the following studies: William L. Sachse, *The Colonial American in Britain* (1956); Raymond P. Stearns "Colonial Fellows of the Royal Society of London, 1661–1798," in *William and Mary Quarterly*, 3rd Series, Vol. III (1946); E. G. Swem, *Brothers of the Spade: Correspondence of Peter Collinson of London, and of John Custis, of Williamsburg, Virginia, 1734–1746* (1947); and Leonard W. Cowie, *Henry Newman, An American in London, 1708–43* (1956). Indeed, this theme of the English and European background can be appreciated best after consulting such a magnificent work as Leslie Stephen's *History of English Thought in the Eighteenth Century* (2 vols., 1876), or a standard history, such as Basil Williams' *The Whig Supremacy* (1939), or the recent contributions of Frank Manuel and A. P. Newton on eighteenth-century English thought. Other studies have long confirmed this interrelationship. Such studies are the following: I. Bernard Cohen, *Franklin and Newton* (1956); Maurice Cranston, *John Locke* (1957); Durand Echeverria, *Mirage in the West: A History of the French Image of American Society to 1815* (1957); and Caroline Robbins, *The Eighteenth Century Commonwealth: Studies in the Transmission, Development, and Circumstance of English Liberal Thought from the Restoration of Charles II until the War with the Thirteen Colonies* (1959).

Two biographies of importance have recently been published that illuminate a number of social-intellectual themes of provincial America. They are Edmund S. Morgan's *The Gentle Puritan, A Life of Ezra Stiles, 1727–1795* (1962) and Lewis L. Tucker's *Puritan Protagonist: President Thomas Clap of Yale College* (1962). See also A. F. Gegeheimer's *William Smith, Educator and Churchman* (1943). George A. Cook's *John Wise, Early American Democrat* (1952) makes the most of the limited materials on that significant figure. *Biographical Sketches of Those Who Attended Harvard College,* edited by Clifford K. Shipton—the recent Volume XII reaches the year 1750—constitutes an invaluable source of social history. Annabelle M. Melville's *John Carroll of Baltimore: Founder of the American Catholic Hierarchy* (1955), Edmond S. Morgan's *Virginians at Home: Family Life in the Eighteenth Century* (1952), and J. C. Spruill's *Women's Life and Work in the Southern Colonies* (1938) are useful sources for social history of the south.

The scholar should see a number of special studies: I. W. Riley, *American Philosophy* (1907); O. G. Sonneck, *Early Concert Life in America, 1731–1800* (1907); St. J. R. Childs, *Malaria and Colonization in the Carolina Low Country* (1940); W. B. Blanton, *Medicine in Virginia in the Eighteenth Century* (1931); Vincent Buranelli, *The Trial of Peter Zenger* (1957); the early chapters of Leonard Levy's provocative book, *Legacy of Suppression: Freedom of Speech and Press in Early American History* (1960); and certain pertinent parts of Oscar and Mary Handlin, *The Dimensions of Liberty* (1961).

Travel accounts provide an insight into social conditions. For a bibliography, see Thomas D. Clark, ed., *Travels in The Old South,* Vol. I (3 vols., 1956). No comparable type of bibliography exists for other areas. Older works, such as those of Esther Singleton's *Social New York under the Georges* (1902) and Mary S. Benson's *Women in the Eighteenth Century* (1935) must be consulted, together with the many volumes of Alice Morse Earle, cited for the seventeenth century. The Diaries of Samuel Sewall of Massachusetts and of William Byrd of Virginia offer an insight into early eighteenth-century oligarchical leadership. For the best introductory essay on William Byrd, see John S. Bassett, ed., *Writings of William Byrd* (1901) or Louis B. Wright and Marion Tinling, eds., *William Byrd of Virginia: The London Diary, 1717–21 and other Writings* (1958).

RELIGION IN PROVINCIAL AMERICA. Religious development involves social, cultural, intellectual, and sometimes political interrelationships. Many of the general works on these aspects of provincial

America discuss religious developments at length, for example, Savelle, *Seeds of Liberty*. A point of departure is provided in a few general volumes: William W. Sweet, *Religion in Colonial America* (1942), which includes a selected bibliography; and James W. Smith and A. Leland Jamison, eds., *Religion in American Life* (4 vols., 1961), the fourth volume of which includes a critical bibliography.

A generalized work extending far beyond the period covered by *The Formative Years* is Anson Phelps Stokes' *Church and State in the United States* (3 vols., 1950). The Great Awakening is covered by the following books: Charles H. Maxson, *The Great Awakening in the Middle Colonies* (1920), which from the point of view of historical writing sets the pattern in approaching this important religious movement, thereby misleading many subsequent scholars; Wesley M. Gewehr, *The Great Awakening in Virginia* (1930); and Edwin S. Gaustad, *The Great Awakening in New England* (1957).

Although there are a number of biographies of Jonathan Edwards, a towering figure in the history of provincial thought and religion, the most readable is Ola Winslow's *Jonathan Edwards, 1703–1758* (1940). Of course, no substitute exists for reading some of Edward's writing, including his sermons.

A number of monographs have recently appeared. A scholar should see the following: Jacob R. Marcus, *Early American Jewry*, previously cited; Dietmar Rothermund, *The Layman's Progress: Religious and Political Experience in Colonial Pennsylvania, 1740–1770* (1962); C. C. Goen, *Revivalism and Separatism in New England, 1740–1800: Strict Congregationalists and Separate Baptists in the Great Awakening* (1962); William Kellaway, *The New England Company, 1649–1776: Missionary Society to the American Indians* (1962); Cyclone Covey, *The American Pilgrimage: The Roots of American History, Religion and Culture* (1962); William L. Lumpkin, *Baptist Foundations in the South: Tracing Through the Separates the Influence of the Great Awakening 1754–1787* (1961); Claude Newlin, *Philosophy and Religion in Colonial America* (1962); Douglas J. Elwood, *The Philosophical Theology of Jonathan Edwards* (1960); Carl Wolf, *Jonathan Edwards the Preacher* (1958); Stuart C. Henry, *George Whitfield: Wayfaring Witness* (1957); Leonard J. Trinterud, *The Forming of An American Tradition: A Re-examination of Colonial Presbyterianism* (1949).

Almost every sect has a history that covers part of this period, and each colony had a wide variety of church records and useful monographs. Good examples of the specialized type of work that is valuable are the following: George MacLaren Brydon, *Virginia's Mother Church* (2 vols., 1947–52); Edgar Pennington, *Apostle of New Jersey, John Talbot, 1645–1727* (1938); Sister Mary Augustina, *American Opinion of Roman Catholicism in the Eighteenth Century* (1936); Reba C. Strickland, *Religion and the State in Georgia in the Eighteenth Century* (1939); Julius Sachse, *The German Sectaries of Pennsylvania, 1708–42: A Critical and Legendary History of the Ephrata Cloister and the Dunkers* (1899); Frank J. Klingberg, *Anglican Humanitarianism in Colonial New York* (1940); and J. S. Klett, *Presbyterianism in Colonial Pennsylvania* (1937).

PROVINCIAL POLITICS. Two general types of monographic studies have been written about provincial politics. One type was written by students under the direction of a past generation of great scholars, such as Osgood and Andrews, whose works are described in the introductory pages of this bibliography. Their approach has been described as political-institutional, which, defined in their terms, means that a particular topic—for example, the jurisdiction of the courts, the operation of a colony's council, the fiscal or judicial systems, or the jurisdiction of legislature—was developed with a minimum regard to time or setting. From these studies scholars gained a general understanding of the structure and machinery of provincial political institutions. But the use of that structure neglected the conflicting power groups, in fact the everyday give and take of political life. The structure existed in isolation.

This group of studies is represented by the following: Charles L. Raper, *North Carolina: A Study in English Colonial Government* (1904); Percy S. Flippen, *The Royal Government of Virginia, 1624–1775* (1919); W. Roy Smith, *South Carolina as a Royal Province* (1903); and W. R. Shepard, *History of Proprietary Government in Pennsylvania* (1891).

The second type of approach to provincial politics has been on a broader level; in such cases, the institutional structure of politics is assumed and attention is concentrated upon the men and groups who struggled to gain control of the political machinery. The results of these investigations have been uneven, often because the authors have not been able, in their analyses, to coordinate persuasively the struggle against royal authority for a greater degree of self-government and the struggle for internal control among competing oligarchical political groups. These studies have, however, added a welcome dimension to the story of provincial politics.

Among the most successful in this category are volumes that are focused upon the oncoming Revolution but which in their early chapters attempt to find more secure footing in investigating the late provincial period. Almost every colony has its monograph: David Lovejoy, *Rhode Island Politics and the American Revolution, 1760–1776* (1958); Oscar Zeichner, *Connecticut's Years of Controversy, 1750–1776* (1940); Theodore Thayer, *Pennsylvania Politics and the Growth of Democracy, 1740–1776* (1954); Charles Barker, *The Background of the Revolution in Maryland* (1940); W. W. Abbot, *The Royal Governors of Georgia, 1754–1775* (1959); and others. Some authors have reached further back to analyze provincial political development. Donald L. Kemmerer's *Path to Freedom; the Struggle for Self-Government in Colonial New Jersey, 1703–1776* (1940) is a good specimen of this type. Robert E. Brown's *Middle Class Democracy and the Revolution in Massachusetts, 1691–1780* (1955) clearly indicates that more people participated in provincial government than most scholars previously believed, but he does not examine the operation of politics and power. Jack P. Greene's *The Quest for Power: The Lower Houses of Assembly in the Southern Royal Colonies, 1689–1776* (1963) is an important volume, but it appeared too late to affect the writing of *The Formative Years*. Unfortunately, several of the most useful investigations of political developments—D. Alan Williams for provincial Virginia, Beverley McAnear for provincial New York, and one of the best political biographies available for the eighteenth century, Milton Klein's William Livingston—remain unpublished. Charles Sydnor's magnificent little book, *Gentlemen Freeholders: Political Practices in Washington's Virginia* (1952), gives a penetrating portrayal of the Virginia political oligarchy. Richard Morton's *Colonial Virginia*, previously cited, deserves mention in this context, and also a number of scattered monographs, such as Charles S. Grant's *Democracy in the Connecticut Frontier Town of Kent* (1961) and George Billias' *The Massachusetts Land Bankers* (1959). A popular account based upon the best scholarly material is Carl Bridenbaugh's essay, *Seat of Empire: The Political Role of Eighteenth-Century Williamsburg* (1958). Mention should be made of a key contemporary source, Hugh Jones' *The Present State of Virginia*, edited with discrimination by Richard L. Morton (1956). A group of essays by Leonard Labaree, *Conservatism in Early American History* (1948), offers a more general view of provincial politics and thought.

A series of biographies have provided in many cases some of the best material on provincial politics. Among the most discriminating and most illuminating biographies are the following: David Mays, *Edmund Pendleton, 1721–1803* (2 vols., 1952), and Aubrey C. Land, *The Dulaneys of Maryland: A Biographical Study of Daniel Dulaney, The Elder (1685–1753) and Daniel Dulaney the Younger (1722–1797)* (1955). But the following are also important biographies: Leonidas Dodson, *Alexander Spotswood, Governor of Colonial Virginia, 1710–22* (1932); Desmond Clarke, *Arthur Dobbs, Esquire, 1689–1765, Surveyor-General of Ireland, Prospector and Governor of North Carolina* (1957); Frederick Tolles, *James Logan,* previously cited; Roy N. Lokken, *David Lloyd, Colonial Lawmaker* (1959); Carl R. Woodward, *Ploughs and Politics: Charles Read of New Jersey and His Notes on Agriculture, 1715–1774* (1941); George M. Waller, *Samuel Vetch, Colonial Enterpriser* (1960); Sophie H. Drinker, *Hannah Penn and the Proprietorship of Pennsylvania* (1958); John A. Schutz, *William Shirley: King's Governor of Massachusetts* (1961) and *Thomas Pownall, British Defender of American Liberty* (1951); and John Cary, *Joseph Warren: Physician, Politician, Patriot* (1961).

Not to be overlooked are the multivolume writings of major revolutionary figures whose roots lie in the provincial period: Franklin (Leonard W. Labaree and Whitefield Bell, eds.), Jefferson (Julian Boyd, ed.), Adams (Lyman Butterfield, ed.), Hamilton (Harold Syrett, ed.), Madison (William T. Hutchinson and William M. E. Rachal, eds.); or the multivolume biographies: Jefferson (Dumas Malone), Washington (Douglas Freeman), Madison (Irving Brant), Hamilton (Broadus Mitchell), John Adams (Page Smith); and the great outpouring of biographical studies of less well known though key revolutionary figures who gained early prominence in provincial America.

Extensive legislative records are available for most of the American provinces, although glaring gaps still exist for Massachusetts and South Carolina, where intensive efforts are being made to publish these invaluable sources. Governors' correspondence, judicial materials, and the like are too extensive to include specifically, but they cast important light upon local, colony-wide, and colony-mother country political life.

A number of volumes, not readily classifiable, make a special contribution: Isaac Sharpless, *History of Quaker Government in Pennsylvania* (2 vols., 1898–99); Dixon Ryan Fox, *Yankees and Yorkers* (1940); Irving Mark, *Agrarian Conflicts in Colonial New York, 1711–1775* (1940); A. L. Cross, *The Anglican Episcopate and the American Colonies* (1902); Kenneth Scott, *Counterfeiting in Colonial Pennsylvania* (1955); Kenneth Ellis, *The Post Office in the Eighteenth Cen-*

tury (1949); George William Edwards, *New York as an Eighteenth Century Municipality, 1731–1776* (1917); Charles P. Keith, *Chronicles of Penn From the English Revolution to the Peace of Aix-la-Chappelle, 1688–1748* (1917); J. F. Burns, *Controversies between Royal Governors and Assemblies in the Northern Colonies* (1923); St. George L. Siousset, *Economics and Politics in Maryland, 1720–50* (1903); Matilda Edgar, *A Colonial Governor in Maryland* (1912); J. D. Ettinger, *James E. Oglethorpe: Imperial Idealist* (1936); Albert B. Saye, *New Viewpoints in Georgia History* (1962); J. R. McCain, *Georgia as a Proprietary Province* (1917); Mary Patterson Clarke, *Parliamentary Privilege in the American Colonies* (1943); Edward McCrady, *The History of South Carolina under the Royal Government, 1719–76* (1899); and Elizabeth Davidson, *The Establishment of the English Church in the Continental American Colonies* (1936).

A definitive, illuminating synthesis has not yet been written of provincial politics.

THE BRITISH EMPIRE AND INTERNATIONAL RIVALRY. The magisterial multivolume work of Lawrence Gipson, *The British Empire Before the American Revolution,* previously cited, and Francis Parkman's *Works,* especially *The Half-Century of Conflict* and *Montcalm and Wolfe,* represent the points of departure. George M. Wrong's *The Rise and Fall of New France* (2 vols., 1928) is an excellent supplement. General studies of the British background and of continental Europe should be consulted, for example, Walter L. Dorn's *Competition for Empire, 1740–63* (1940). In addition to the British bibliographies cited earlier, Henry P. Beers' *The French in North America: A Bibliographical Guide to French Archives, Reproductions, and Research Missions* (1957) is valuable for this subject.

A popular and accurate account of the international rivalry is given in Edward P. Hamilton's *The French and Indian Wars* (1962). Howard Peckham will soon publish an excellent summary of the Indian Wars, and see also his *Pontiac and the Indian Uprising* (1947). As background, Paul Quattlebaum's *The Land Called Chicora: The Carolinas under Spanish Rule with French Intrusions, 1520–1670* (1956) is useful. Standard works, such as Stanley Pargellis' *Lord Loudoun in North America* (1933), Hayes Baker Crothers' *Virginia and the French and Indian Wars* (1928), J. D. Ettinger's *James E. Oglethorpe,* previously cited, and John T. Lanning's *The Diplomatic History of Georgia* (1936), contribute significantly to the full story of international rivalry.

A number of recent monographs cast light on separate incidents. They are as follows: Charles W. Arnade, *The Siege of St. Augustine in 1702* (1959); Gerald S. Graham, ed., *The Walker Expedition to Quebec, 1711* (1953); Marshall Smelser, *The Campaign for the Sugar Islands, 1759: A Study of Amphibious Warfare* (1955); Robert C. Newbold, *The Albany Congress and Plan of Union, 1754* (1955); C. P. Stacey, *Quebec, 1759: The Siege and the Battle* (1959); Christopher Lloyd, *The Capture of Quebec* (1959); and Christopher Hibbert, *Wolfe at Quebec* (1959).

But these studies fail to visualize the impact of the diplomatic revolution of the eighteenth century as it touched the American colonies. In this respect, Max Savelle, "The American Balance of Power and European Diplomacy, 1713–78," in *The Era of the American Revolution* (1939), edited by R. B. Morris, remains a pioneer piece of work. In addition, Max Savelle's *The Diplomatic History of the Canadian Boundary, 1749–63* (1940) must be consulted.

Certain recent general works also have their value: Harrison Bird, *Navies in the Mountains: The Battles on the Waters of Lake Champlain and Lake George, 1609–1814* (1962); Joseph Lister Rutledge, *Century of Conflict: The Struggle between the French and British in Colonial America* (1956); Paul Walden Bamford, *Forests and French Sea Power, 1660–1789* (1956); Bernard Knollenberg, *Origin of the American Revolution, 1759–1766* (1960); Harold L. Peterson, *Arms and Armor in Colonial America, 1526–1783* (1956); and Wilbur R. Jacobs, *Diplomacy and Gifts* (1950).

No study, unfortunately, properly explores the intimate interrelationship between England's internal evolution, the diplomatic revolution in Europe, and the development of an inner-oriented political system within the British colonies in North America.

Index

Printed in Great Britain by
Lowe & Brydone (Printers) Ltd, London